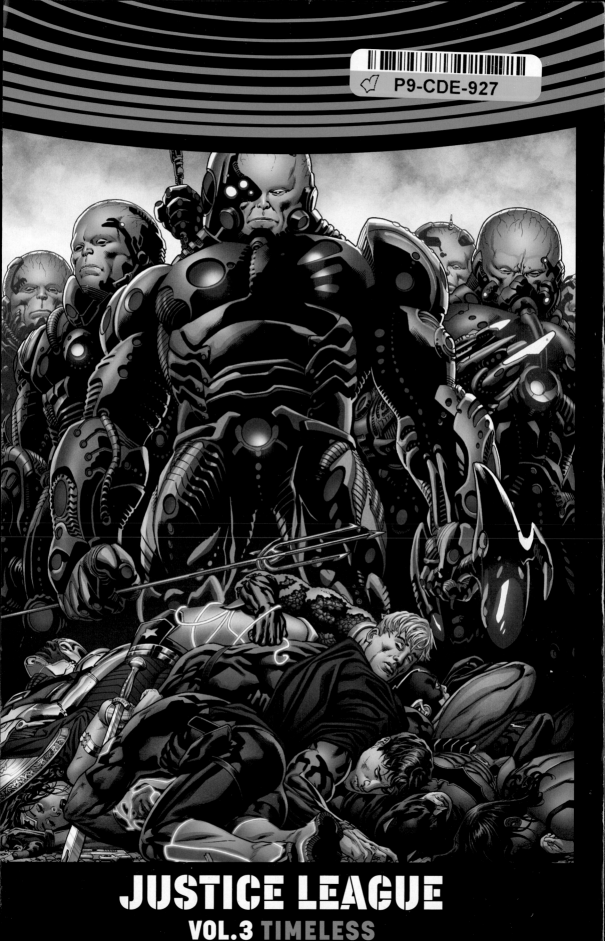

JUSTICE LEAGUE
VOL.3 TIMELESS

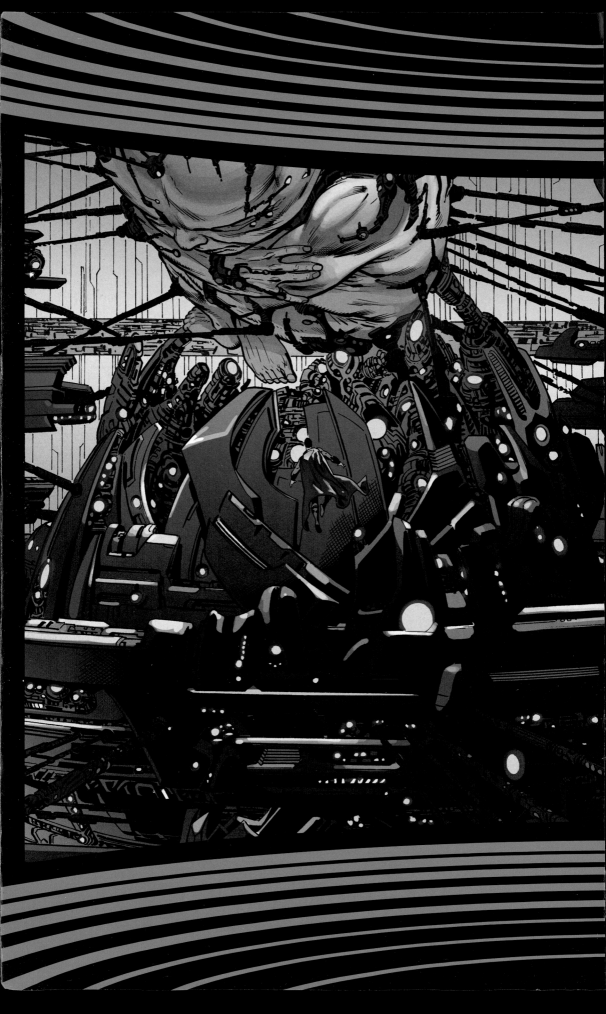

JUSTICE LEAGUE

VOL.3 TIMELESS

BRYAN HITCH
writer

FERNANDO PASARIN
BRYAN HITCH
pencillers

MATT RYAN
DANIEL HENRIQUES
inkers

BRAD ANDERSON
ALEX SINCLAIR
colorists

RICHARD STARKINGS & COMICRAFT
letterers

FERNANDO PASARIN, MATT RYAN & BRAD ANDERSON
collection cover artists

SUPERMAN created by **JERRY SIEGEL** and **JOE SHUSTER**
By special arrangement with the Jerry Siegel family

BRIAN CUNNINGHAM Editor - Original Series ＊ **AMEDEO TURTURRO DIEGO LOPEZ** Assistant Editors - Original Series
JEB WOODARD Group Editor - Collected Editions ＊ **ROBIN WILDMAN** Editor - Collected Edition
STEVE COOK Design Director - Books ＊ **MONIQUE GRUSPE** Publication Design

BOB HARRAS Senior VP - Editor-in-Chief, DC Comics

DIANE NELSON President ＊ **DAN DiDIO** Publisher ＊ **JIM LEE** Publisher ＊ **GEOFF JOHNS** President & Chief Creative Officer
AMIT DESAI Executive VP - Business & Marketing Strategy, Direct to Consumer & Global Franchise Management ＊ **SAM ADES** Senior VP - Direct to Consumer
BOBBIE CHASE VP - Talent Development ＊ **MARK CHIARELLO** Senior VP - Art, Design & Collected Editions
JOHN CUNNINGHAM Senior VP - Sales & Trade Marketing ＊ **ANNE DePIES** Senior VP - Business Strategy, Finance & Administration
DON FALLETTI VP - Manufacturing Operations ＊ **LAWRENCE GANEM** VP - Editorial Administration & Talent Relations
ALISON GILL Senior VP - Manufacturing & Operations ＊ **HANK KANALZ** Senior VP - Editorial Strategy & Administration
JAY KOGAN VP - Legal Affairs ＊ **THOMAS LOFTUS** VP - Business Affairs
JACK MAHAN VP - Business Affairs ＊ **NICK J. NAPOLITANO** VP - Manufacturing Administration
EDDIE SCANNELL VP - Consumer Marketing ＊ **COURTNEY SIMMONS** Senior VP - Publicity & Communications
JIM (SKI) SOKOLOWSKI VP - Comic Book Specialty Sales & Trade Marketing ＊ **NANCY SPEARS** VP - Mass, Book, Digital Sales & Trade Marketing

JUSTICE LEAGUE VOL. 3: TIMELESS

Published by DC Comics. Compilation and all new material Copyright © 2017 DC Comics. All Rights Reserved.
Originally published in single magazine form in JUSTICE LEAGUE 14-19. Copyright © 2017 DC Comics. All Rights Reserved.
All characters, their distinctive likenesses and related elements featured in this publication are trademarks of DC Comics.
The stories, characters and incidents featured in this publication are entirely fictional.
DC Comics does not read or accept unsolicited submissions of ideas, stories or artwork.

DC Comics, 2900 West Alameda Ave., Burbank, CA 91505.
Printed by LSC Communications, Salem, VA, USA. 6/9/17. First Printing.
ISBN: 978-1-4012-7112-1

Library of Congress Cataloging-in-Publication Data is available.

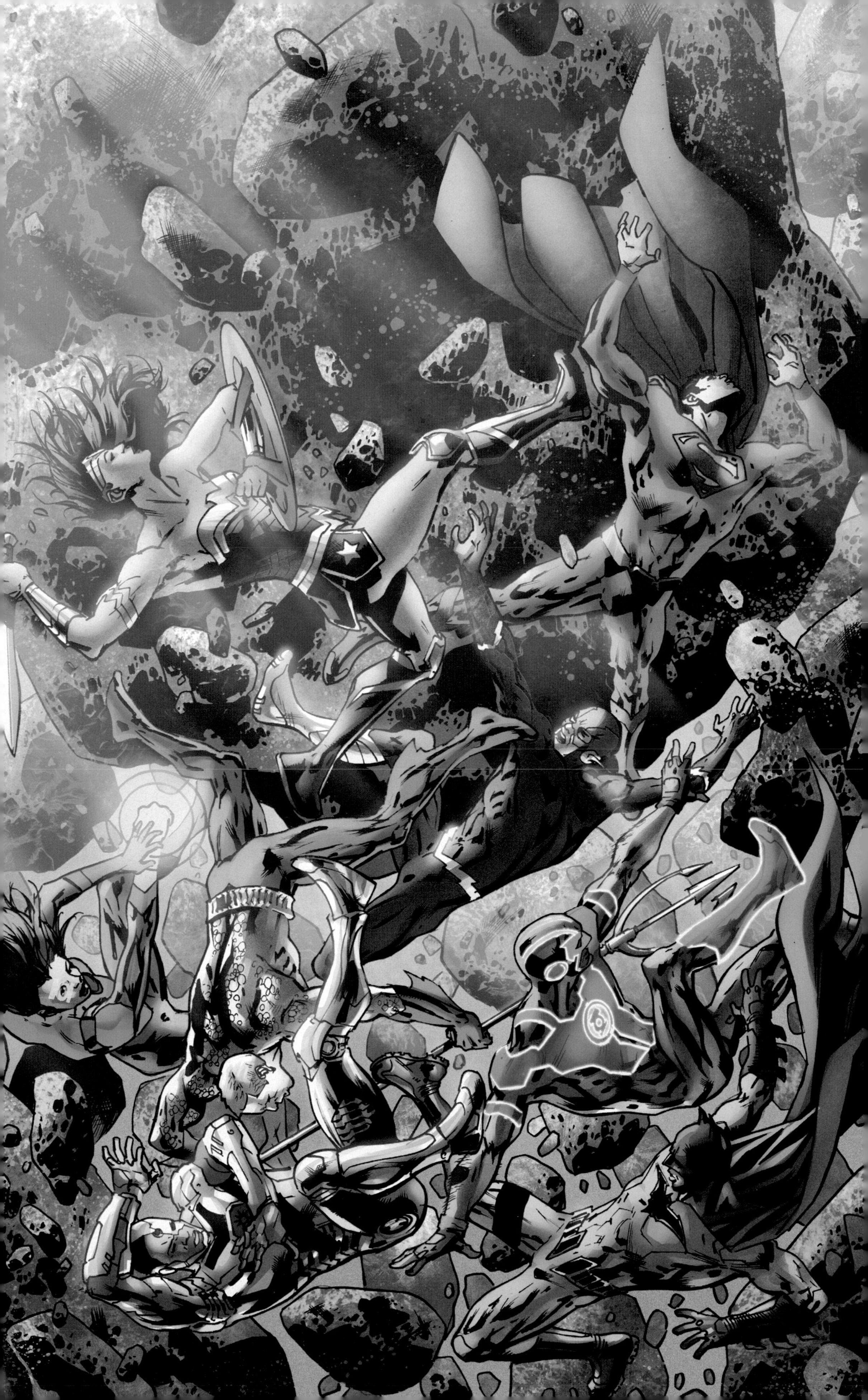

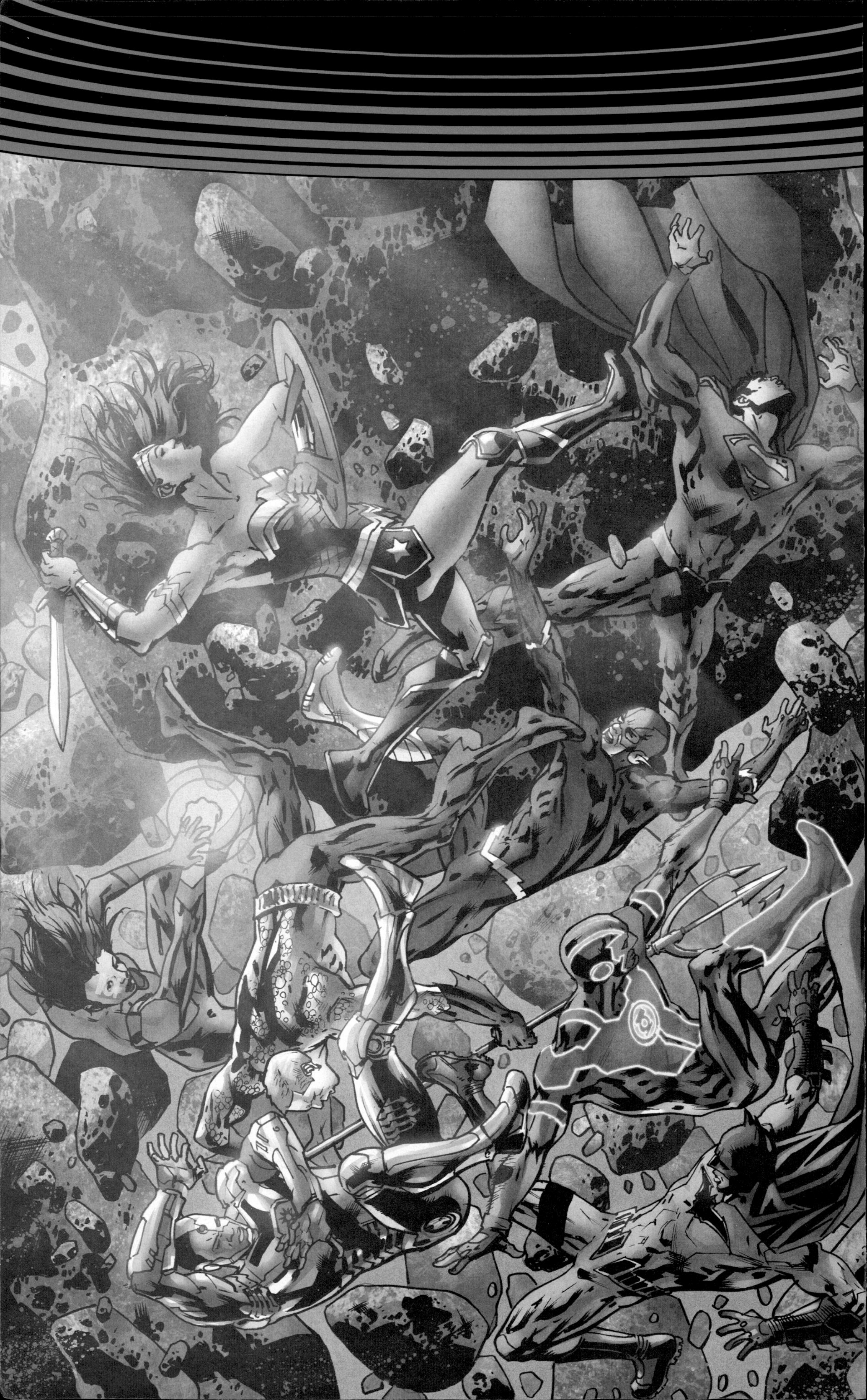

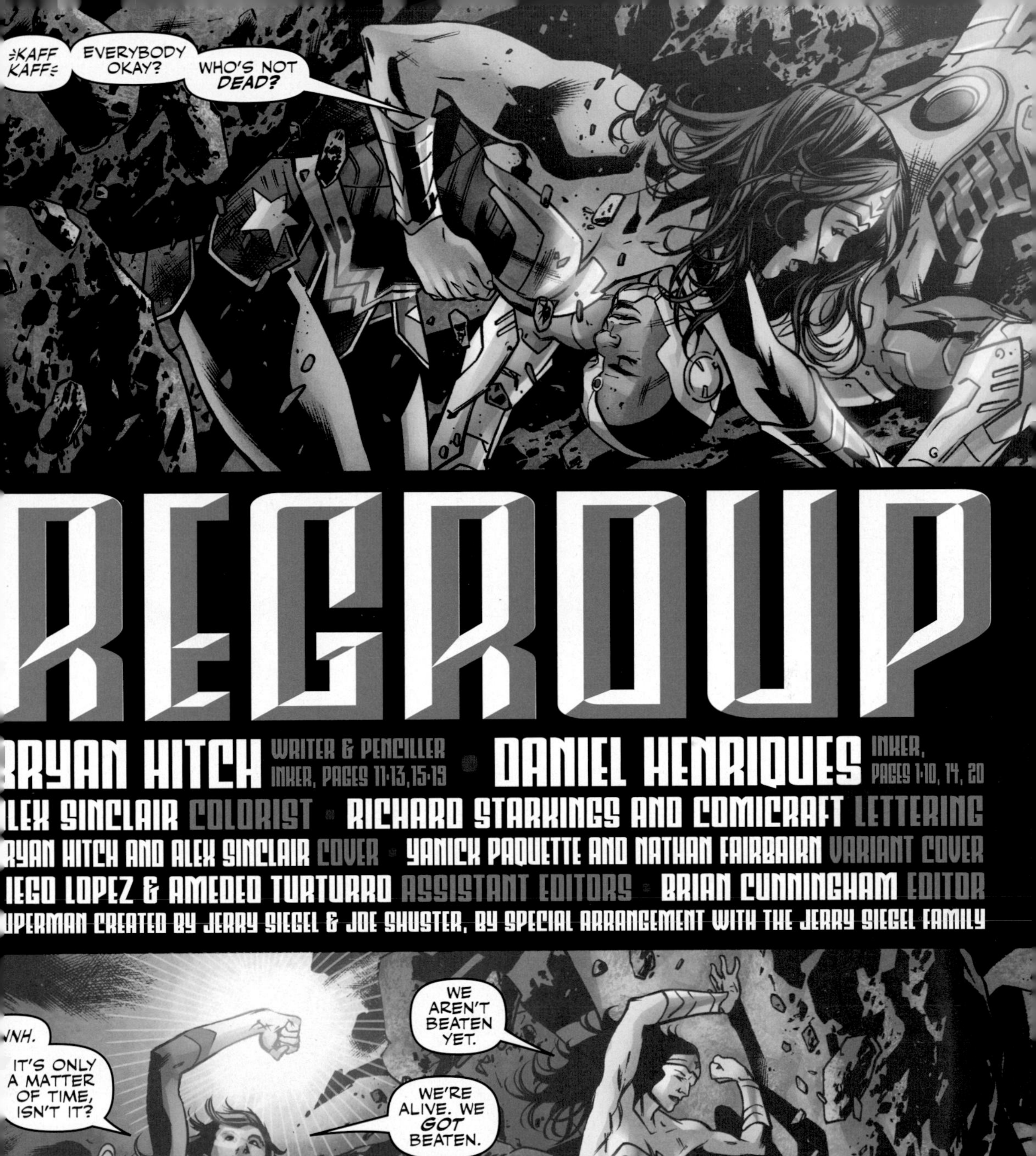

KAFF KAFF
EVERYBODY OKAY?
WHO'S NOT *DEAD?*

REGROUP

RYAN HITCH WRITER & PENCILLER INKER, PAGES 11-13, 15-19 • DANIEL HENRIQUES INKER, PAGES 1-10, 14, 20
LEX SINCLAIR COLORIST • RICHARD STARKINGS AND COMICRAFT LETTERING
RYAN HITCH AND ALEX SINCLAIR COVER • YANICK PAQUETTE AND NATHAN FAIRBAIRN VARIANT COVER
IEGO LOPEZ & AMEDEO TURTURRO ASSISTANT EDITORS • BRIAN CUNNINGHAM EDITOR
UPERMAN CREATED BY JERRY SIEGEL & JOE SHUSTER, BY SPECIAL ARRANGEMENT WITH THE JERRY SIEGEL FAMILY

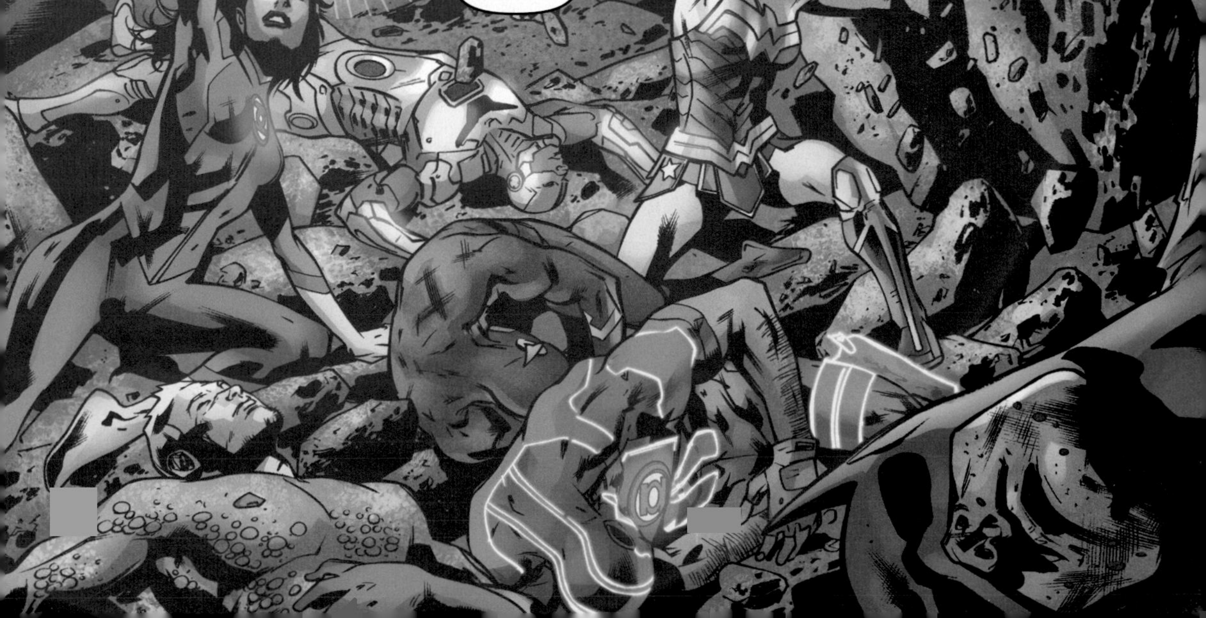

NH.
IT'S ONLY A MATTER OF TIME, ISN'T IT?
WE'RE ALIVE. WE *GOT* BEATEN.
WE AREN'T BEATEN YET.

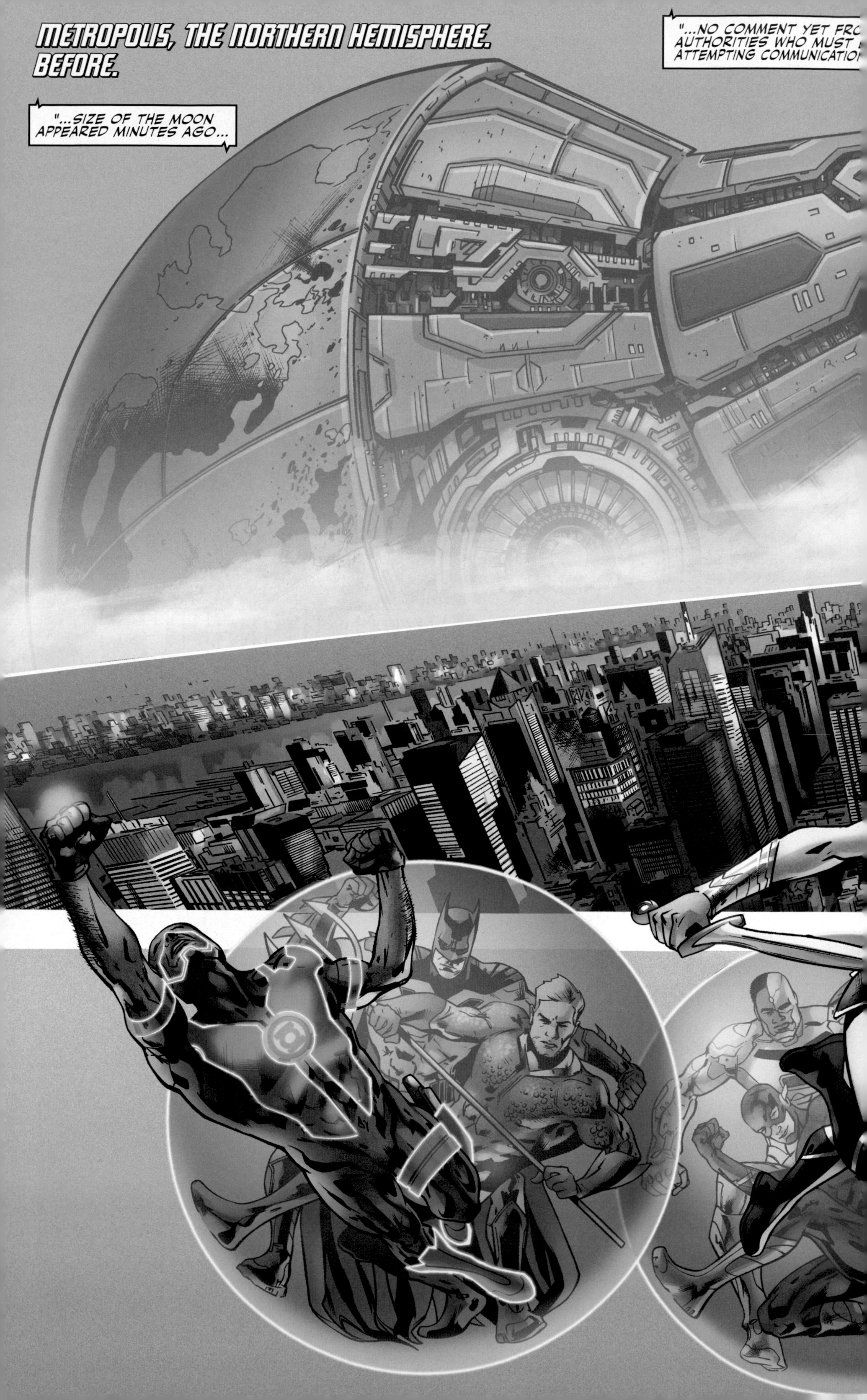
METROPOLIS, THE NORTHERN HEMISPHERE. BEFORE.
"...SIZE OF THE MOON APPEARED MINUTES AGO...
"...NO COMMENT YET FRO AUTHORITIES WHO MUST ATTEMPTING COMMUNICATIO

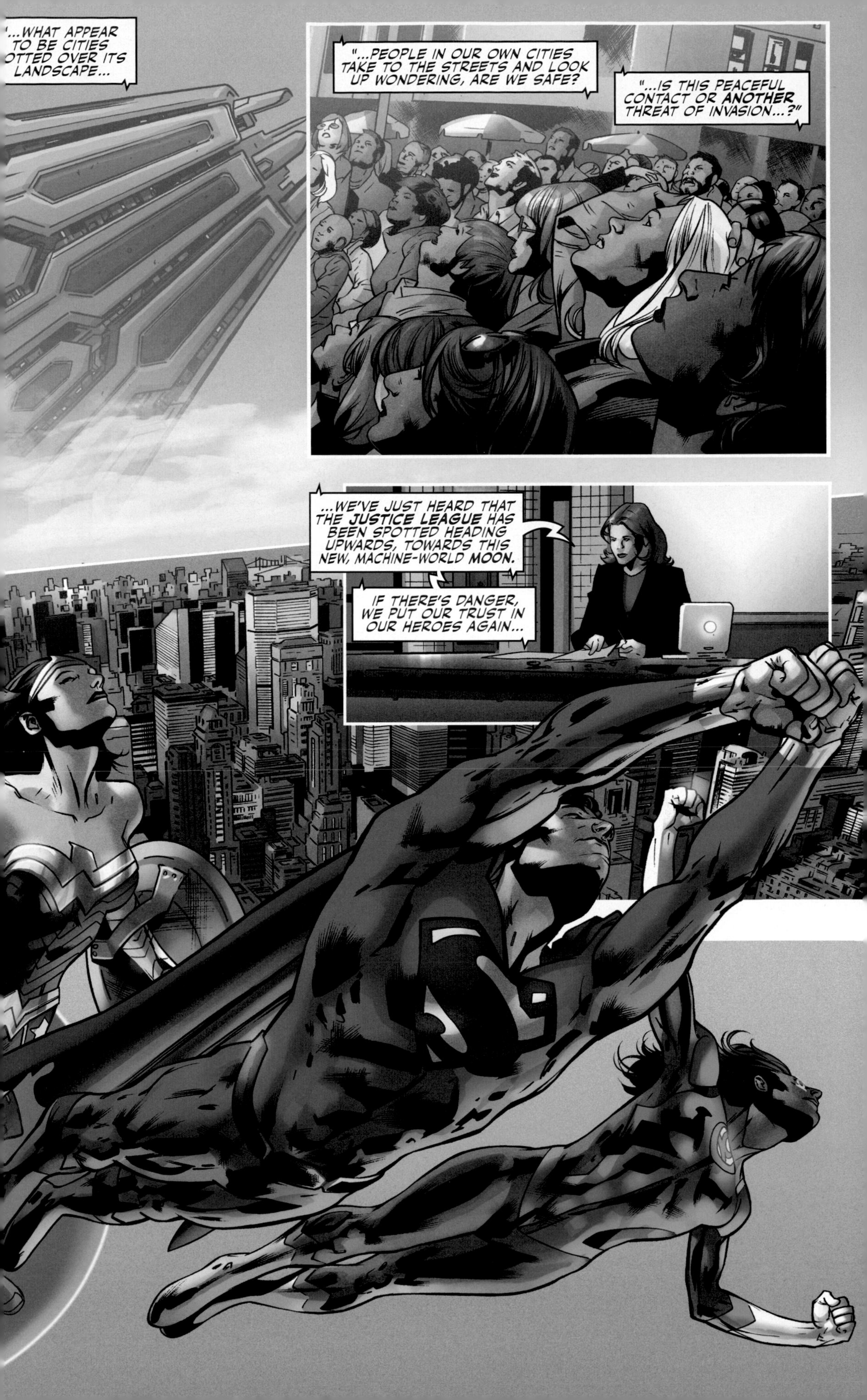
"...WHAT APPEAR TO BE CITIES DOTTED OVER ITS LANDSCAPE...
"...PEOPLE IN OUR OWN CITIES TAKE TO THE STREETS AND LOOK UP WONDERING, ARE WE SAFE?
"...IS THIS PEACEFUL CONTACT OR ANOTHER THREAT OF INVASION...?"
...WE'VE JUST HEARD THAT THE JUSTICE LEAGUE HAS BEEN SPOTTED HEADING UPWARDS, TOWARDS THIS NEW, MACHINE-WORLD MOON.
IF THERE'S DANGER, WE PUT OUR TRUST IN OUR HEROES AGAIN...

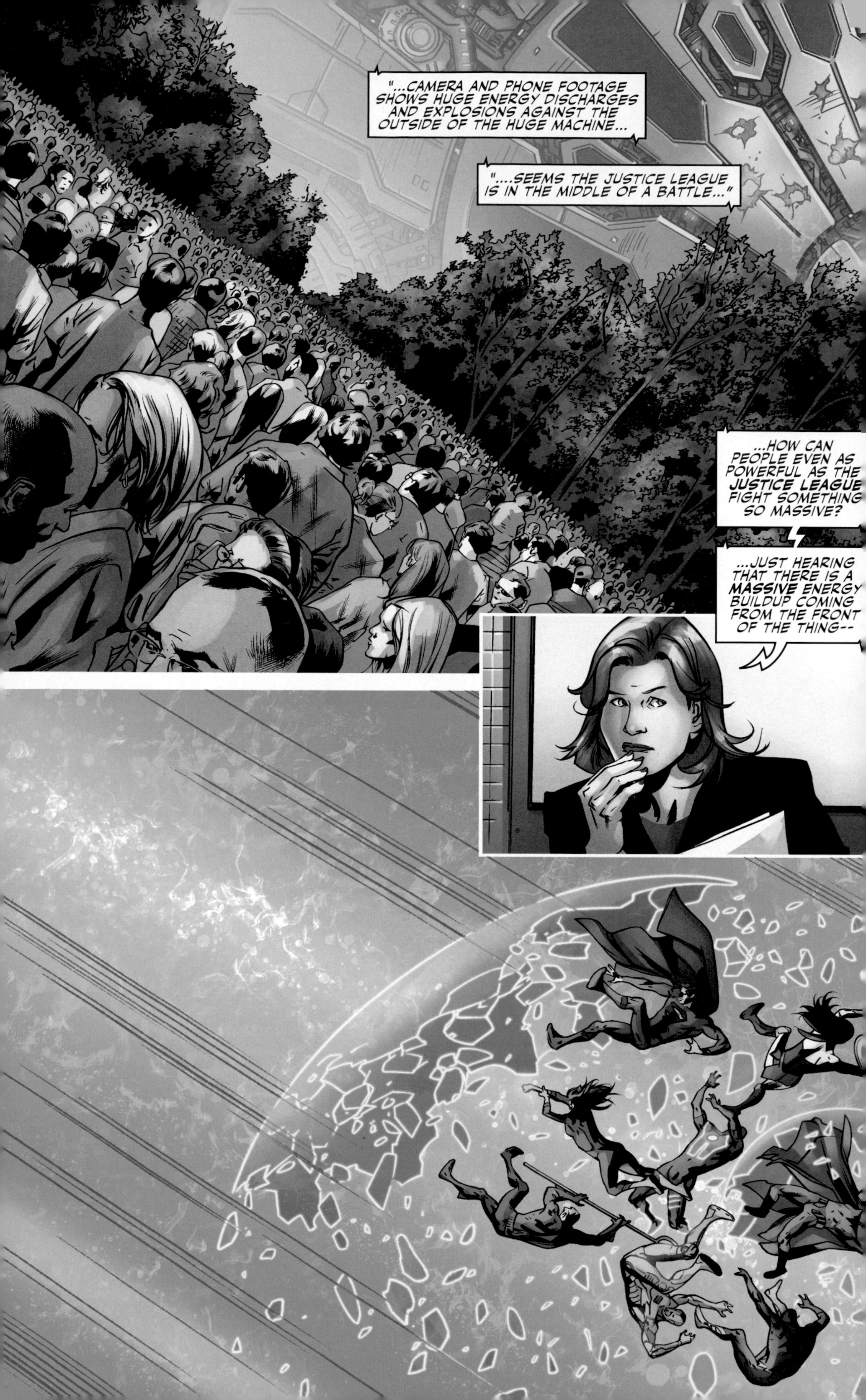
"...CAMERA AND PHONE FOOTAGE SHOWS HUGE ENERGY DISCHARGES AND EXPLOSIONS AGAINST THE OUTSIDE OF THE HUGE MACHINE...
"....SEEMS THE JUSTICE LEAGUE IS IN THE MIDDLE OF A BATTLE..."
...HOW CAN PEOPLE EVEN AS POWERFUL AS THE JUSTICE LEAGUE FIGHT SOMETHING SO MASSIVE?
...JUST HEARING THAT THERE IS A MASSIVE ENERGY BUILDUP COMING FROM THE FRONT OF THE THING--

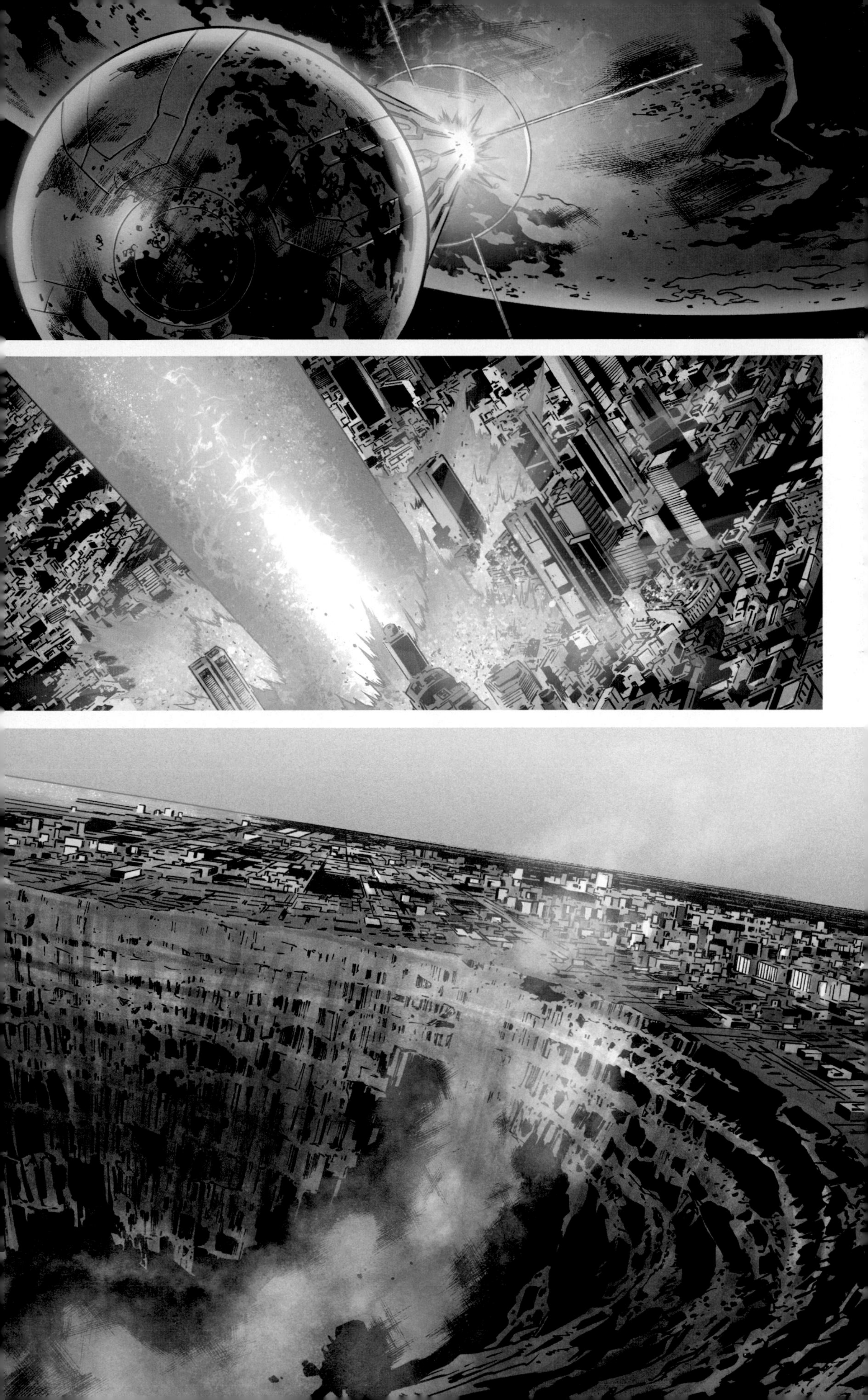

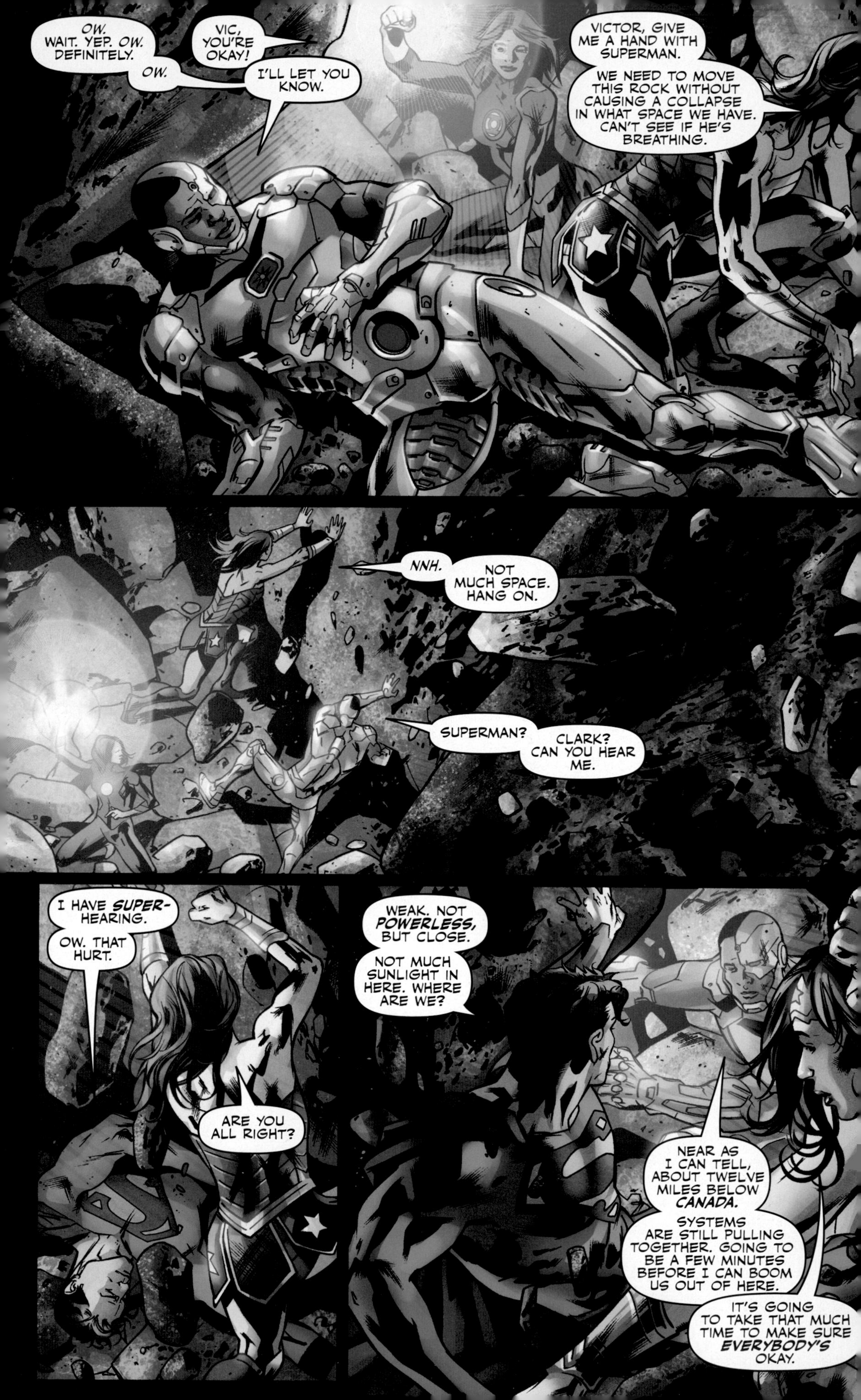
OW. WAIT. YEP. OW. DEFINITELY.
OW.
VIC, YOU'RE OKAY!
I'LL LET YOU KNOW.
VICTOR, GIVE ME A HAND WITH SUPERMAN.
WE NEED TO MOVE THIS ROCK WITHOUT CAUSING A COLLAPSE IN WHAT SPACE WE HAVE. CAN'T SEE IF HE'S BREATHING.
NNH.
NOT MUCH SPACE. HANG ON.
SUPERMAN?
CLARK? CAN YOU HEAR ME.
I HAVE SUPER-HEARING.
OW. THAT HURT.
ARE YOU ALL RIGHT?
WEAK. NOT POWERLESS, BUT CLOSE.
NOT MUCH SUNLIGHT IN HERE. WHERE ARE WE?
NEAR AS I CAN TELL, ABOUT TWELVE MILES BELOW CANADA.
SYSTEMS ARE STILL PULLING TOGETHER. GOING TO BE A FEW MINUTES BEFORE I CAN BOOM US OUT OF HERE.
IT'S GOING TO TAKE THAT MUCH TIME TO MAKE SURE EVERYBODY'S OKAY.

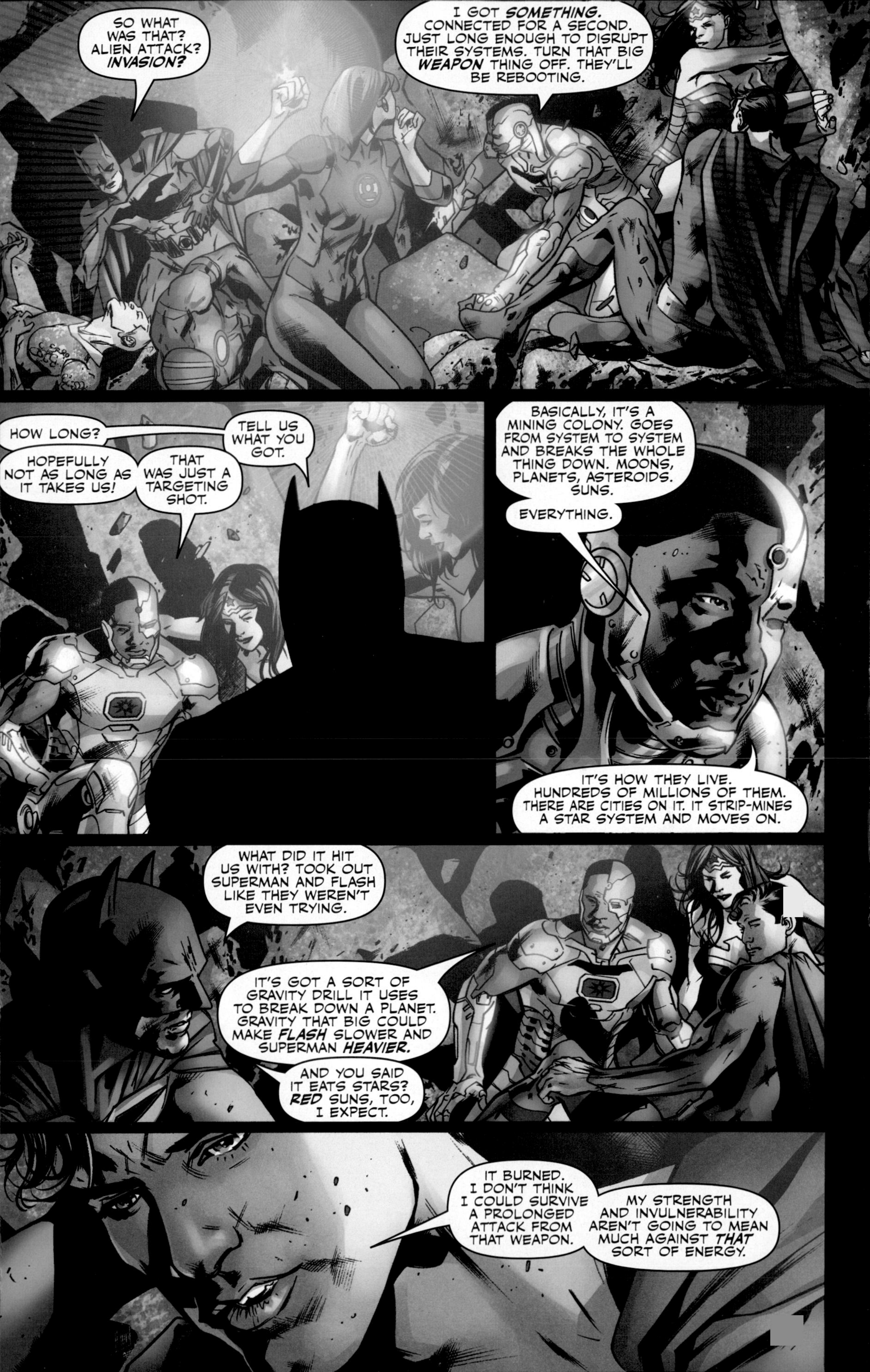
SO WHAT WAS THAT? ALIEN ATTACK? *INVASION?*
I GOT *SOMETHING.* CONNECTED FOR A SECOND. JUST LONG ENOUGH TO DISRUPT THEIR SYSTEMS. TURN THAT BIG *WEAPON* THING OFF. THEY'LL BE REBOOTING.
HOW LONG?
TELL US WHAT YOU GOT.
HOPEFULLY NOT AS LONG AS IT TAKES US!
THAT WAS JUST A TARGETING SHOT.
BASICALLY, IT'S A MINING COLONY. GOES FROM SYSTEM TO SYSTEM AND BREAKS THE WHOLE THING DOWN. MOONS, PLANETS, ASTEROIDS. SUNS.
EVERYTHING.
IT'S HOW THEY LIVE. HUNDREDS OF MILLIONS OF THEM. THERE ARE CITIES ON IT. IT STRIP-MINES A STAR SYSTEM AND MOVES ON.
WHAT DID IT HIT US WITH? TOOK OUT SUPERMAN AND FLASH LIKE THEY WEREN'T EVEN TRYING.
IT'S GOT A SORT OF GRAVITY DRILL IT USES TO BREAK DOWN A PLANET. GRAVITY THAT BIG COULD MAKE *FLASH* SLOWER AND SUPERMAN *HEAVIER.*
AND YOU SAID IT EATS STARS? *RED* SUNS, TOO, I EXPECT.
IT BURNED. I DON'T THINK I COULD SURVIVE A PROLONGED ATTACK FROM THAT WEAPON.
MY STRENGTH AND INVULNERABILITY AREN'T GOING TO MEAN MUCH AGAINST *THAT* SORT OF ENERGY.

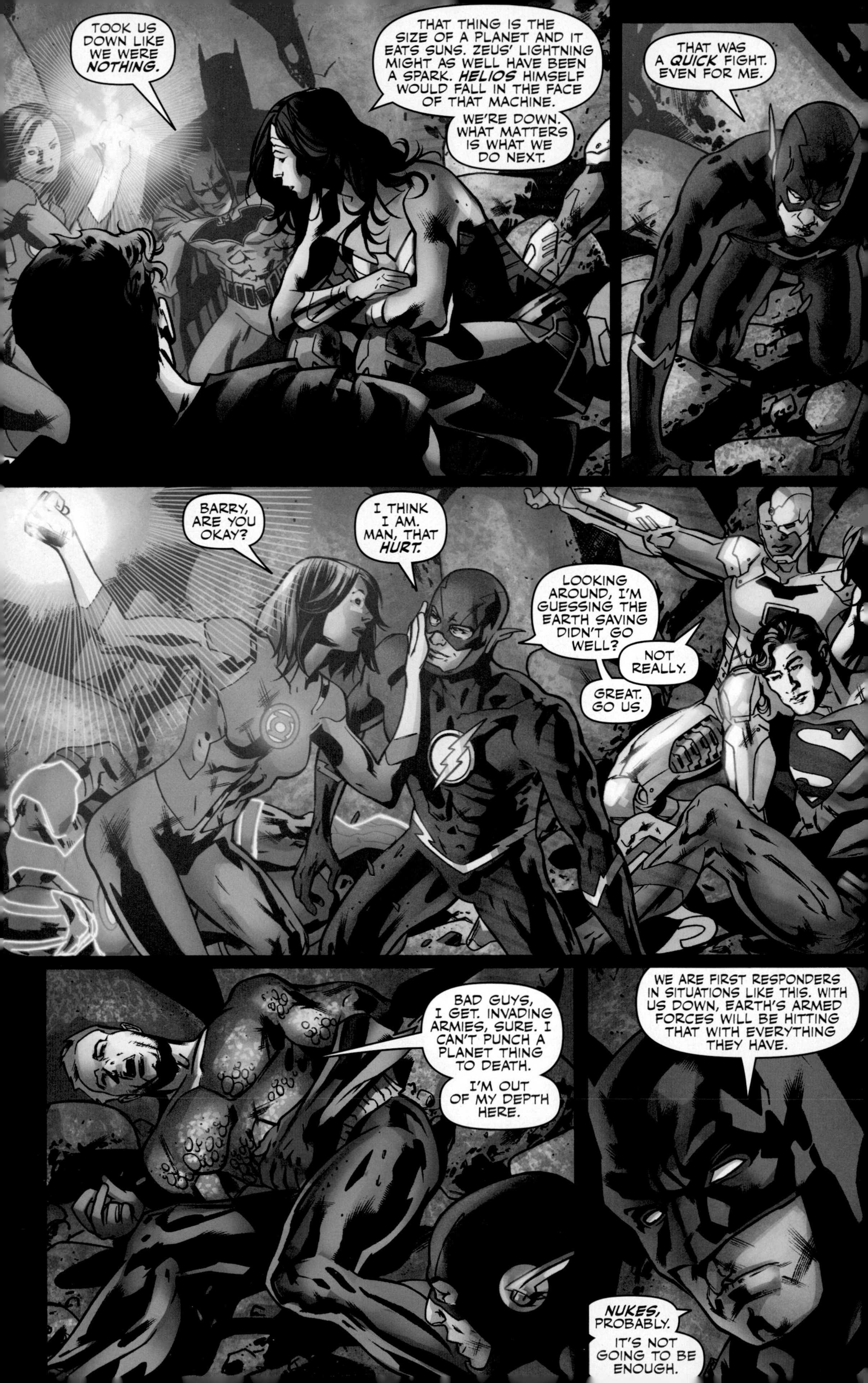
TOOK US DOWN LIKE WE WERE *NOTHING*.
THAT THING IS THE SIZE OF A PLANET AND IT EATS SUNS. ZEUS' LIGHTNING MIGHT AS WELL HAVE BEEN A SPARK. *HELIOS* HIMSELF WOULD FALL IN THE FACE OF THAT MACHINE.
WE'RE DOWN. WHAT MATTERS IS WHAT WE DO NEXT.
THAT WAS A *QUICK* FIGHT. EVEN FOR ME.
BARRY, ARE YOU OKAY?
I THINK I AM. MAN, THAT *HURT.*
LOOKING AROUND, I'M GUESSING THE EARTH SAVING DIDN'T GO WELL?
NOT REALLY.
GREAT. GO US.
BAD GUYS, I GET. INVADING ARMIES, SURE. I CAN'T PUNCH A PLANET THING TO DEATH.
I'M OUT OF MY DEPTH HERE.
WE ARE FIRST RESPONDERS IN SITUATIONS LIKE THIS. WITH US DOWN, EARTH'S ARMED FORCES WILL BE HITTING THAT WITH EVERYTHING THEY HAVE.
NUKES, PROBABLY.
IT'S NOT GOING TO BE ENOUGH.

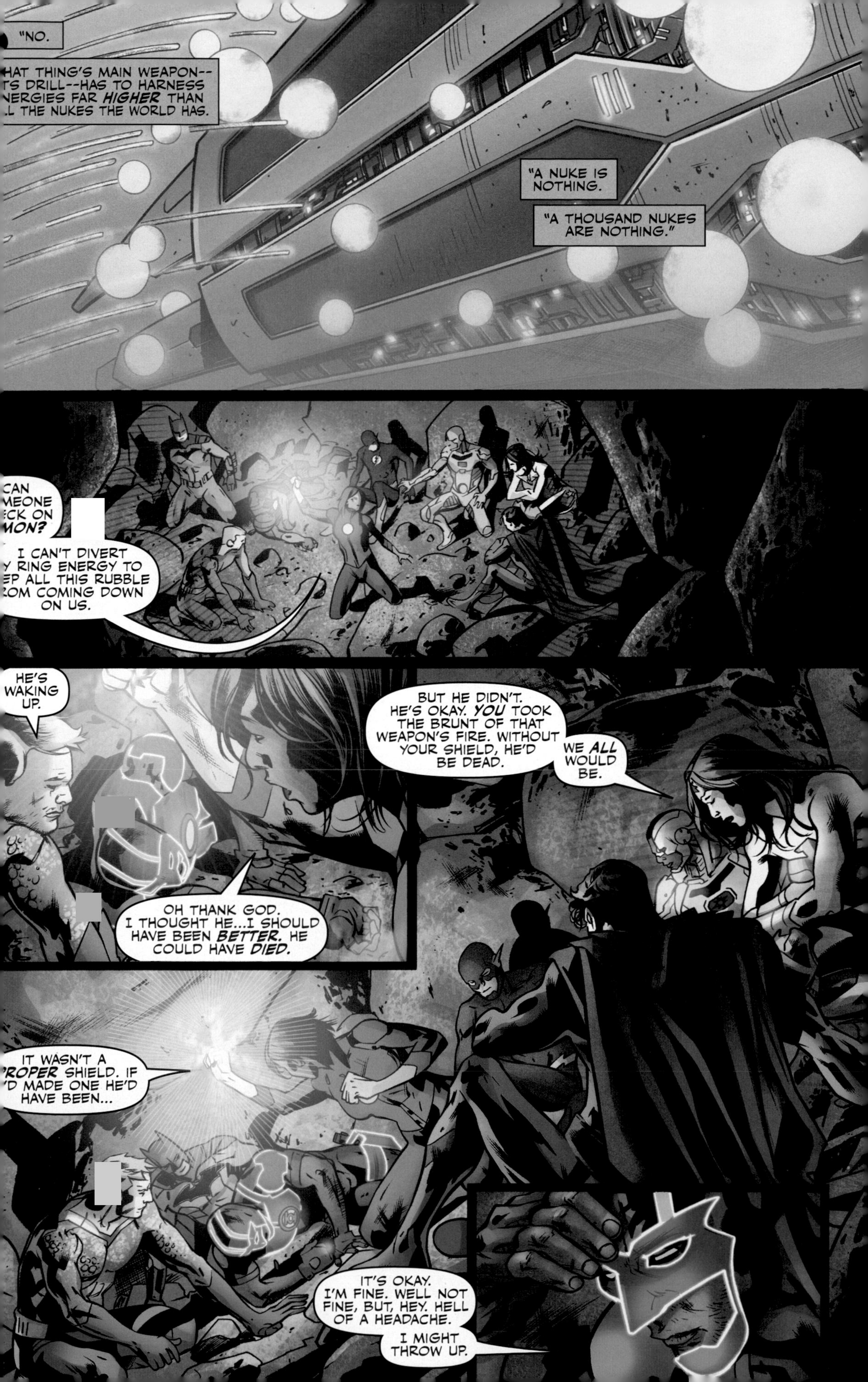
"NO.
HAT THING'S MAIN WEAPON-- TS DRILL--HAS TO HARNESS NERGIES FAR HIGHER THAN L THE NUKES THE WORLD HAS.
"A NUKE IS NOTHING.
"A THOUSAND NUKES ARE NOTHING."
CAN MEONE ECK ON MON?
I CAN'T DIVERT Y RING ENERGY TO EP ALL THIS RUBBLE ROM COMING DOWN ON US.
HE'S WAKING UP.
OH THANK GOD. I THOUGHT HE...I SHOULD HAVE BEEN BETTER. HE COULD HAVE DIED.
BUT HE DIDN'T. HE'S OKAY. YOU TOOK THE BRUNT OF THAT WEAPON'S FIRE. WITHOUT YOUR SHIELD, HE'D BE DEAD.
WE ALL WOULD BE.
IT WASN'T A ROPER SHIELD. IF 'D MADE ONE HE'D HAVE BEEN...
IT'S OKAY. I'M FINE. WELL NOT FINE, BUT, HEY. HELL OF A HEADACHE.
I MIGHT THROW UP.

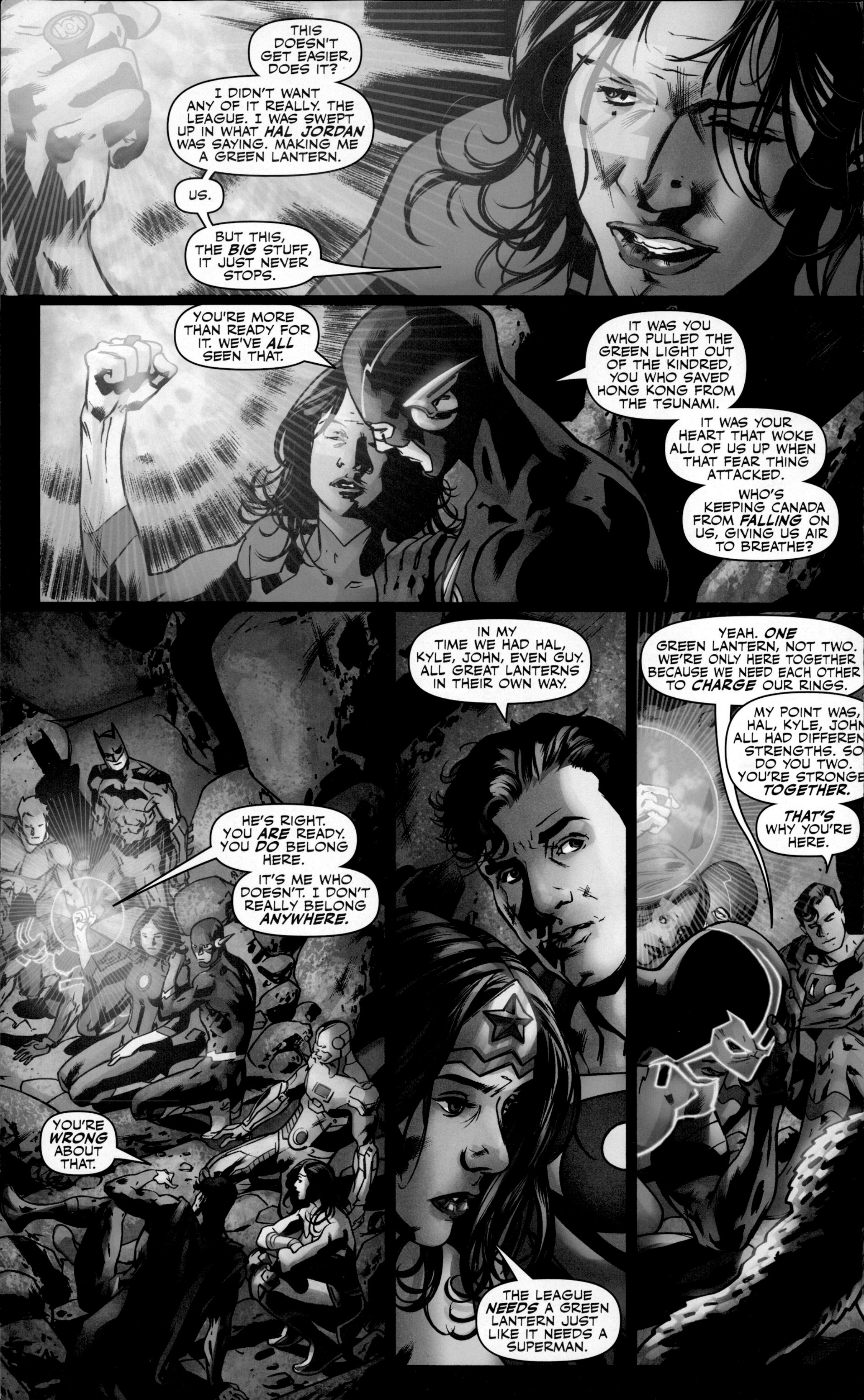
THIS DOESN'T GET EASIER, DOES IT?
I DIDN'T WANT ANY OF IT REALLY. THE LEAGUE. I WAS SWEPT UP IN WHAT HAL JORDAN WAS SAYING. MAKING ME A GREEN LANTERN.
US.
BUT THIS, THE BIG STUFF, IT JUST NEVER STOPS.
YOU'RE MORE THAN READY FOR IT. WE'VE ALL SEEN THAT.
IT WAS YOU WHO PULLED THE GREEN LIGHT OUT OF THE KINDRED, YOU WHO SAVED HONG KONG FROM THE TSUNAMI.
IT WAS YOUR HEART THAT WOKE ALL OF US UP WHEN THAT FEAR THING ATTACKED.
WHO'S KEEPING CANADA FROM FALLING ON US, GIVING US AIR TO BREATHE?
HE'S RIGHT. YOU ARE READY. YOU DO BELONG HERE.
IT'S ME WHO DOESN'T. I DON'T REALLY BELONG ANYWHERE.
YOU'RE WRONG ABOUT THAT.
IN MY TIME WE HAD HAL, KYLE, JOHN, EVEN GUY. ALL GREAT LANTERNS IN THEIR OWN WAY.
THE LEAGUE NEEDS A GREEN LANTERN JUST LIKE IT NEEDS A SUPERMAN.
YEAH. ONE GREEN LANTERN, NOT TWO. WE'RE ONLY HERE TOGETHER BECAUSE WE NEED EACH OTHER TO CHARGE OUR RINGS.
MY POINT WAS, HAL, KYLE, JOHN ALL HAD DIFFEREN STRENGTHS. SO DO YOU TWO. YOU'RE STRONGE TOGETHER.
THAT'S WHY YOU'RE HERE.

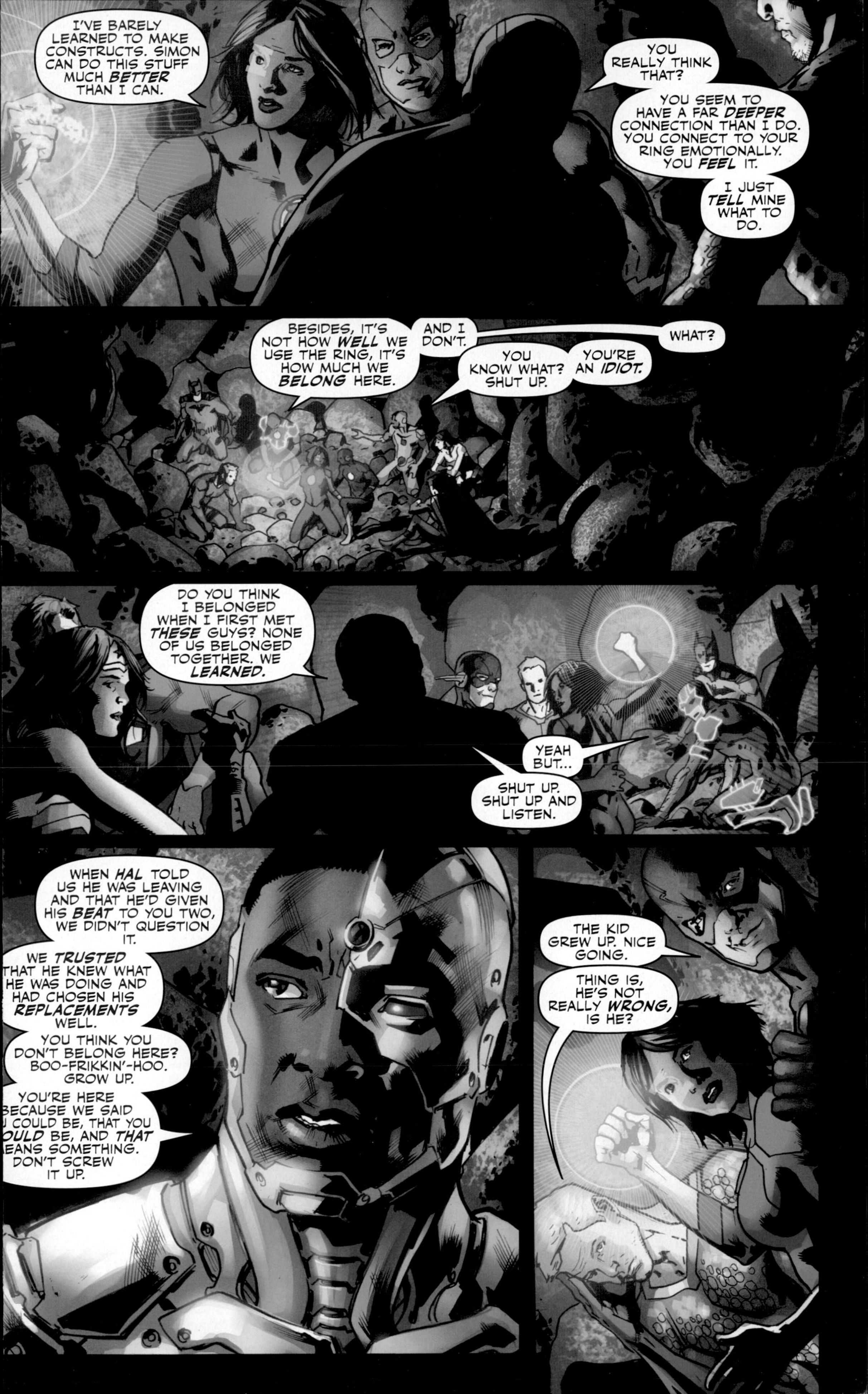
I'VE BARELY LEARNED TO MAKE CONSTRUCTS. SIMON CAN DO THIS STUFF MUCH BETTER THAN I CAN.
YOU REALLY THINK THAT?
YOU SEEM TO HAVE A FAR DEEPER CONNECTION THAN I DO. YOU CONNECT TO YOUR RING EMOTIONALLY. YOU FEEL IT.
I JUST TELL MINE WHAT TO DO.
BESIDES, IT'S NOT HOW WELL WE USE THE RING, IT'S HOW MUCH WE BELONG HERE.
AND I DON'T.
WHAT?
YOU KNOW WHAT? SHUT UP.
YOU'RE AN IDIOT.
DO YOU THINK I BELONGED WHEN I FIRST MET THESE GUYS? NONE OF US BELONGED TOGETHER. WE LEARNED.
YEAH BUT...
SHUT UP. SHUT UP AND LISTEN.
WHEN HAL TOLD US HE WAS LEAVING AND THAT HE'D GIVEN HIS BEAT TO YOU TWO, WE DIDN'T QUESTION IT.
WE TRUSTED THAT HE KNEW WHAT HE WAS DOING AND HAD CHOSEN HIS REPLACEMENTS WELL.
YOU THINK YOU DON'T BELONG HERE? BOO-FRIKKIN'-HOO. GROW UP.
YOU'RE HERE BECAUSE WE SAID U COULD BE, THAT YOU OULD BE, AND THAT EANS SOMETHING. DON'T SCREW IT UP.
THE KID GREW UP. NICE GOING.
THING IS, HE'S NOT REALLY WRONG, IS HE?

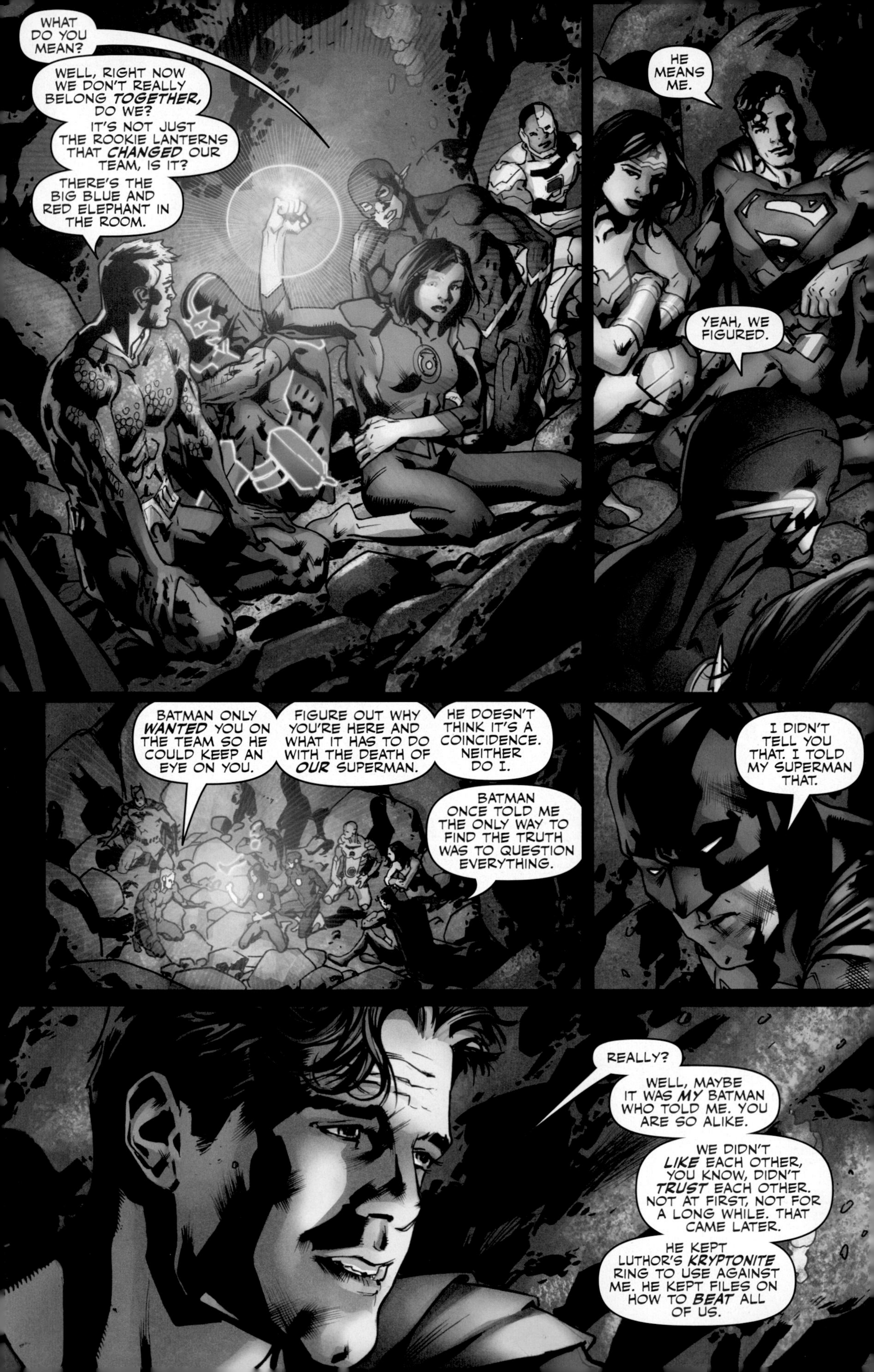
WHAT DO YOU MEAN?
WELL, RIGHT NOW WE DON'T REALLY BELONG *TOGETHER,* DO WE?
IT'S NOT JUST THE ROOKIE LANTERNS THAT *CHANGED* OUR TEAM, IS IT?
THERE'S THE BIG BLUE AND RED ELEPHANT IN THE ROOM.
HE MEANS ME.
YEAH, WE FIGURED.
BATMAN ONLY *WANTED* YOU ON THE TEAM SO HE COULD KEEP AN EYE ON YOU.
FIGURE OUT WHY YOU'RE HERE AND WHAT IT HAS TO DO WITH THE DEATH OF *OUR* SUPERMAN.
HE DOESN'T THINK IT'S A COINCIDENCE. NEITHER DO I.
BATMAN ONCE TOLD ME THE ONLY WAY TO FIND THE TRUTH WAS TO QUESTION EVERYTHING.
I DIDN'T TELL YOU THAT. I TOLD MY SUPERMAN THAT.
REALLY?
WELL, MAYBE IT WAS *MY* BATMAN WHO TOLD ME. YOU ARE SO ALIKE.
WE DIDN'T *LIKE* EACH OTHER, YOU KNOW, DIDN'T *TRUST* EACH OTHER. NOT AT FIRST, NOT FOR A LONG WHILE. THAT CAME LATER.
HE KEPT LUTHOR'S *KRYPTONITE* RING TO USE AGAINST ME. HE KEPT FILES ON HOW TO *BEAT* ALL OF US.

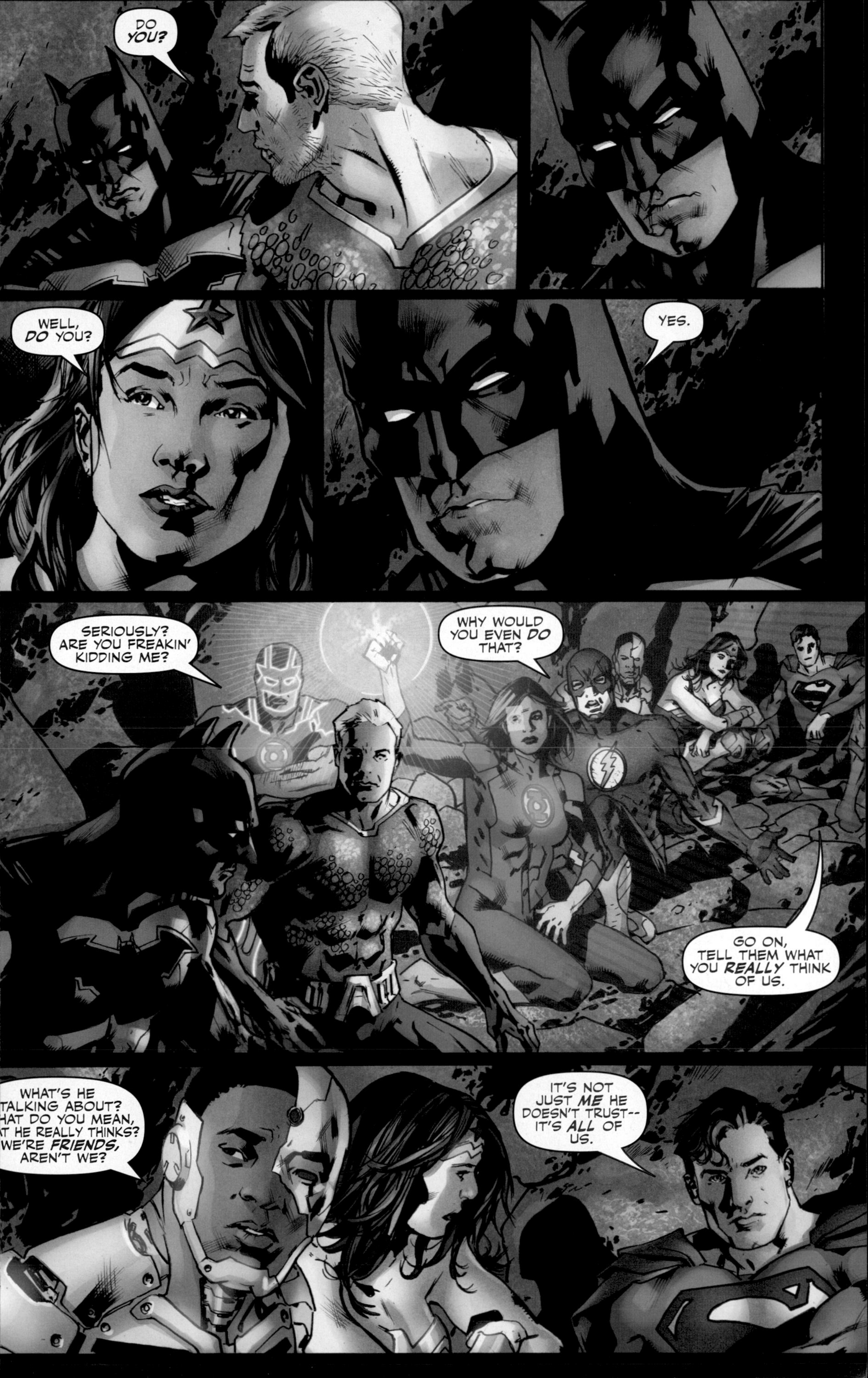
DO YOU?
WELL, DO YOU?
YES.
SERIOUSLY? ARE YOU FREAKIN' KIDDING ME?
WHY WOULD YOU EVEN DO THAT?
GO ON, TELL THEM WHAT YOU REALLY THINK OF US.
WHAT'S HE TALKING ABOUT? HAT DO YOU MEAN, AT HE REALLY THINKS? WE'RE FRIENDS, AREN'T WE?
IT'S NOT JUST ME HE DOESN'T TRUST-- IT'S ALL OF US.

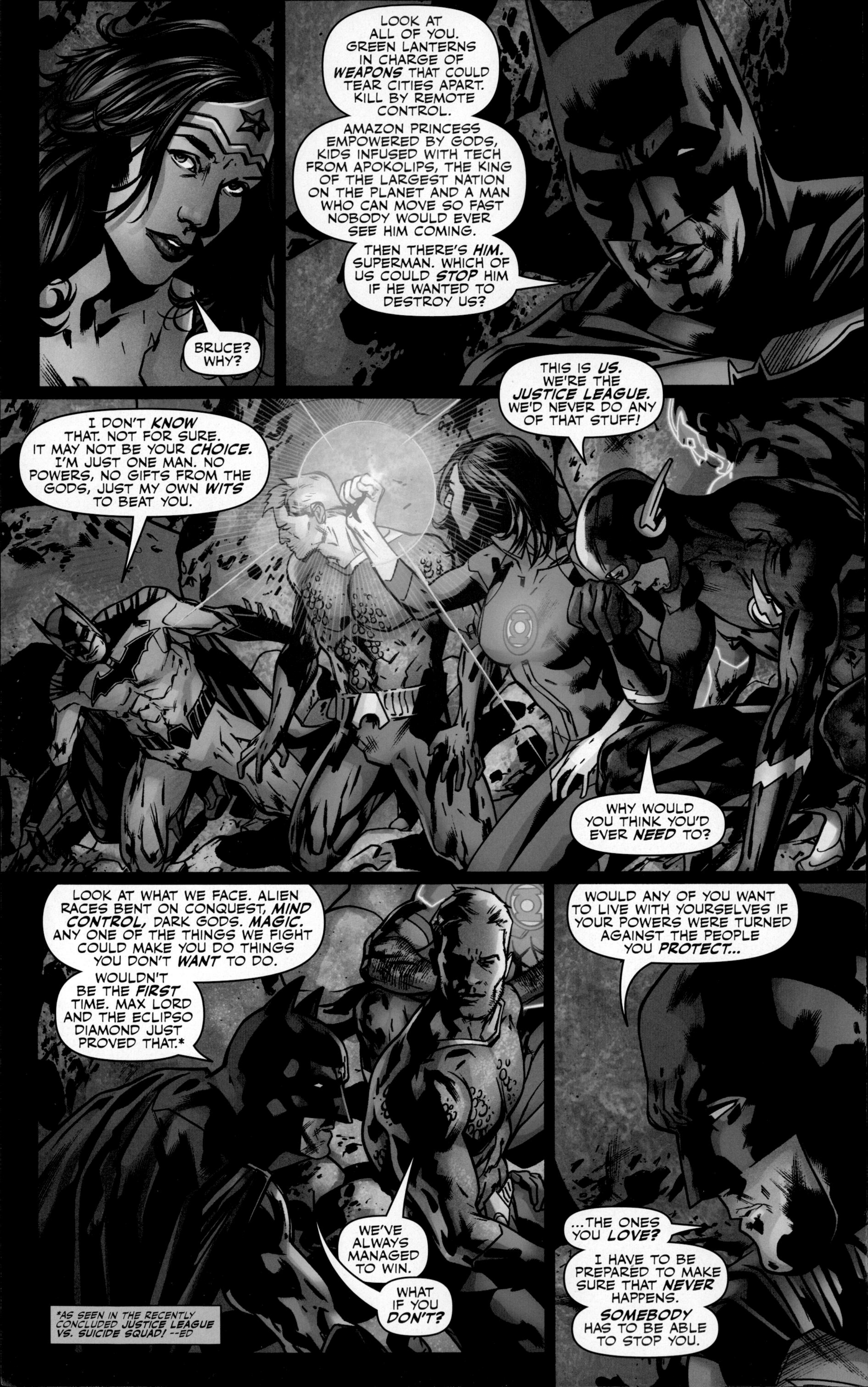
LOOK AT ALL OF YOU. GREEN LANTERNS IN CHARGE OF WEAPONS THAT COULD TEAR CITIES APART. KILL BY REMOTE CONTROL.
AMAZON PRINCESS EMPOWERED BY GODS, KIDS INFUSED WITH TECH FROM APOKOLIPS, THE KING OF THE LARGEST NATION ON THE PLANET AND A MAN WHO CAN MOVE SO FAST NOBODY WOULD EVER SEE HIM COMING.
THEN THERE'S HIM. SUPERMAN. WHICH OF US COULD STOP HIM IF HE WANTED TO DESTROY US?
BRUCE? WHY?
THIS IS US. WE'RE THE JUSTICE LEAGUE. WE'D NEVER DO ANY OF THAT STUFF!
I DON'T KNOW THAT. NOT FOR SURE. IT MAY NOT BE YOUR CHOICE. I'M JUST ONE MAN. NO POWERS, NO GIFTS FROM THE GODS, JUST MY OWN WITS TO BEAT YOU.
WHY WOULD YOU THINK YOU'D EVER NEED TO?
LOOK AT WHAT WE FACE. ALIEN RACES BENT ON CONQUEST, MIND CONTROL, DARK GODS. MAGIC. ANY ONE OF THE THINGS WE FIGHT COULD MAKE YOU DO THINGS YOU DON'T WANT TO DO.
WOULDN'T BE THE FIRST TIME. MAX LORD AND THE ECLIPSO DIAMOND JUST PROVED THAT.*
WE'VE ALWAYS MANAGED TO WIN.
WHAT IF YOU DON'T?
*AS SEEN IN THE RECENTLY CONCLUDED JUSTICE LEAGUE VS. SUICIDE SQUAD! --ED
WOULD ANY OF YOU WANT TO LIVE WITH YOURSELVES IF YOUR POWERS WERE TURNED AGAINST THE PEOPLE YOU PROTECT...
...THE ONES YOU LOVE?
I HAVE TO BE PREPARED TO MAKE SURE THAT NEVER HAPPENS.
SOMEBODY HAS TO BE ABLE TO STOP YOU.

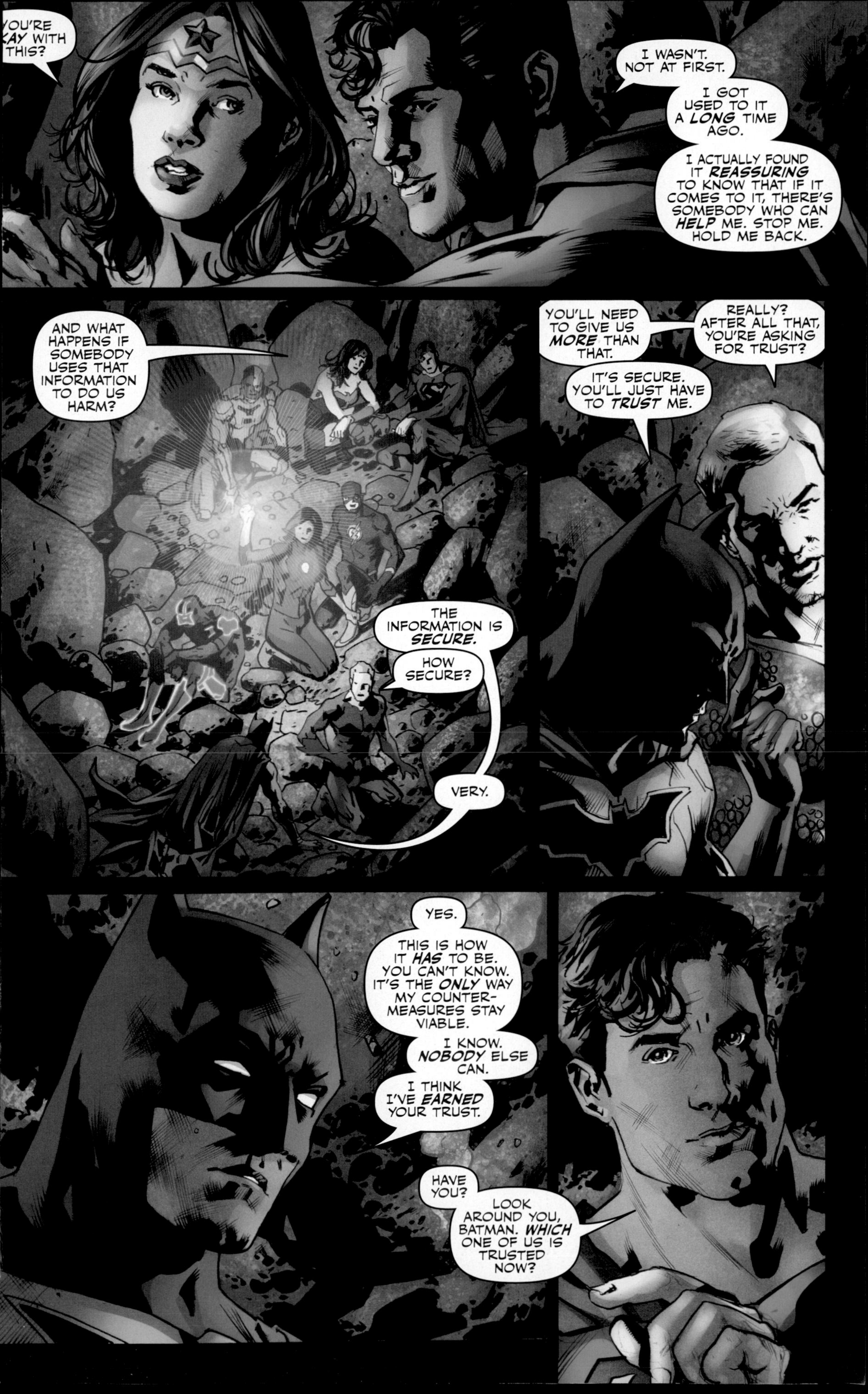

YOU'RE
KAY WITH THIS?
I WASN'T. NOT AT FIRST.
I GOT USED TO IT A LONG TIME AGO.
I ACTUALLY FOUND IT REASSURING TO KNOW THAT IF IT COMES TO IT, THERE'S SOMEBODY WHO CAN HELP ME. STOP ME. HOLD ME BACK.
AND WHAT HAPPENS IF SOMEBODY USES THAT INFORMATION TO DO US HARM?
THE INFORMATION IS SECURE.
HOW SECURE?
VERY.
YOU'LL NEED TO GIVE US MORE THAN THAT.
REALLY? AFTER ALL THAT, YOU'RE ASKING FOR TRUST?
IT'S SECURE. YOU'LL JUST HAVE TO TRUST ME.
YES.
THIS IS HOW IT HAS TO BE. YOU CAN'T KNOW. IT'S THE ONLY WAY MY COUNTER-MEASURES STAY VIABLE.
I KNOW. NOBODY ELSE CAN.
I THINK I'VE EARNED YOUR TRUST.
HAVE YOU?
LOOK AROUND YOU, BATMAN. WHICH ONE OF US IS TRUSTED NOW?

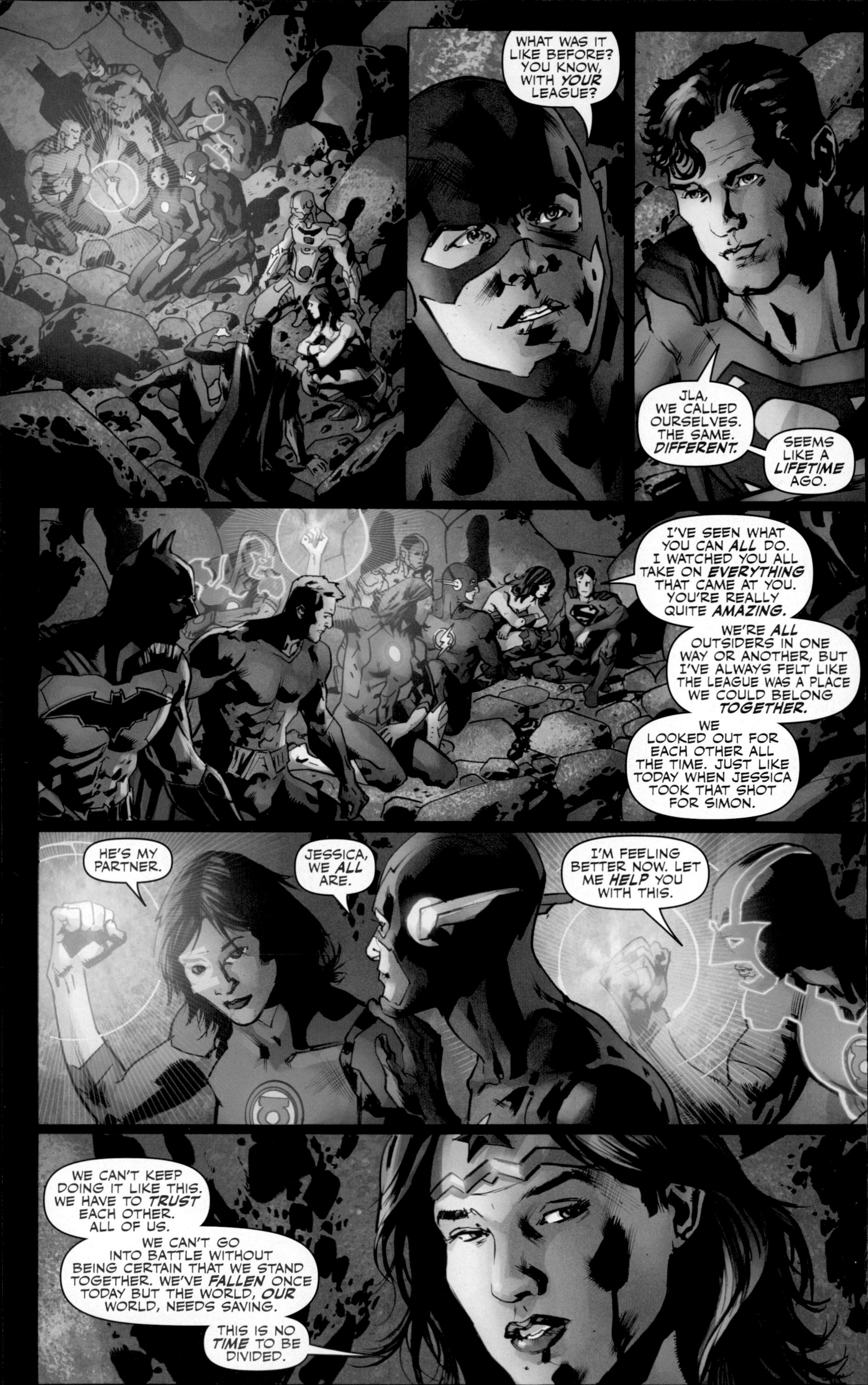
WHAT WAS IT LIKE BEFORE? YOU KNOW, WITH YOUR LEAGUE?
JLA, WE CALLED OURSELVES. THE SAME. DIFFERENT.
SEEMS LIKE A LIFETIME AGO.
I'VE SEEN WHAT YOU CAN ALL DO. I WATCHED YOU ALL TAKE ON EVERYTHING THAT CAME AT YOU. YOU'RE REALLY QUITE AMAZING.
WE'RE ALL OUTSIDERS IN ONE WAY OR ANOTHER, BUT I'VE ALWAYS FELT LIKE THE LEAGUE WAS A PLACE WE COULD BELONG TOGETHER.
WE LOOKED OUT FOR EACH OTHER ALL THE TIME. JUST LIKE TODAY WHEN JESSICA TOOK THAT SHOT FOR SIMON.
HE'S MY PARTNER.
JESSICA, WE ALL ARE.
I'M FEELING BETTER NOW. LET ME HELP YOU WITH THIS.
WE CAN'T KEEP DOING IT LIKE THIS. WE HAVE TO TRUST EACH OTHER. ALL OF US.
WE CAN'T GO INTO BATTLE WITHOUT BEING CERTAIN THAT WE STAND TOGETHER. WE'VE FALLEN ONCE TODAY BUT THE WORLD, OUR WORLD, NEEDS SAVING.
THIS IS NO TIME TO BE DIVIDED.

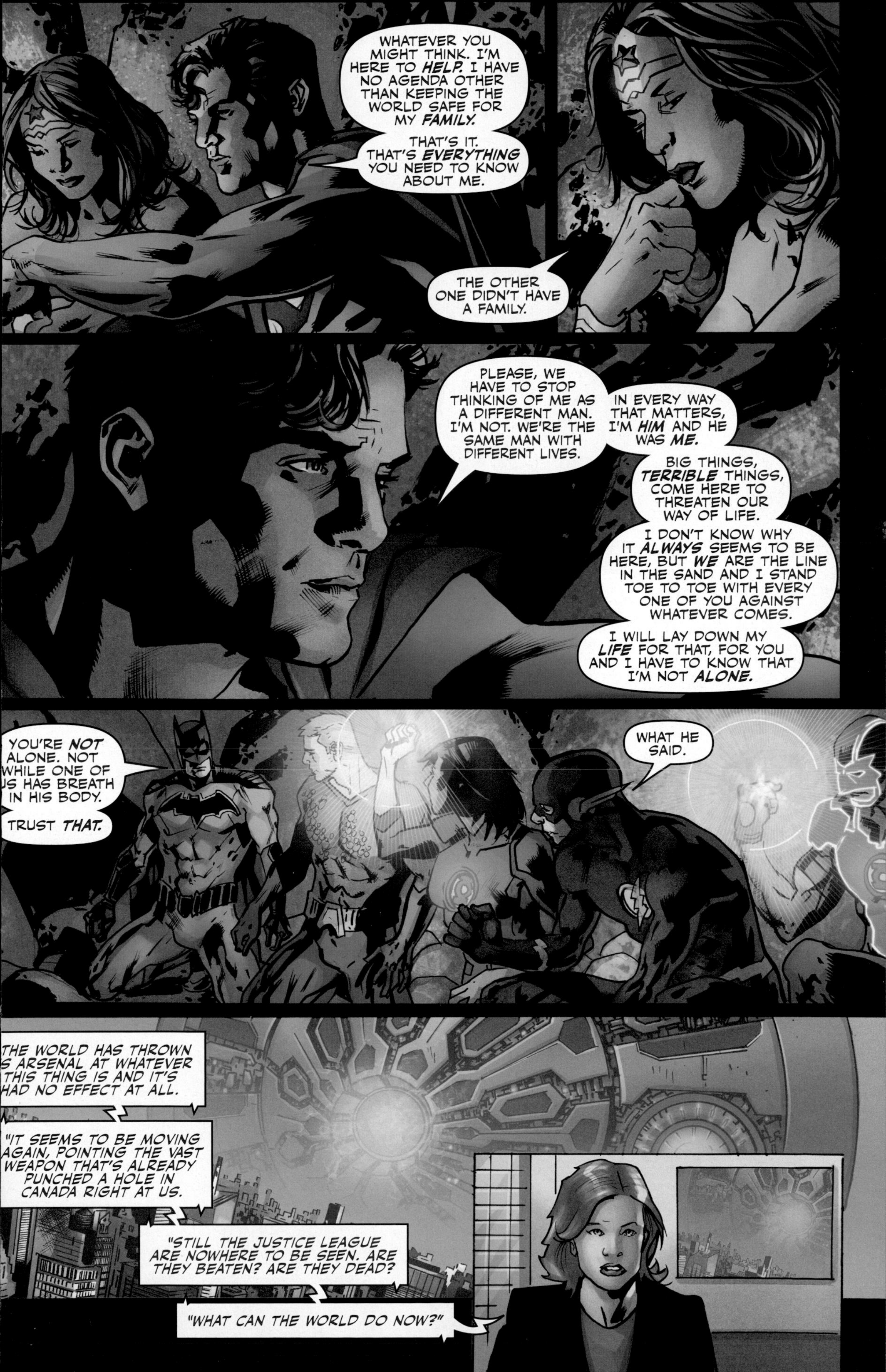
WHATEVER YOU MIGHT THINK. I'M HERE TO HELP. I HAVE NO AGENDA OTHER THAN KEEPING THE WORLD SAFE FOR MY FAMILY.
THAT'S IT. THAT'S EVERYTHING YOU NEED TO KNOW ABOUT ME.
THE OTHER ONE DIDN'T HAVE A FAMILY.
PLEASE, WE HAVE TO STOP THINKING OF ME AS A DIFFERENT MAN. I'M NOT. WE'RE THE SAME MAN WITH DIFFERENT LIVES.
IN EVERY WAY THAT MATTERS, I'M HIM AND HE WAS ME.
BIG THINGS, TERRIBLE THINGS, COME HERE TO THREATEN OUR WAY OF LIFE.
I DON'T KNOW WHY IT ALWAYS SEEMS TO BE HERE, BUT WE ARE THE LINE IN THE SAND AND I STAND TOE TO TOE WITH EVERY ONE OF YOU AGAINST WHATEVER COMES.
I WILL LAY DOWN MY LIFE FOR THAT, FOR YOU AND I HAVE TO KNOW THAT I'M NOT ALONE.
YOU'RE NOT ALONE. NOT WHILE ONE OF US HAS BREATH IN HIS BODY.
TRUST THAT.
WHAT HE SAID.
THE WORLD HAS THROWN ITS ARSENAL AT WHATEVER THIS THING IS AND IT'S HAD NO EFFECT AT ALL.
"IT SEEMS TO BE MOVING AGAIN, POINTING THE VAST WEAPON THAT'S ALREADY PUNCHED A HOLE IN CANADA RIGHT AT US.
"STILL THE JUSTICE LEAGUE ARE NOWHERE TO BE SEEN. ARE THEY BEATEN? ARE THEY DEAD?
"WHAT CAN THE WORLD DO NOW?"

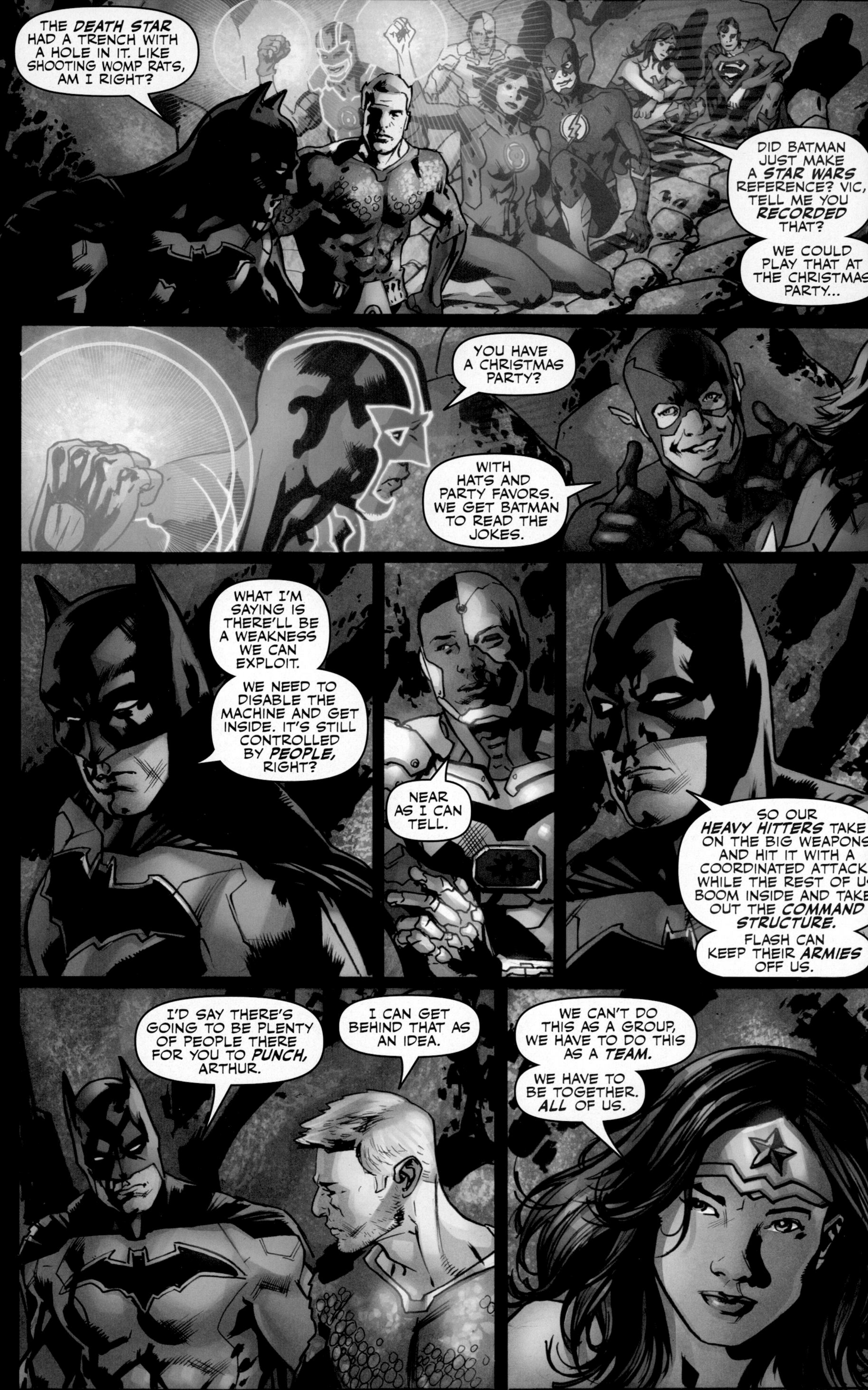
THE DEATH STAR HAD A TRENCH WITH A HOLE IN IT. LIKE SHOOTING WOMP RATS, AM I RIGHT?
DID BATMAN JUST MAKE A STAR WARS REFERENCE? VIC, TELL ME YOU RECORDED THAT?
WE COULD PLAY THAT AT THE CHRISTMAS PARTY...
YOU HAVE A CHRISTMAS PARTY?
WITH HATS AND PARTY FAVORS. WE GET BATMAN TO READ THE JOKES.
WHAT I'M SAYING IS THERE'LL BE A WEAKNESS WE CAN EXPLOIT.
WE NEED TO DISABLE THE MACHINE AND GET INSIDE. IT'S STILL CONTROLLED BY PEOPLE, RIGHT?
NEAR AS I CAN TELL.
SO OUR HEAVY HITTERS TAKE ON THE BIG WEAPONS AND HIT IT WITH A COORDINATED ATTACK WHILE THE REST OF US BOOM INSIDE AND TAKE OUT THE COMMAND STRUCTURE.
FLASH CAN KEEP THEIR ARMIES OFF US.
I'D SAY THERE'S GOING TO BE PLENTY OF PEOPLE THERE FOR YOU TO PUNCH, ARTHUR.
I CAN GET BEHIND THAT AS AN IDEA.
WE CAN'T DO THIS AS A GROUP, WE HAVE TO DO THIS AS A TEAM.
WE HAVE TO BE TOGETHER. ALL OF US.

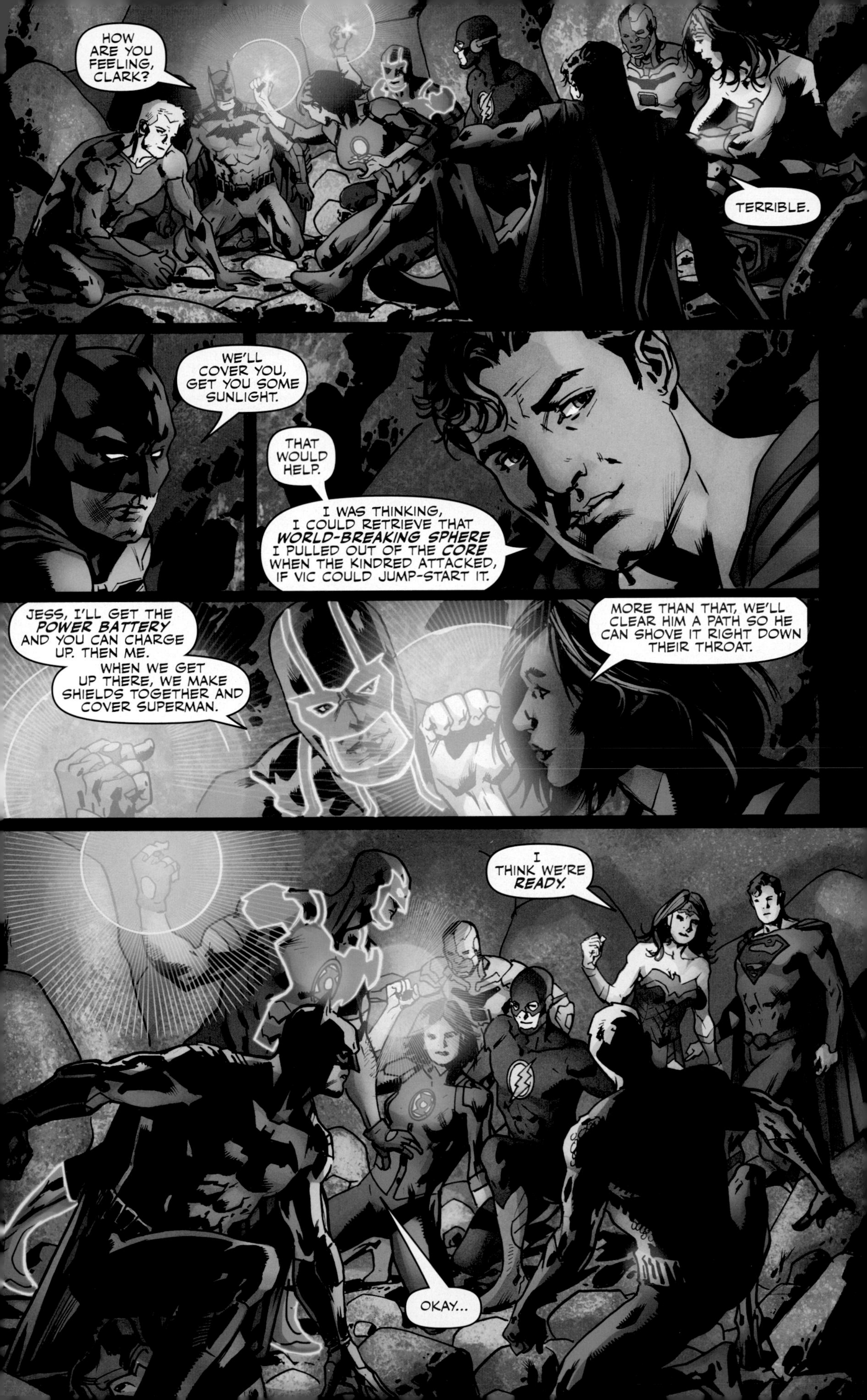
HOW ARE YOU FEELING, CLARK?
TERRIBLE.
WE'LL COVER YOU, GET YOU SOME SUNLIGHT.
THAT WOULD HELP.
I WAS THINKING, I COULD RETRIEVE THAT WORLD-BREAKING SPHERE I PULLED OUT OF THE CORE WHEN THE KINDRED ATTACKED, IF VIC COULD JUMP-START IT.
JESS, I'LL GET THE POWER BATTERY AND YOU CAN CHARGE UP. THEN ME.
WHEN WE GET UP THERE, WE MAKE SHIELDS TOGETHER AND COVER SUPERMAN.
MORE THAN THAT, WE'LL CLEAR HIM A PATH SO HE CAN SHOVE IT RIGHT DOWN THEIR THROAT.
I THINK WE'RE READY.
OKAY...

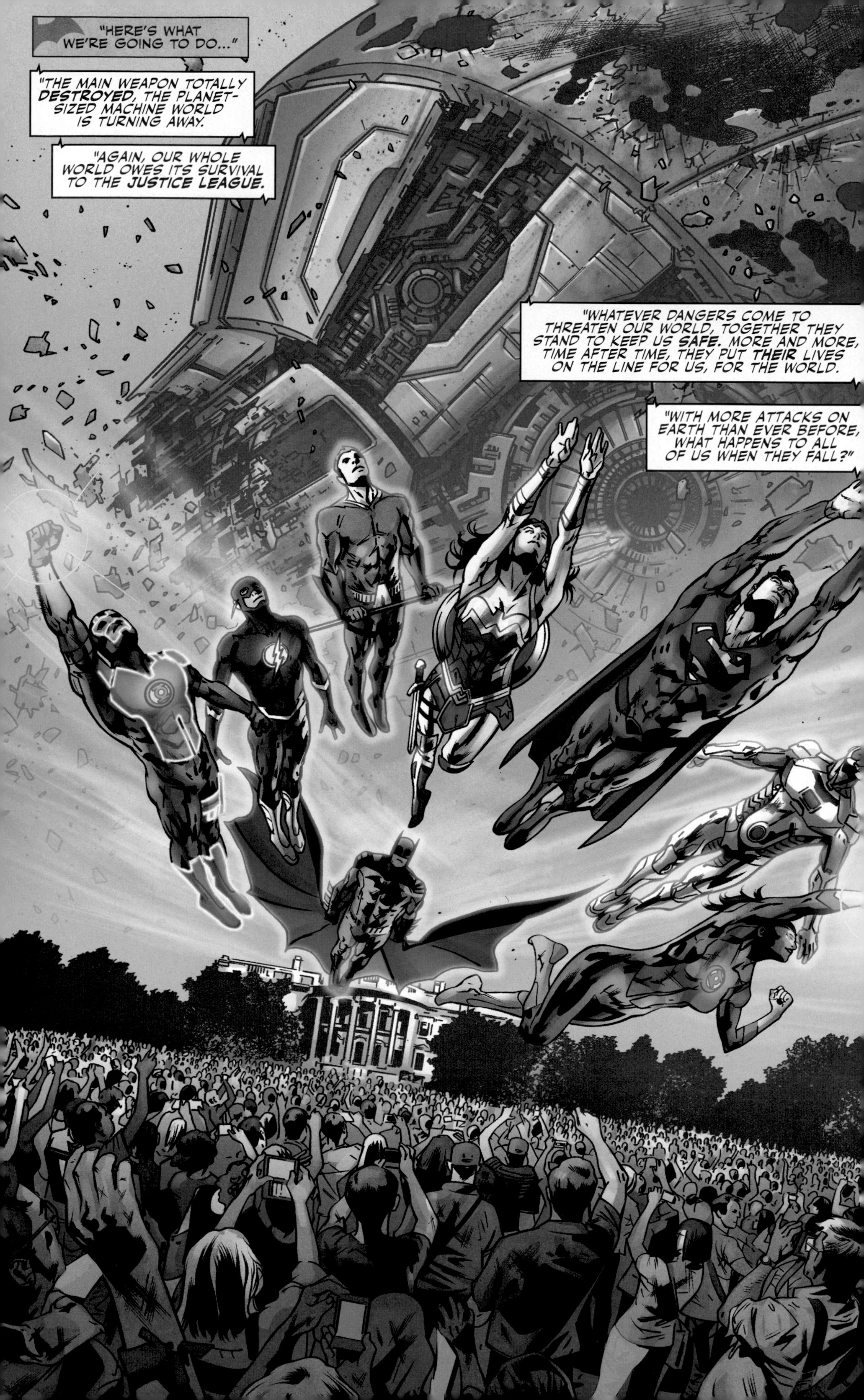
"HERE'S WHAT WE'RE GOING TO DO..."
"THE MAIN WEAPON TOTALLY DESTROYED, THE PLANET-SIZED MACHINE WORLD IS TURNING AWAY.
"AGAIN, OUR WHOLE WORLD OWES ITS SURVIVAL TO THE JUSTICE LEAGUE.
"WHATEVER DANGERS COME TO THREATEN OUR WORLD, TOGETHER THEY STAND TO KEEP US SAFE. MORE AND MORE, TIME AFTER TIME, THEY PUT THEIR LIVES ON THE LINE FOR US, FOR THE WORLD.
"WITH MORE ATTACKS ON EARTH THAN EVER BEFORE, WHAT HAPPENS TO ALL OF US WHEN THEY FALL?"

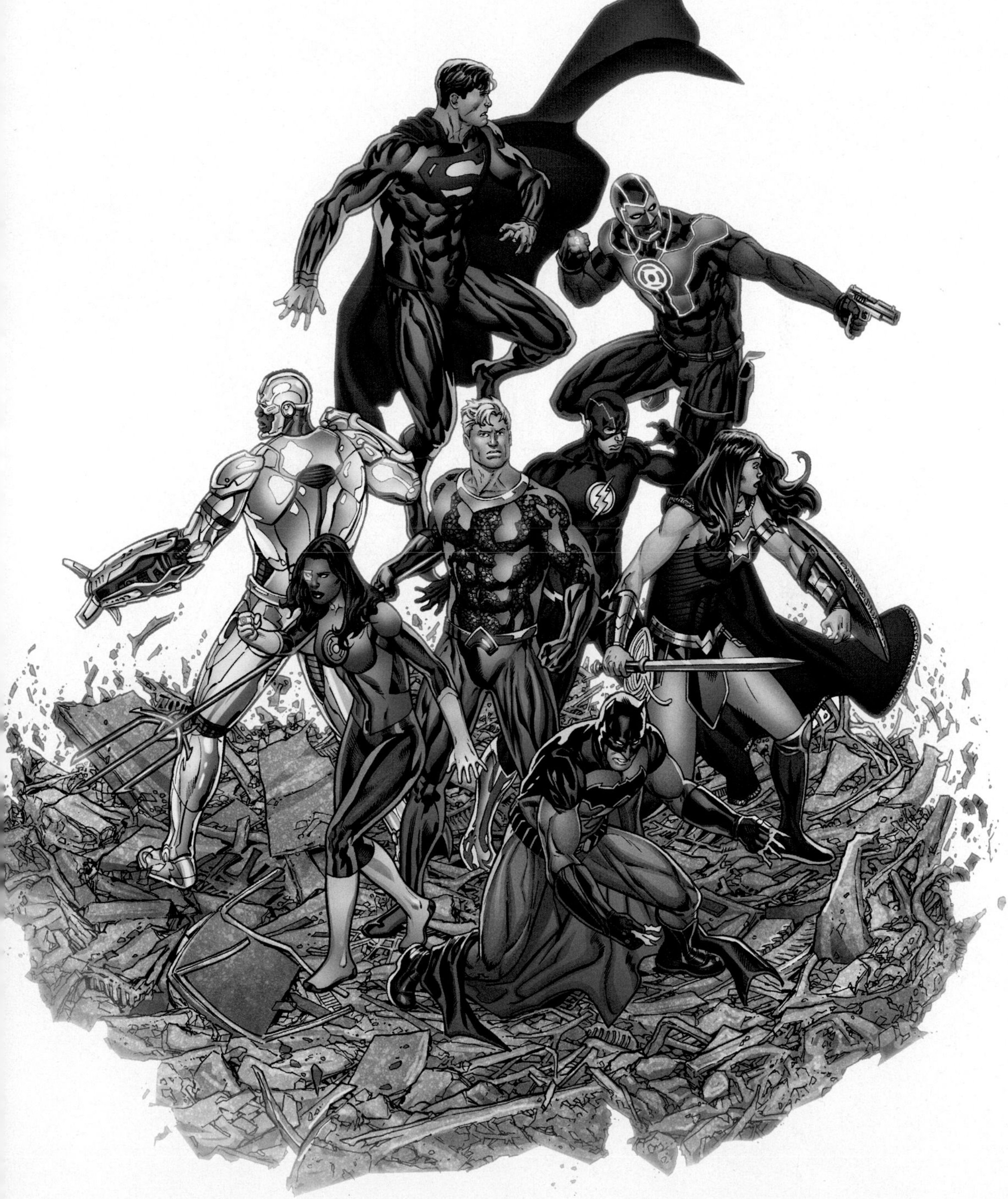

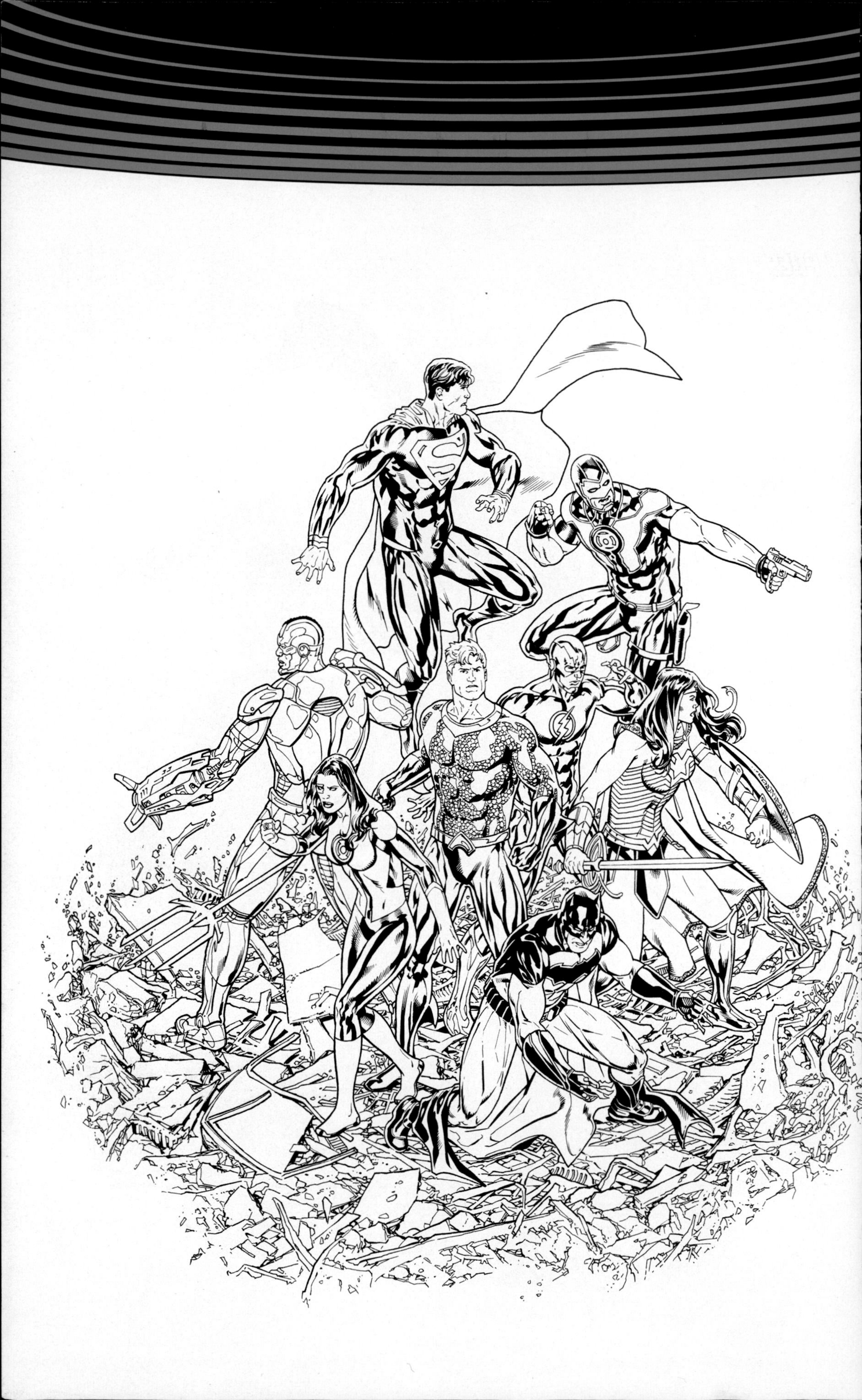

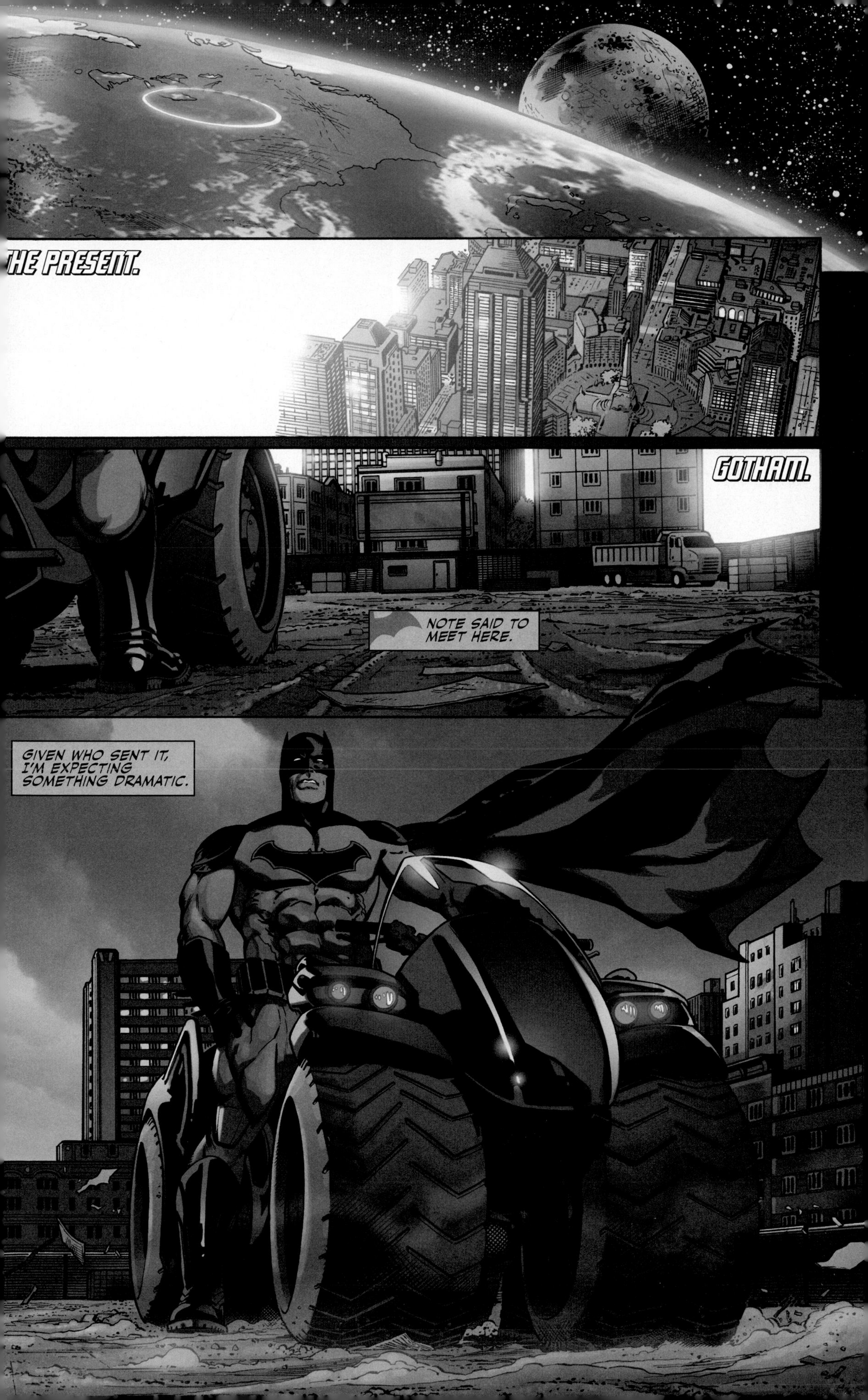
THE PRESENT.
GOTHAM.
NOTE SAID TO MEET HERE.
GIVEN WHO SENT IT, I'M EXPECTING SOMETHING DRAMATIC.

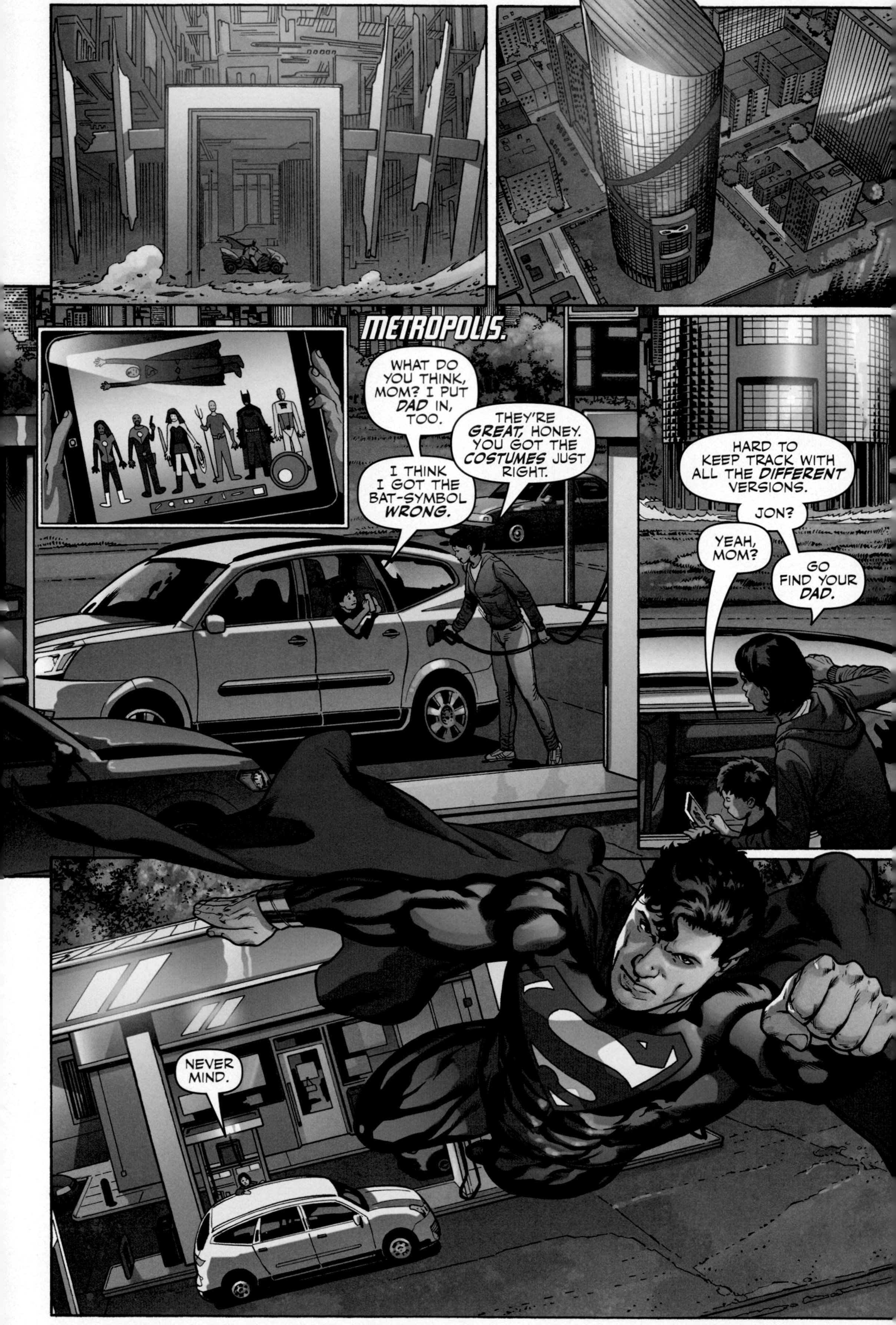
METROPOLIS.
WHAT DO YOU THINK, MOM? I PUT DAD IN, TOO.
I THINK I GOT THE BAT-SYMBOL WRONG.
THEY'RE GREAT, HONEY. YOU GOT THE COSTUMES JUST RIGHT.
HARD TO KEEP TRACK WITH ALL THE DIFFERENT VERSIONS.
JON?
YEAH, MOM?
GO FIND YOUR DAD.
NEVER MIND.

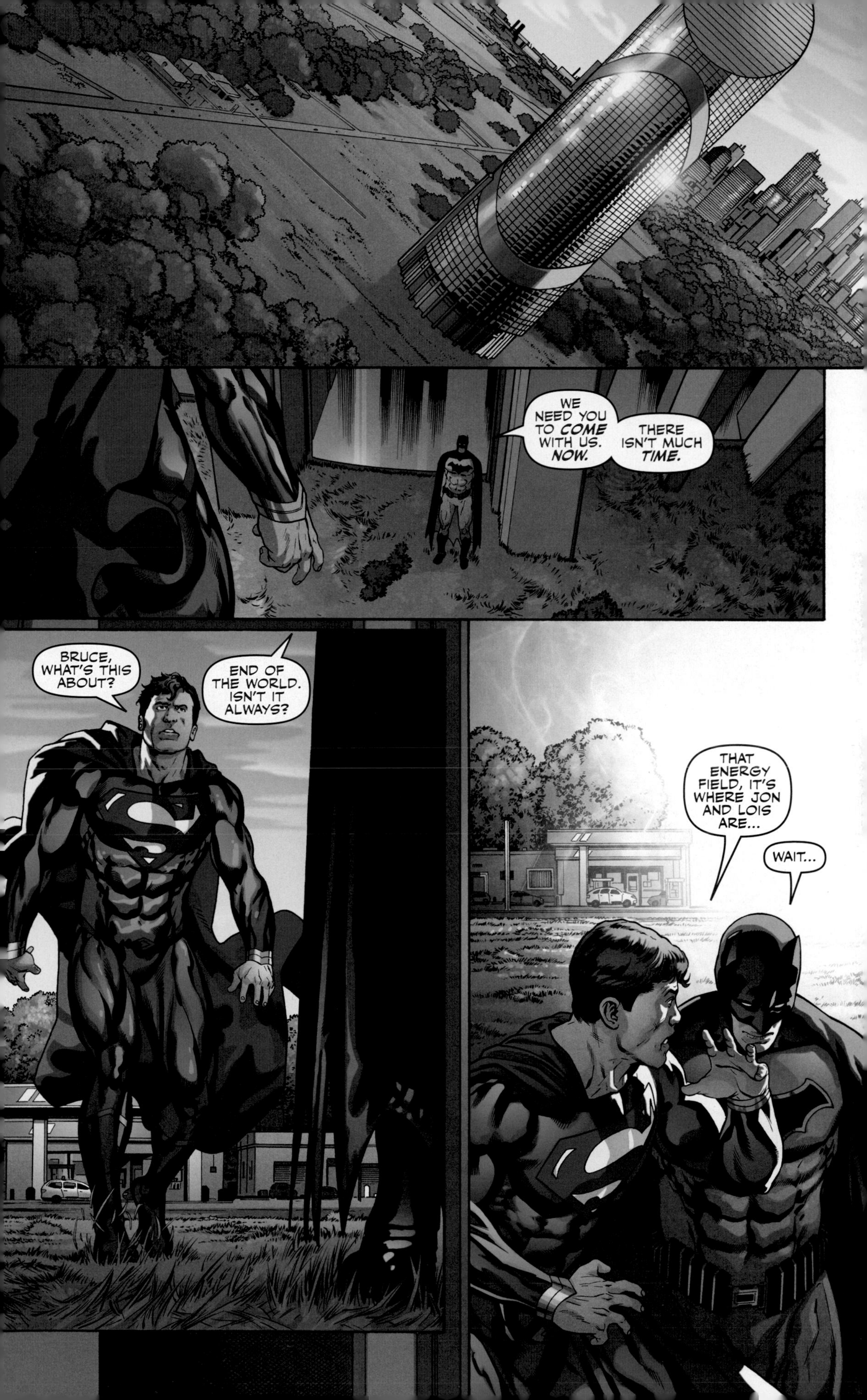
WE NEED YOU TO COME WITH US. NOW.
THERE ISN'T MUCH TIME.
BRUCE, WHAT'S THIS ABOUT?
END OF THE WORLD. ISN'T IT ALWAYS?
THAT ENERGY FIELD, IT'S WHERE JON AND LOIS ARE...
WAIT...

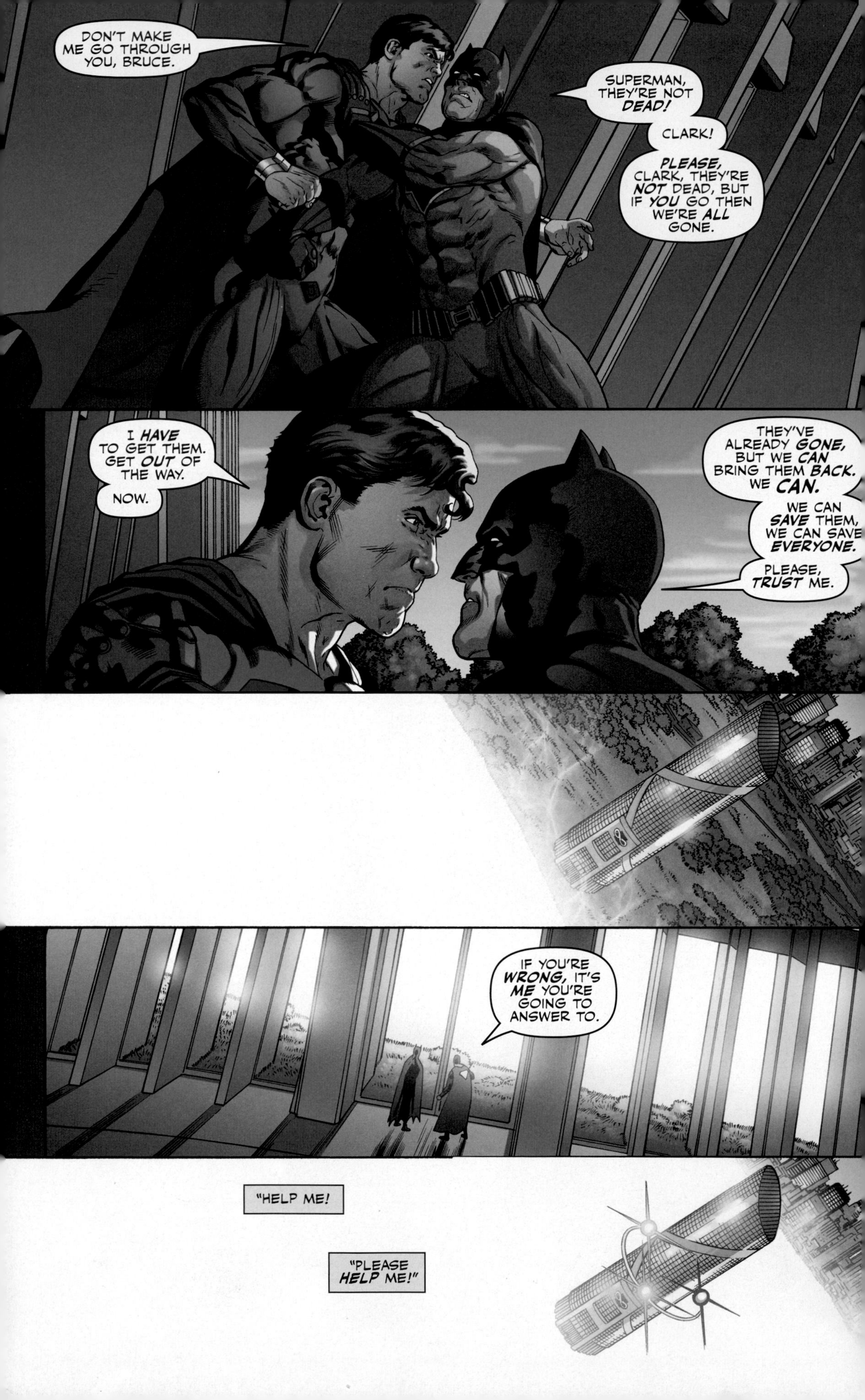
DON'T MAKE ME GO THROUGH YOU, BRUCE.
SUPERMAN, THEY'RE NOT DEAD!
CLARK!
PLEASE, CLARK, THEY'RE NOT DEAD, BUT IF YOU GO THEN WE'RE ALL GONE.
I HAVE TO GET THEM. GET OUT OF THE WAY.
NOW.
THEY'VE ALREADY GONE, BUT WE CAN BRING THEM BACK. WE CAN.
WE CAN SAVE THEM, WE CAN SAVE EVERYONE.
PLEASE, TRUST ME.
IF YOU'RE WRONG, IT'S ME YOU'RE GOING TO ANSWER TO.
"HELP ME!
"PLEASE HELP ME!"

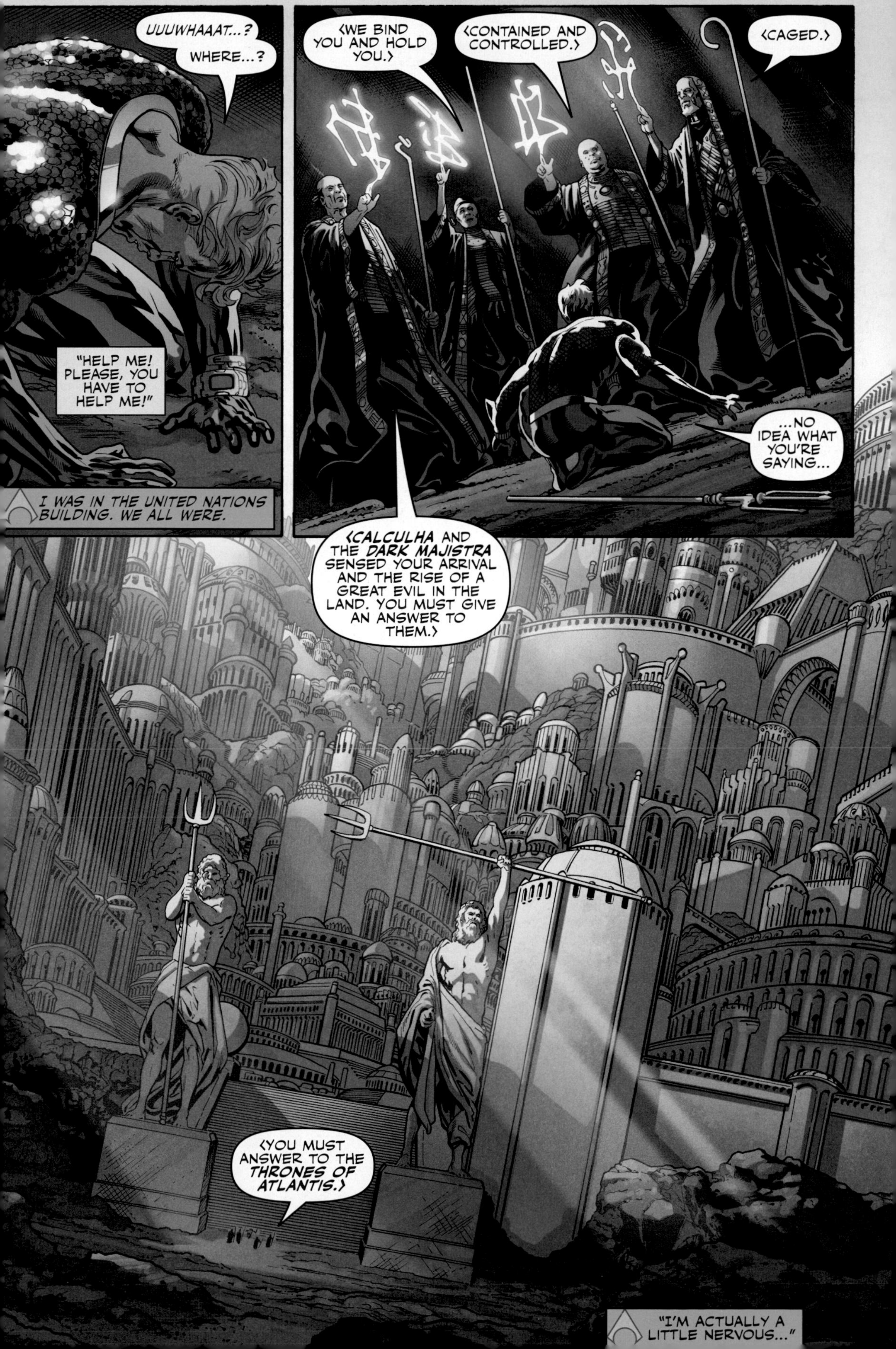
UUUWHAAAT...?
WHERE...?
"HELP ME! PLEASE, YOU HAVE TO HELP ME!"
I WAS IN THE UNITED NATIONS BUILDING. WE ALL WERE.
‹WE BIND YOU AND HOLD YOU.›
‹CONTAINED AND CONTROLLED.›
‹CAGED.›
...NO IDEA WHAT YOU'RE SAYING...
‹CALCULHA AND THE DARK MAJISTRA SENSED YOUR ARRIVAL AND THE RISE OF A GREAT EVIL IN THE LAND. YOU MUST GIVE AN ANSWER TO THEM.›
‹YOU MUST ANSWER TO THE THRONES OF ATLANTIS.›
"I'M ACTUALLY A LITTLE NERVOUS..."

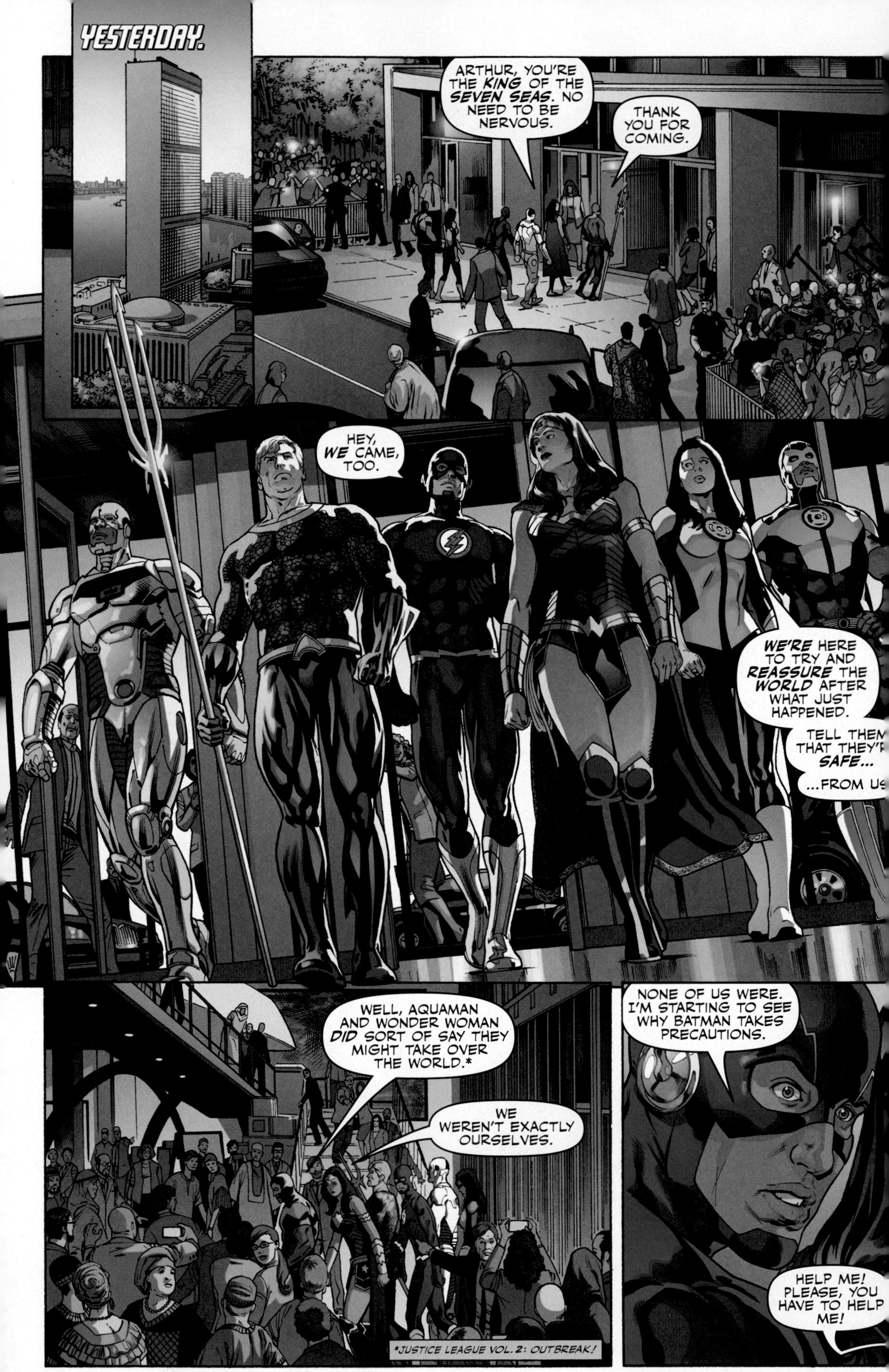
YESTERDAY.
ARTHUR, YOU'RE THE KING OF THE SEVEN SEAS. NO NEED TO BE NERVOUS.
THANK YOU FOR COMING.
HEY, WE CAME, TOO.
WE'RE HERE TO TRY AND REASSURE THE WORLD AFTER WHAT JUST HAPPENED.
TELL THEM THAT THEY'R SAFE...
...FROM US
WELL, AQUAMAN AND WONDER WOMAN DID SORT OF SAY THEY MIGHT TAKE OVER THE WORLD.*
WE WEREN'T EXACTLY OURSELVES.
*JUSTICE LEAGUE VOL. 2: OUTBREAK!
NONE OF US WERE. I'M STARTING TO SEE WHY BATMAN TAKES PRECAUTIONS.
HELP ME! PLEASE, YOU HAVE TO HELP ME!

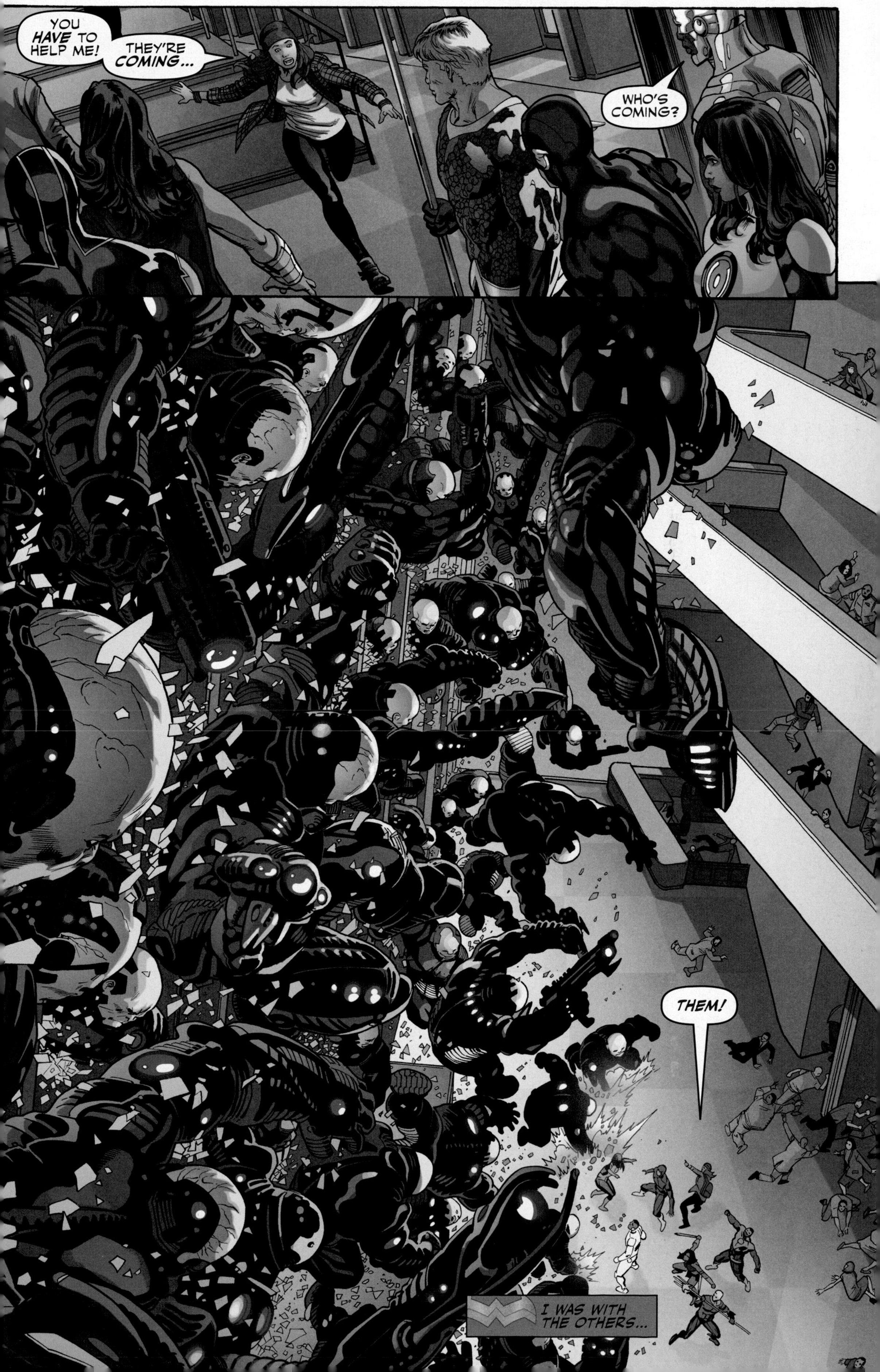
YOU *HAVE* TO HELP ME!
THEY'RE *COMING*...
WHO'S COMING?
THEM!
I WAS WITH THE OTHERS...

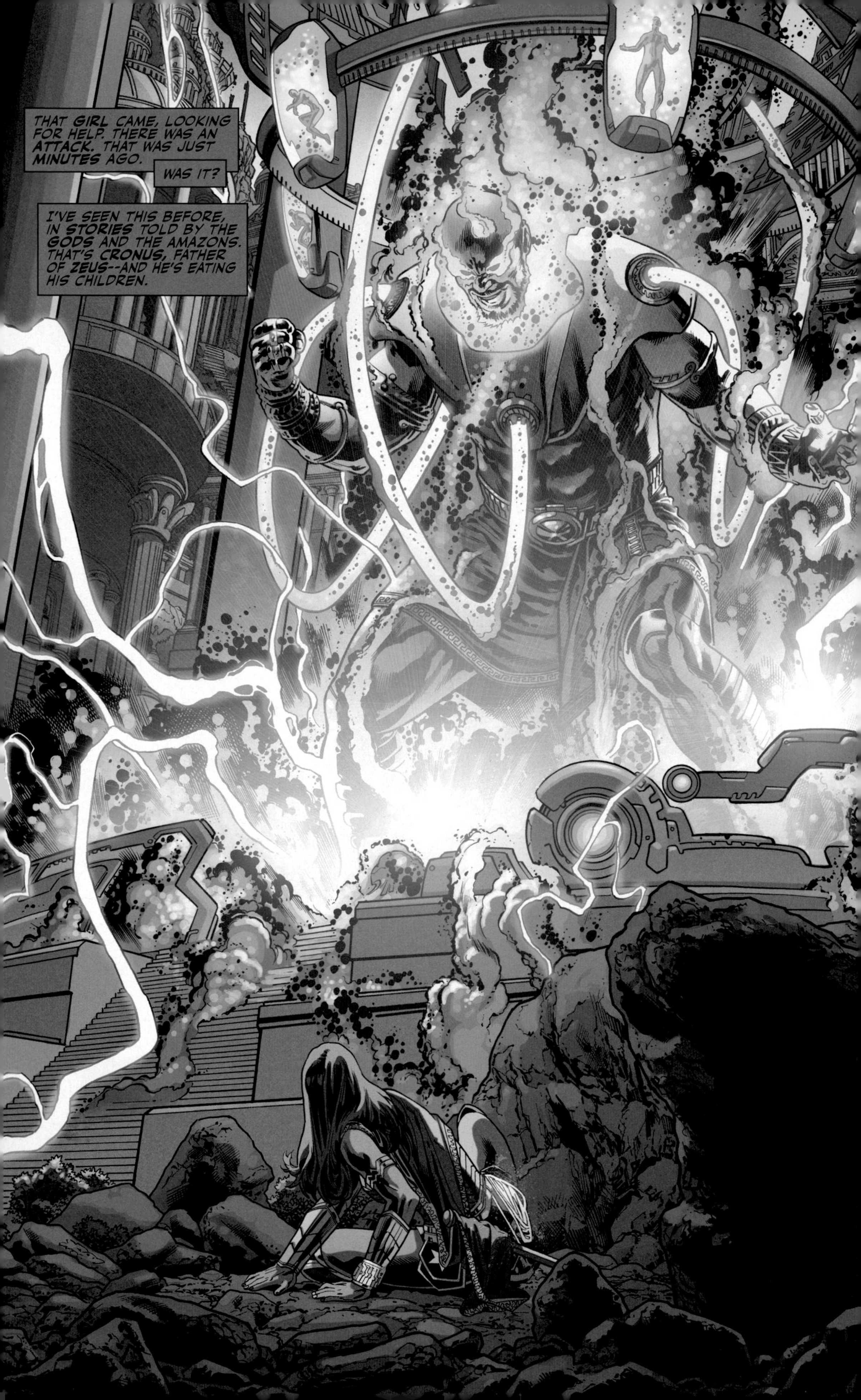
THAT GIRL CAME, LOOKING FOR HELP. THERE WAS AN ATTACK. THAT WAS JUST MINUTES AGO.
WAS IT?
I'VE SEEN THIS BEFORE, IN STORIES TOLD BY THE GODS AND THE AMAZONS. THAT'S CRONUS, FATHER OF ZEUS--AND HE'S EATING HIS CHILDREN.

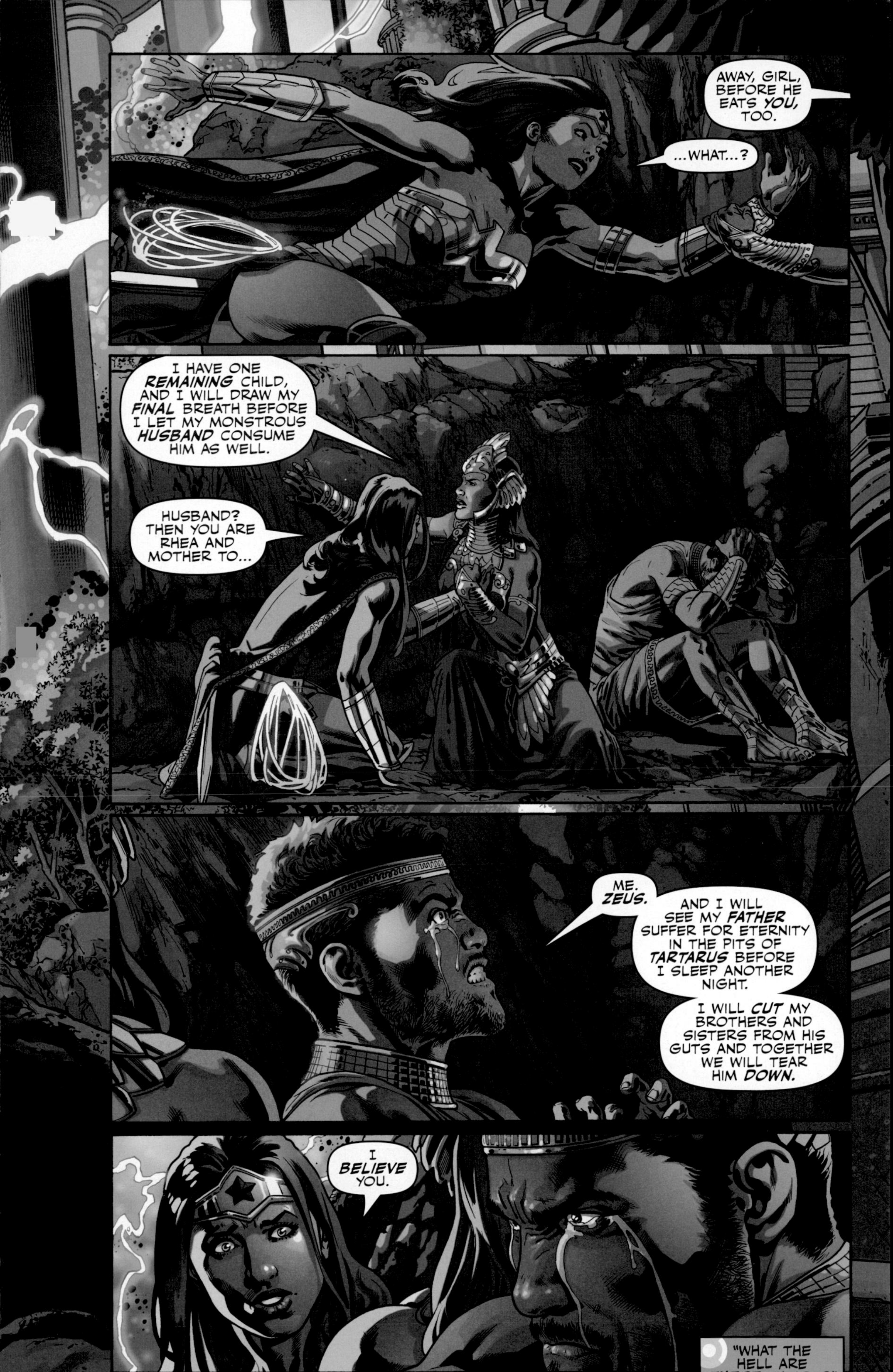
AWAY, GIRL, BEFORE HE EATS YOU, TOO.
...WHAT...?
I HAVE ONE REMAINING CHILD, AND I WILL DRAW MY FINAL BREATH BEFORE I LET MY MONSTROUS HUSBAND CONSUME HIM AS WELL.
HUSBAND? THEN YOU ARE RHEA AND MOTHER TO...
ME. ZEUS.
AND I WILL SEE MY FATHER SUFFER FOR ETERNITY IN THE PITS OF TARTARUS BEFORE I SLEEP ANOTHER NIGHT.
I WILL CUT MY BROTHERS AND SISTERS FROM HIS GUTS AND TOGETHER WE WILL TEAR HIM DOWN.
I BELIEVE YOU.
"WHAT THE HELL ARE

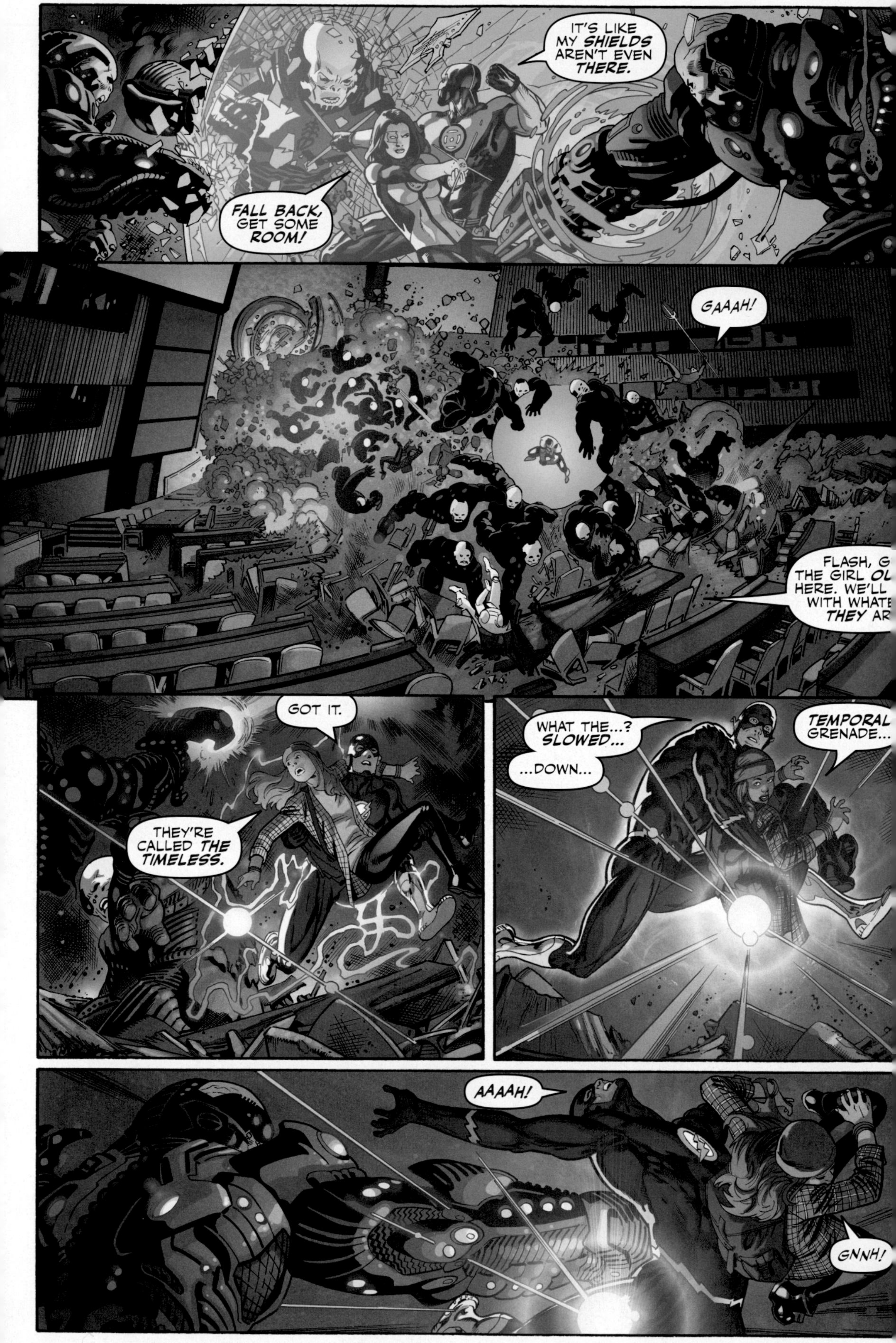
IT'S LIKE MY *SHIELDS* AREN'T EVEN *THERE.*
FALL BACK, GET SOME *ROOM!*
GAAAH!
FLASH, G THE GIRL *OU* HERE. WE'LL WITH WHATE *THEY* AR
GOT IT.
THEY'RE CALLED *THE TIMELESS.*
WHAT THE...? *SLOWED...*
...DOWN...
TEMPORAL GRENADE...
AAAAH!
GNNH!

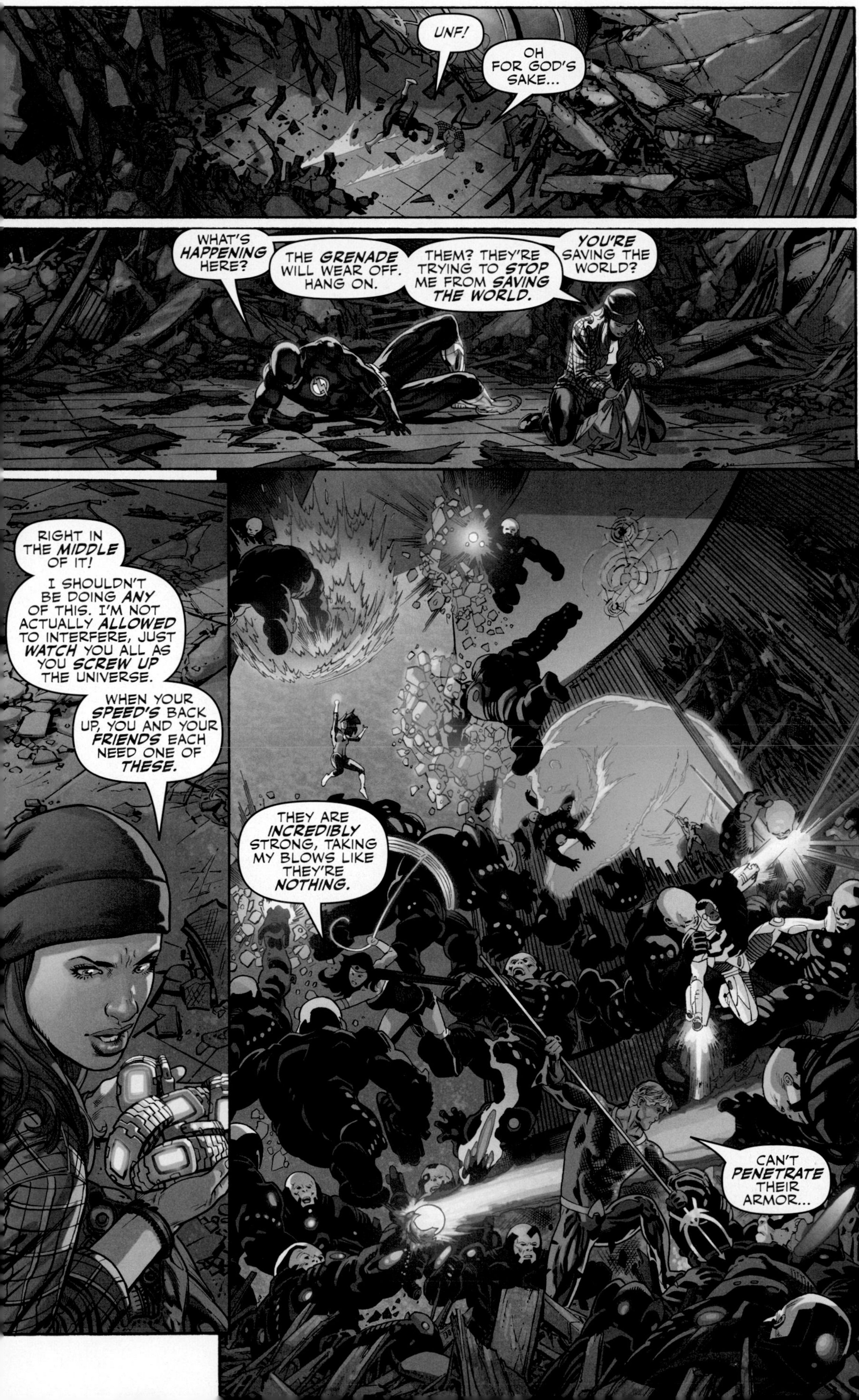
UNF!
OH FOR GOD'S SAKE...
WHAT'S HAPPENING HERE?
THE GRENADE WILL WEAR OFF. HANG ON.
THEM? THEY'RE TRYING TO STOP ME FROM SAVING THE WORLD.
YOU'RE SAVING THE WORLD?
RIGHT IN THE MIDDLE OF IT!
I SHOULDN'T BE DOING ANY OF THIS. I'M NOT ACTUALLY ALLOWED TO INTERFERE, JUST WATCH YOU ALL AS YOU SCREW UP THE UNIVERSE.
WHEN YOUR SPEED'S BACK UP, YOU AND YOUR FRIENDS EACH NEED ONE OF THESE.
THEY ARE INCREDIBLY STRONG, TAKING MY BLOWS LIKE THEY'RE NOTHING.
CAN'T PENETRATE THEIR ARMOR...

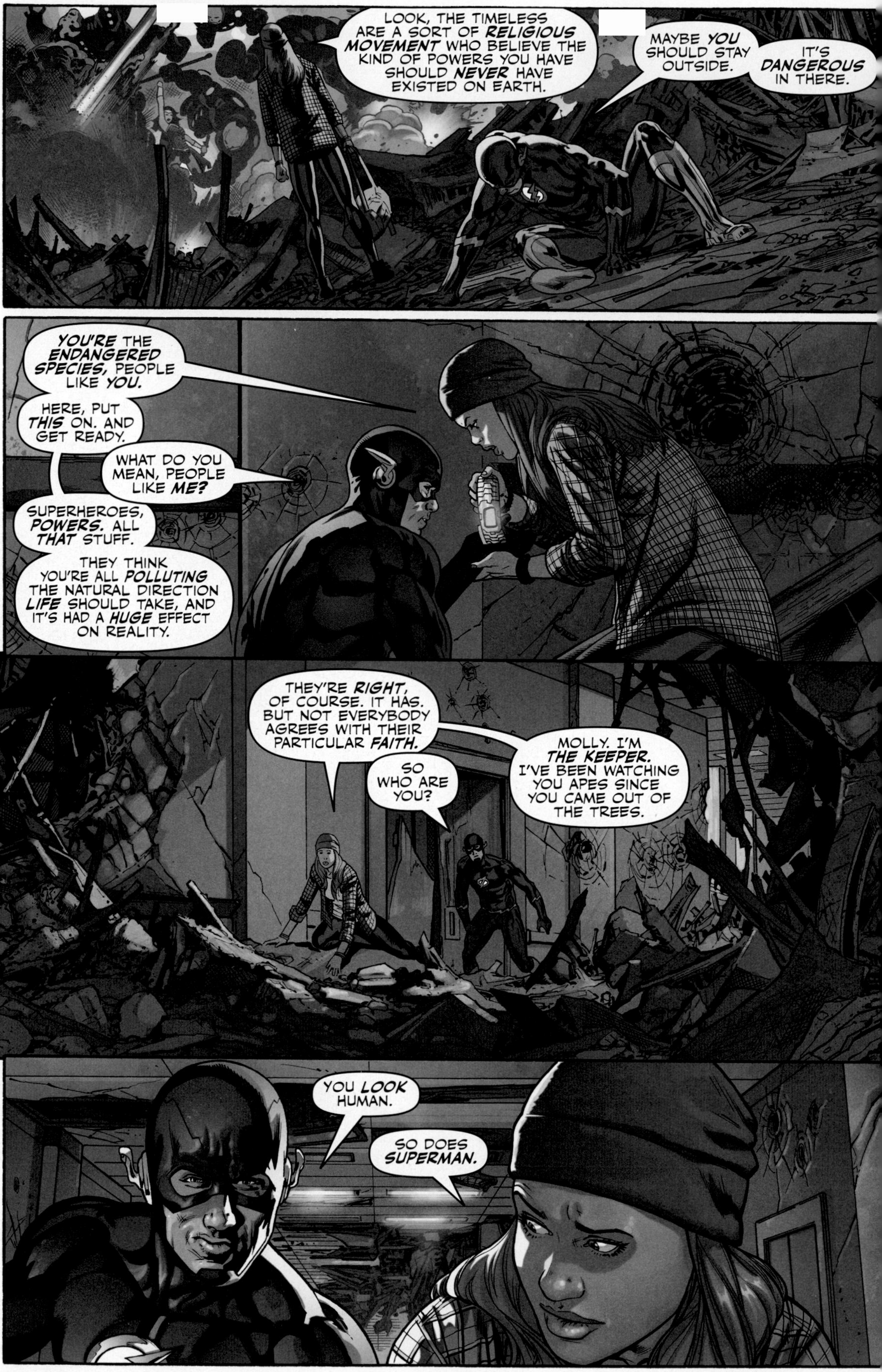
LOOK, THE TIMELESS ARE A SORT OF RELIGIOUS MOVEMENT WHO BELIEVE THE KIND OF POWERS YOU HAVE SHOULD NEVER HAVE EXISTED ON EARTH.
MAYBE YOU SHOULD STAY OUTSIDE.
IT'S DANGEROUS IN THERE.
YOU'RE THE ENDANGERED SPECIES, PEOPLE LIKE YOU.
HERE, PUT THIS ON. AND GET READY.
WHAT DO YOU MEAN, PEOPLE LIKE ME?
SUPERHEROES, POWERS. ALL THAT STUFF.
THEY THINK YOU'RE ALL POLLUTING THE NATURAL DIRECTION LIFE SHOULD TAKE, AND IT'S HAD A HUGE EFFECT ON REALITY.
THEY'RE RIGHT, OF COURSE. IT HAS. BUT NOT EVERYBODY AGREES WITH THEIR PARTICULAR FAITH.
SO WHO ARE YOU?
MOLLY. I'M THE KEEPER. I'VE BEEN WATCHING YOU APES SINCE YOU CAME OUT OF THE TREES.
YOU LOOK HUMAN.
SO DOES SUPERMAN.

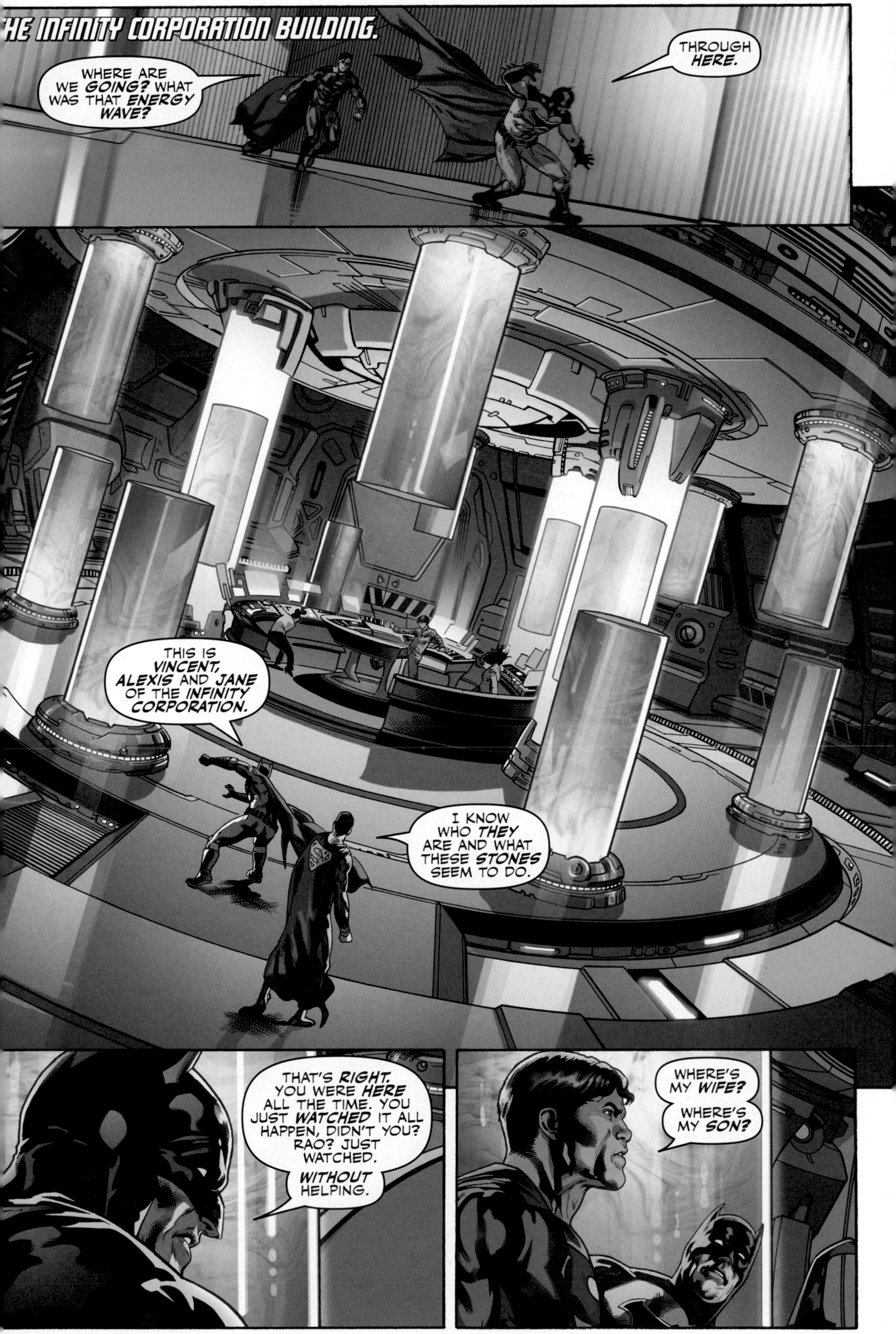
THE INFINITY CORPORATION BUILDING.
WHERE ARE WE GOING? WHAT WAS THAT ENERGY WAVE?
THROUGH HERE.
THIS IS VINCENT, ALEXIS AND JANE OF THE INFINITY CORPORATION.
I KNOW WHO THEY ARE AND WHAT THESE STONES SEEM TO DO.
THAT'S RIGHT. YOU WERE HERE ALL THE TIME. YOU JUST WATCHED IT ALL HAPPEN, DIDN'T YOU? RAO? JUST WATCHED.
WITHOUT HELPING.
WHERE'S MY WIFE?
WHERE'S MY SON?

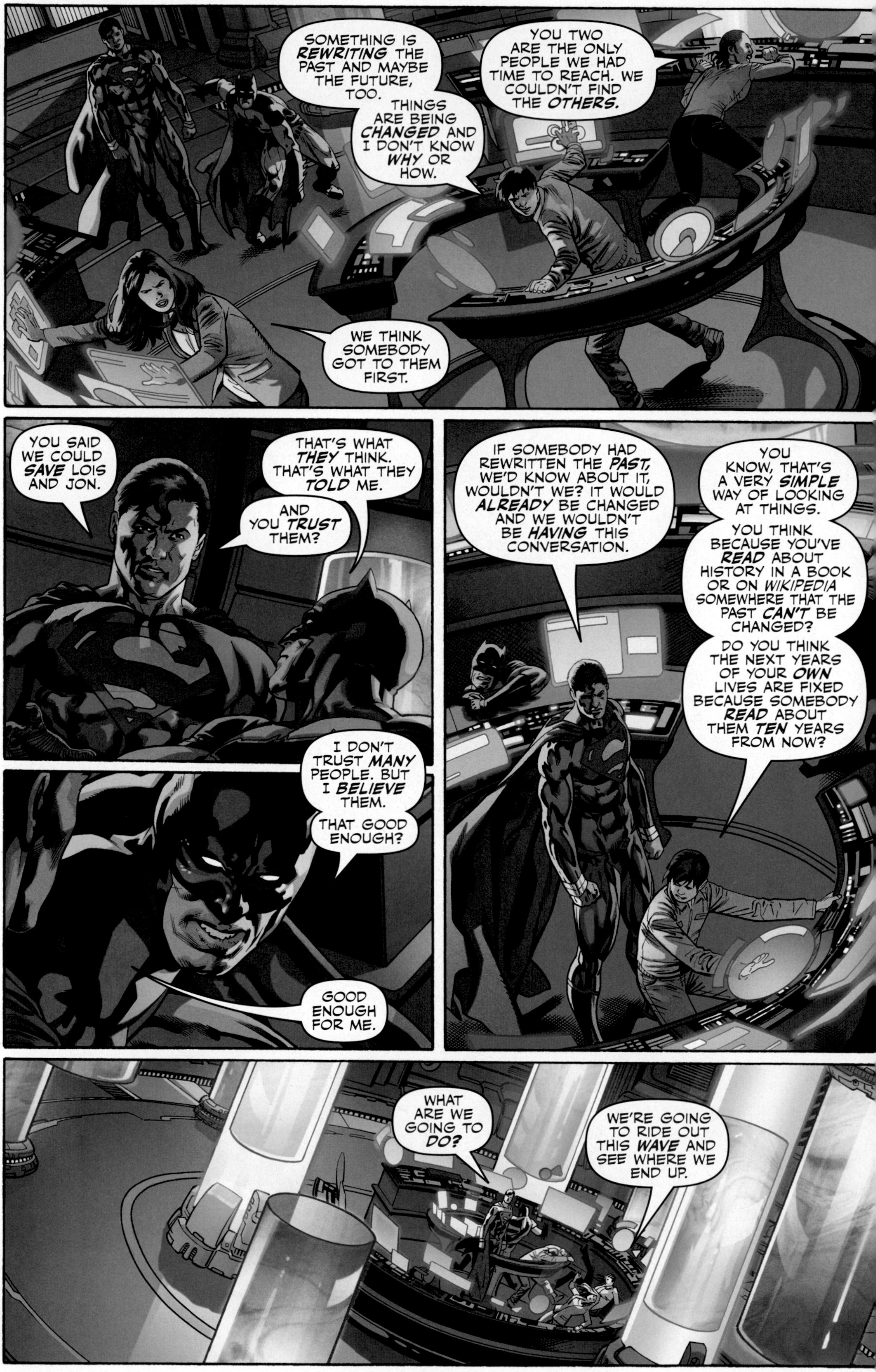
SOMETHING IS REWRITING THE PAST AND MAYBE THE FUTURE, TOO.
THINGS ARE BEING CHANGED AND I DON'T KNOW WHY OR HOW.
YOU TWO ARE THE ONLY PEOPLE WE HAD TIME TO REACH. WE COULDN'T FIND THE OTHERS.
WE THINK SOMEBODY GOT TO THEM FIRST.
YOU SAID WE COULD SAVE LOIS AND JON.
THAT'S WHAT THEY THINK. THAT'S WHAT THEY TOLD ME.
AND YOU TRUST THEM?
I DON'T TRUST MANY PEOPLE. BUT I BELIEVE THEM.
THAT GOOD ENOUGH?
GOOD ENOUGH FOR ME.
IF SOMEBODY HAD REWRITTEN THE PAST, WE'D KNOW ABOUT IT, WOULDN'T WE? IT WOULD ALREADY BE CHANGED AND WE WOULDN'T BE HAVING THIS CONVERSATION.
YOU KNOW, THAT'S A VERY SIMPLE WAY OF LOOKING AT THINGS.
YOU THINK BECAUSE YOU'VE READ ABOUT HISTORY IN A BOOK OR ON WIKIPEDIA SOMEWHERE THAT THE PAST CAN'T BE CHANGED?
DO YOU THINK THE NEXT YEARS OF YOUR OWN LIVES ARE FIXED BECAUSE SOMEBODY READ ABOUT THEM TEN YEARS FROM NOW?
WHAT ARE WE GOING TO DO?
WE'RE GOING TO RIDE OUT THIS WAVE AND SEE WHERE WE END UP.

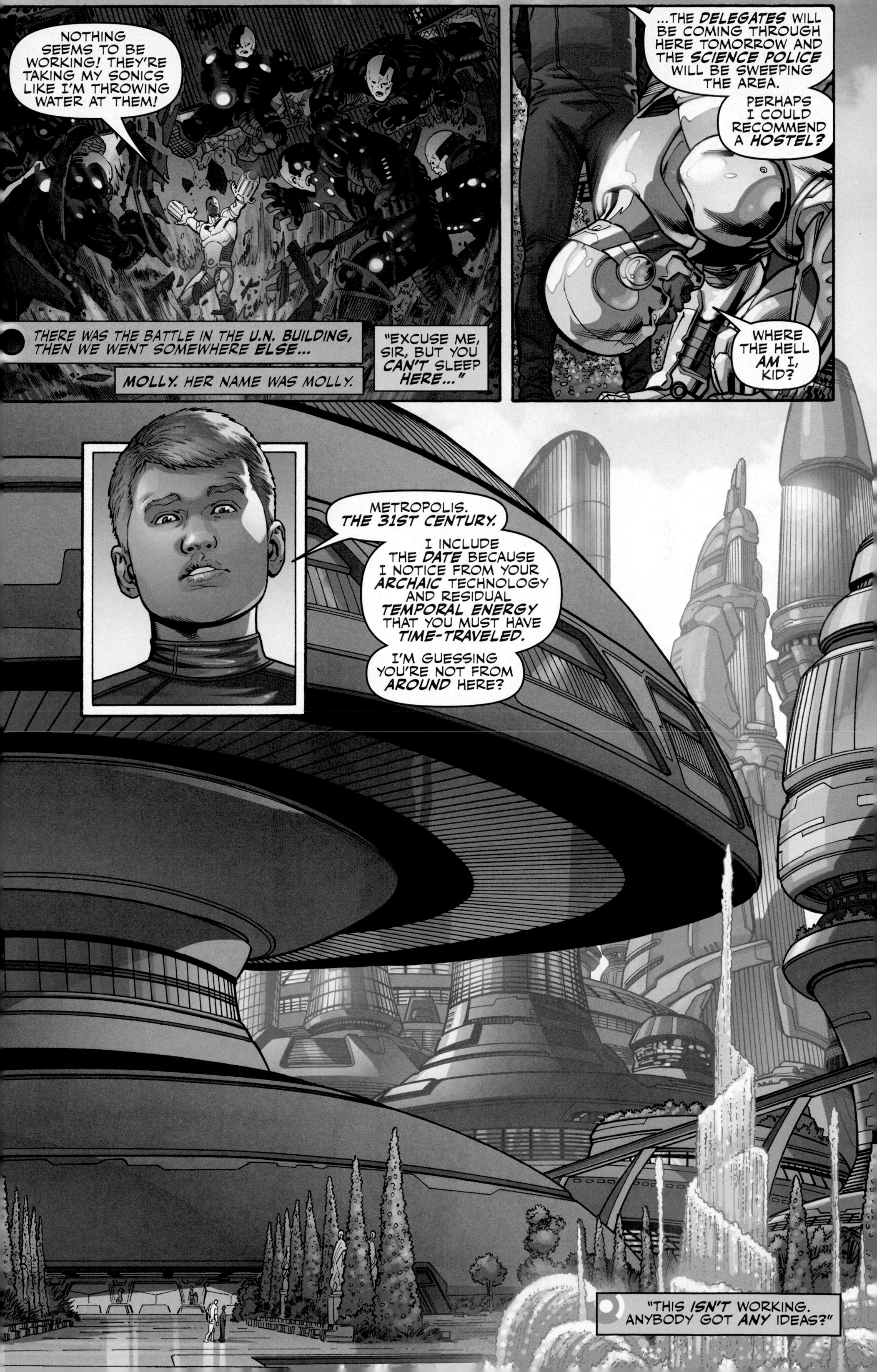
NOTHING SEEMS TO BE WORKING! THEY'RE TAKING MY SONICS LIKE I'M THROWING WATER AT THEM!
THERE WAS THE BATTLE IN THE U.N. BUILDING, THEN WE WENT SOMEWHERE ELSE...
MOLLY. HER NAME WAS MOLLY.
"EXCUSE ME, SIR, BUT YOU CAN'T SLEEP HERE..."
...THE DELEGATES WILL BE COMING THROUGH HERE TOMORROW AND THE SCIENCE POLICE WILL BE SWEEPING THE AREA.
PERHAPS I COULD RECOMMEND A HOSTEL?
WHERE THE HELL AM I, KID?
METROPOLIS. THE 31ST CENTURY.
I INCLUDE THE DATE BECAUSE I NOTICE FROM YOUR ARCHAIC TECHNOLOGY AND RESIDUAL TEMPORAL ENERGY THAT YOU MUST HAVE TIME-TRAVELED.
I'M GUESSING YOU'RE NOT FROM AROUND HERE?
"THIS ISN'T WORKING. ANYBODY GOT ANY IDEAS?"

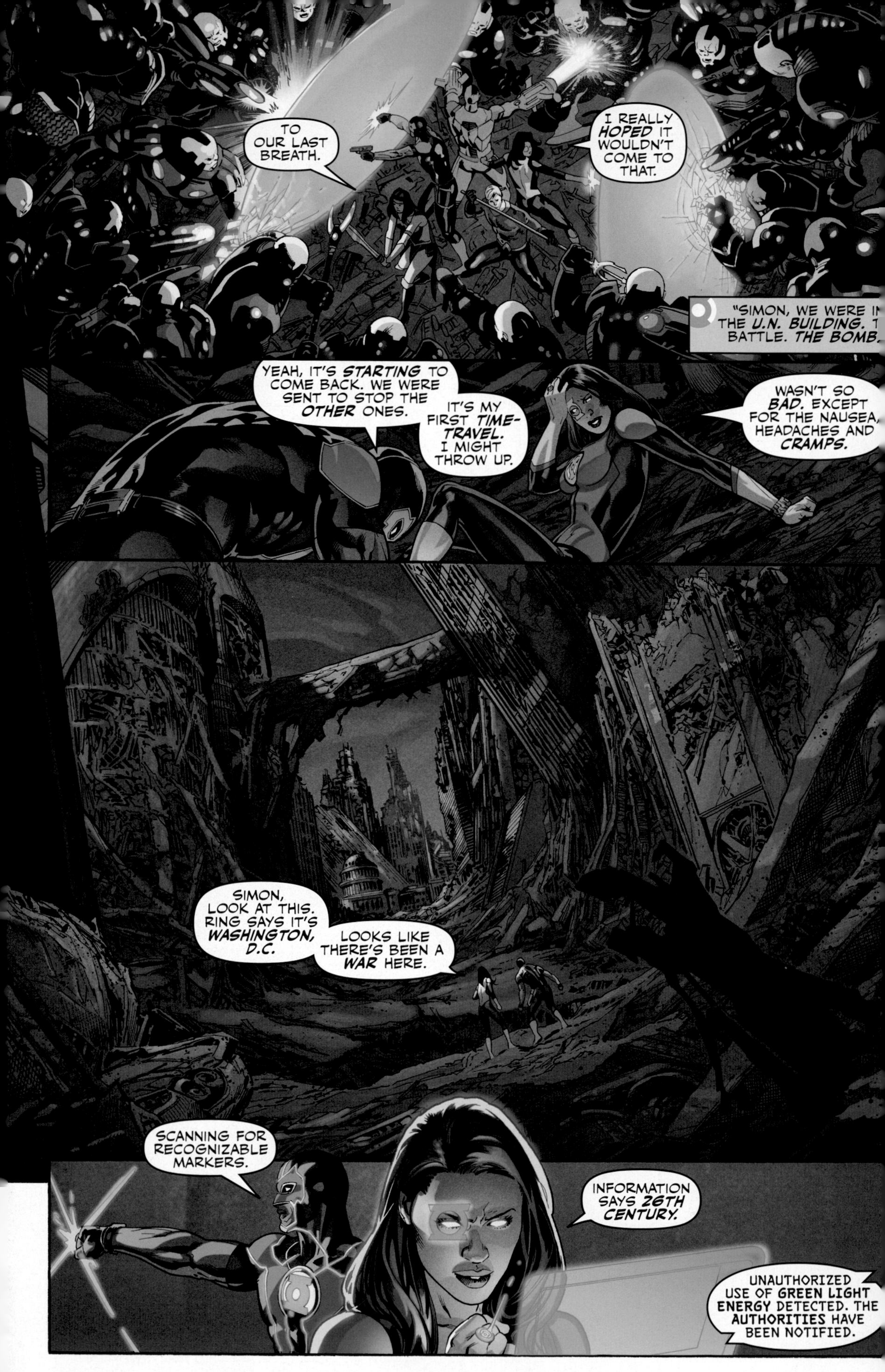
TO OUR LAST BREATH.
I REALLY HOPED IT WOULDN'T COME TO THAT.
"SIMON, WE WERE IN THE U.N. BUILDING. T BATTLE. THE BOMB.
YEAH, IT'S STARTING TO COME BACK. WE WERE SENT TO STOP THE OTHER ONES.
IT'S MY FIRST TIME-TRAVEL. I MIGHT THROW UP.
WASN'T SO BAD. EXCEPT FOR THE NAUSEA, HEADACHES AND CRAMPS.
SIMON, LOOK AT THIS. RING SAYS IT'S WASHINGTON, D.C.
LOOKS LIKE THERE'S BEEN A WAR HERE.
SCANNING FOR RECOGNIZABLE MARKERS.
INFORMATION SAYS 26TH CENTURY.
UNAUTHORIZED USE OF GREEN LIGHT ENERGY DETECTED. THE AUTHORITIES HAVE BEEN NOTIFIED.

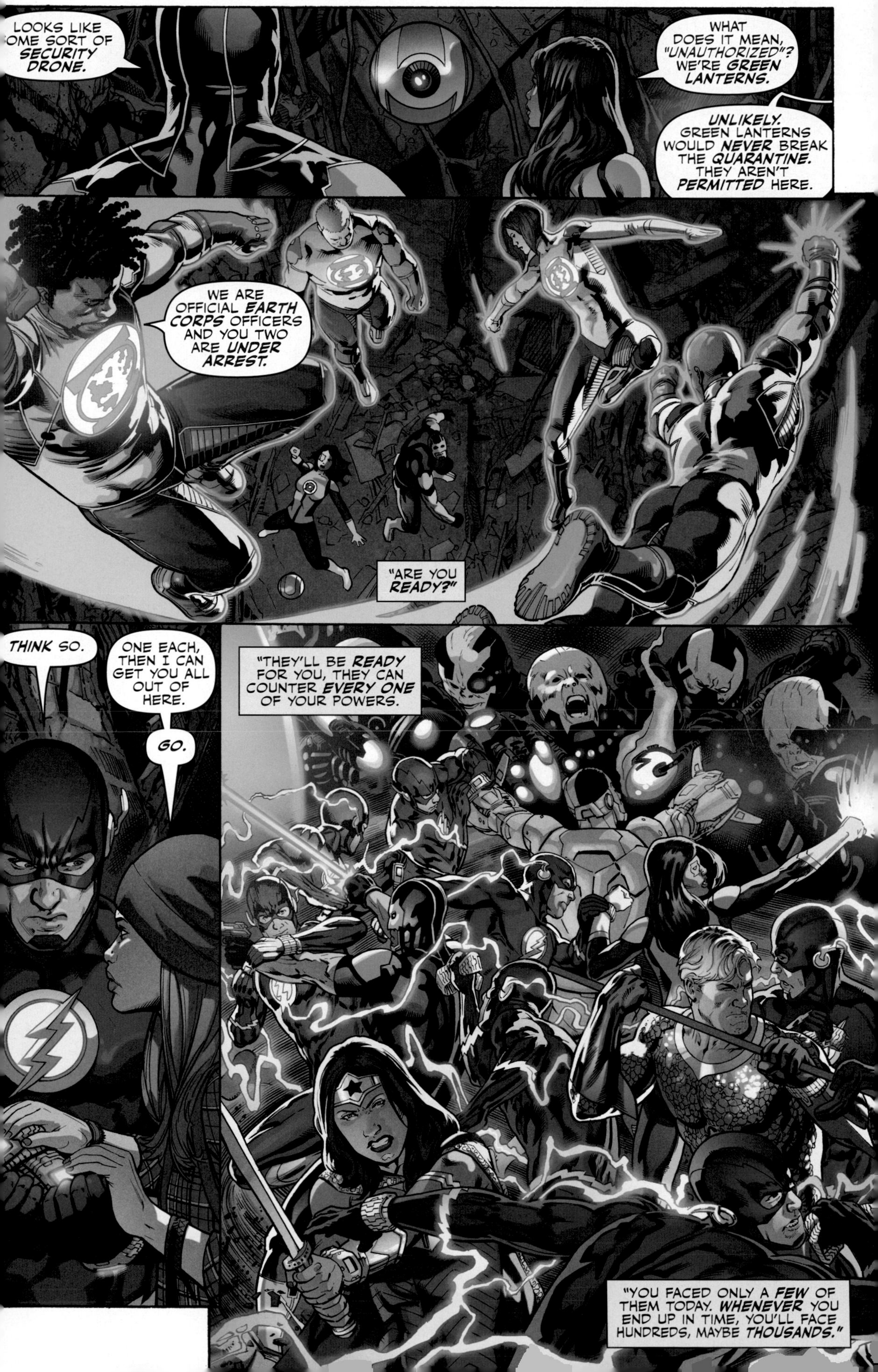
LOOKS LIKE SOME SORT OF SECURITY DRONE.
WHAT DOES IT MEAN, "UNAUTHORIZED"? WE'RE GREEN LANTERNS.
UNLIKELY. GREEN LANTERNS WOULD NEVER BREAK THE QUARANTINE. THEY AREN'T PERMITTED HERE.
WE ARE OFFICIAL EARTH CORPS OFFICERS AND YOU TWO ARE UNDER ARREST.
"ARE YOU READY?"
THINK SO.
ONE EACH, THEN I CAN GET YOU ALL OUT OF HERE.
GO.
"THEY'LL BE READY FOR YOU, THEY CAN COUNTER EVERY ONE OF YOUR POWERS.
"YOU FACED ONLY A FEW OF THEM TODAY. WHENEVER YOU END UP IN TIME, YOU'LL FACE HUNDREDS, MAYBE THOUSANDS."

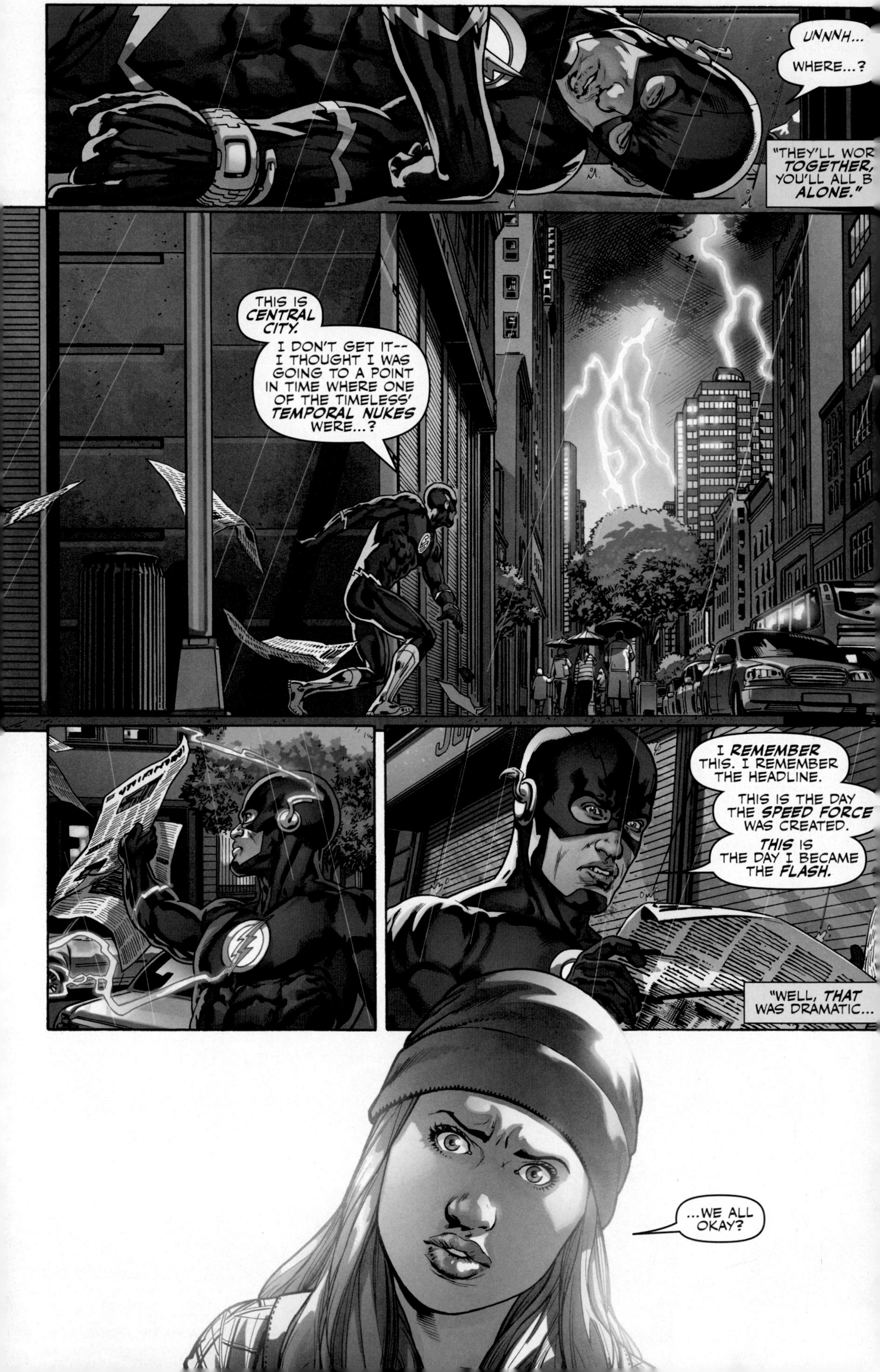
UNNNH...
WHERE...?
"THEY'LL WOR TOGETHER, YOU'LL ALL B ALONE."
THIS IS CENTRAL CITY.
I DON'T GET IT-- I THOUGHT I WAS GOING TO A POINT IN TIME WHERE ONE OF THE TIMELESS' TEMPORAL NUKES WERE...?
I REMEMBER THIS. I REMEMBER THE HEADLINE.
THIS IS THE DAY THE SPEED FORCE WAS CREATED.
THIS IS THE DAY I BECAME THE FLASH.
"WELL, THAT WAS DRAMATIC...
...WE ALL OKAY?

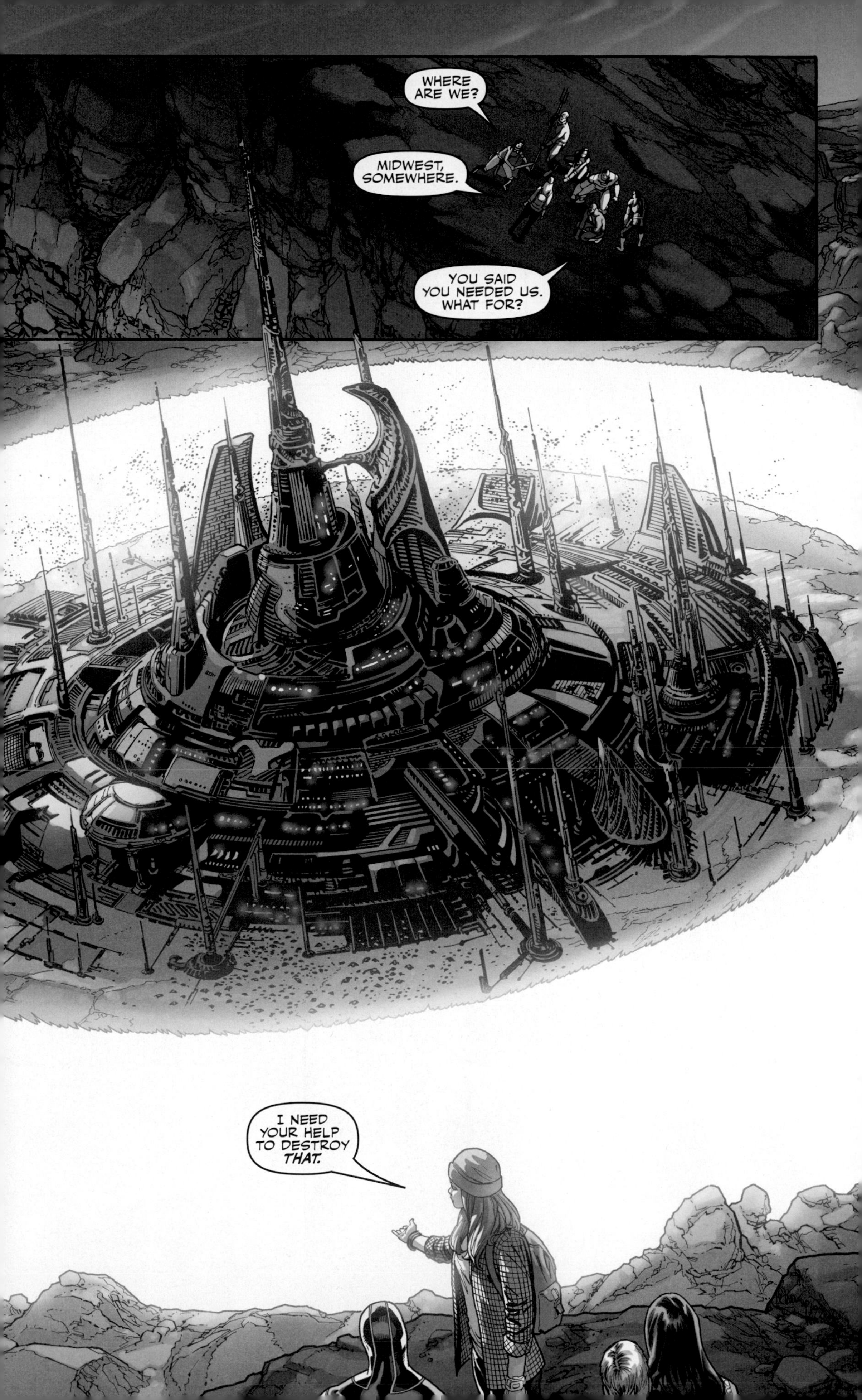
WHERE ARE WE?
MIDWEST, SOMEWHERE.
YOU SAID YOU NEEDED US. WHAT FOR?
I NEED YOUR HELP TO DESTROY *THAT.*

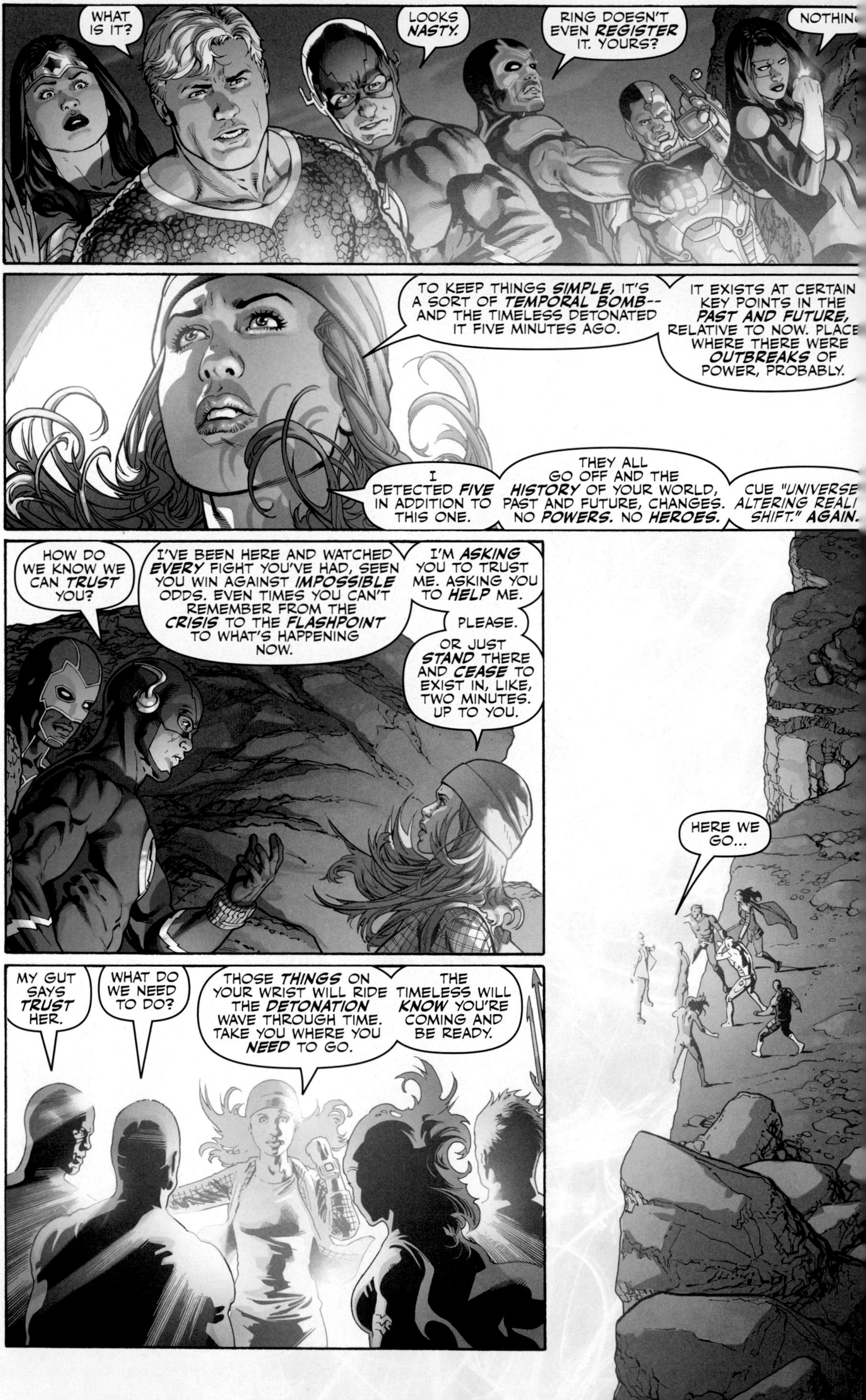
WHAT IS IT?
LOOKS NASTY.
RING DOESN'T EVEN REGISTER IT. YOURS?
NOTHIN
TO KEEP THINGS SIMPLE, IT'S A SORT OF TEMPORAL BOMB-- AND THE TIMELESS DETONATED IT FIVE MINUTES AGO.
IT EXISTS AT CERTAIN KEY POINTS IN THE PAST AND FUTURE, RELATIVE TO NOW. PLACE WHERE THERE WERE OUTBREAKS OF POWER, PROBABLY.
I DETECTED FIVE IN ADDITION TO THIS ONE.
THEY ALL GO OFF AND THE HISTORY OF YOUR WORLD, PAST AND FUTURE, CHANGES. NO POWERS. NO HEROES.
CUE "UNIVERSE ALTERING REALI SHIFT." AGAIN.
HOW DO WE KNOW WE CAN TRUST YOU?
I'VE BEEN HERE AND WATCHED EVERY FIGHT YOU'VE HAD, SEEN YOU WIN AGAINST IMPOSSIBLE ODDS. EVEN TIMES YOU CAN'T REMEMBER FROM THE CRISIS TO THE FLASHPOINT TO WHAT'S HAPPENING NOW.
I'M ASKING YOU TO TRUST ME. ASKING YOU TO HELP ME.
PLEASE.
OR JUST STAND THERE AND CEASE TO EXIST IN, LIKE, TWO MINUTES. UP TO YOU.
MY GUT SAYS TRUST HER.
WHAT DO WE NEED TO DO?
THOSE THINGS ON YOUR WRIST WILL RIDE THE DETONATION WAVE THROUGH TIME. TAKE YOU WHERE YOU NEED TO GO.
THE TIMELESS WILL KNOW YOU'RE COMING AND BE READY.
HERE WE GO...

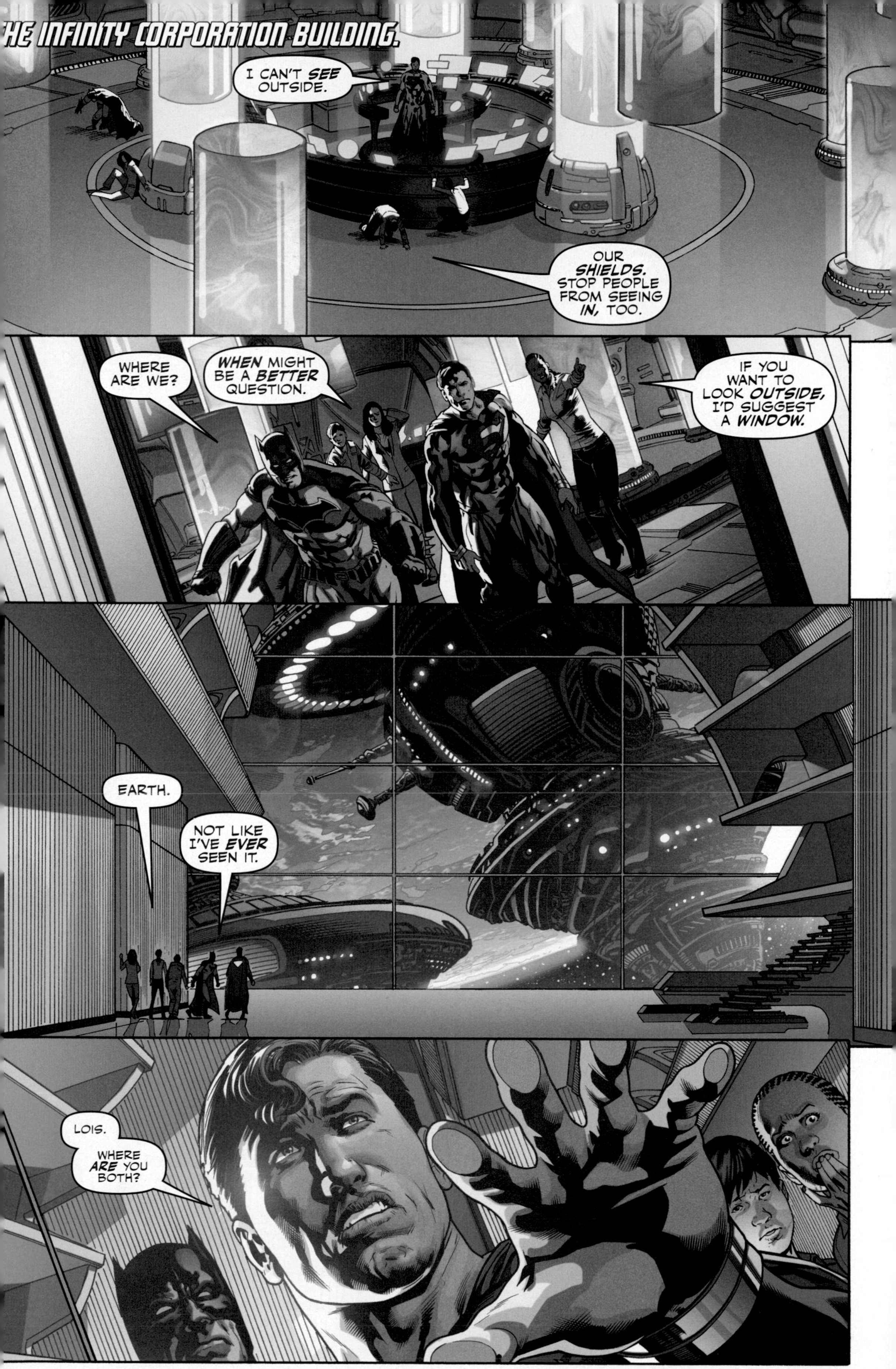
HE INFINITY CORPORATION BUILDING.
I CAN'T SEE OUTSIDE.
OUR SHIELDS. STOP PEOPLE FROM SEEING IN, TOO.
WHERE ARE WE?
WHEN MIGHT BE A BETTER QUESTION.
IF YOU WANT TO LOOK OUTSIDE, I'D SUGGEST A WINDOW.
EARTH.
NOT LIKE I'VE EVER SEEN IT.
LOIS.
WHERE ARE YOU BOTH?

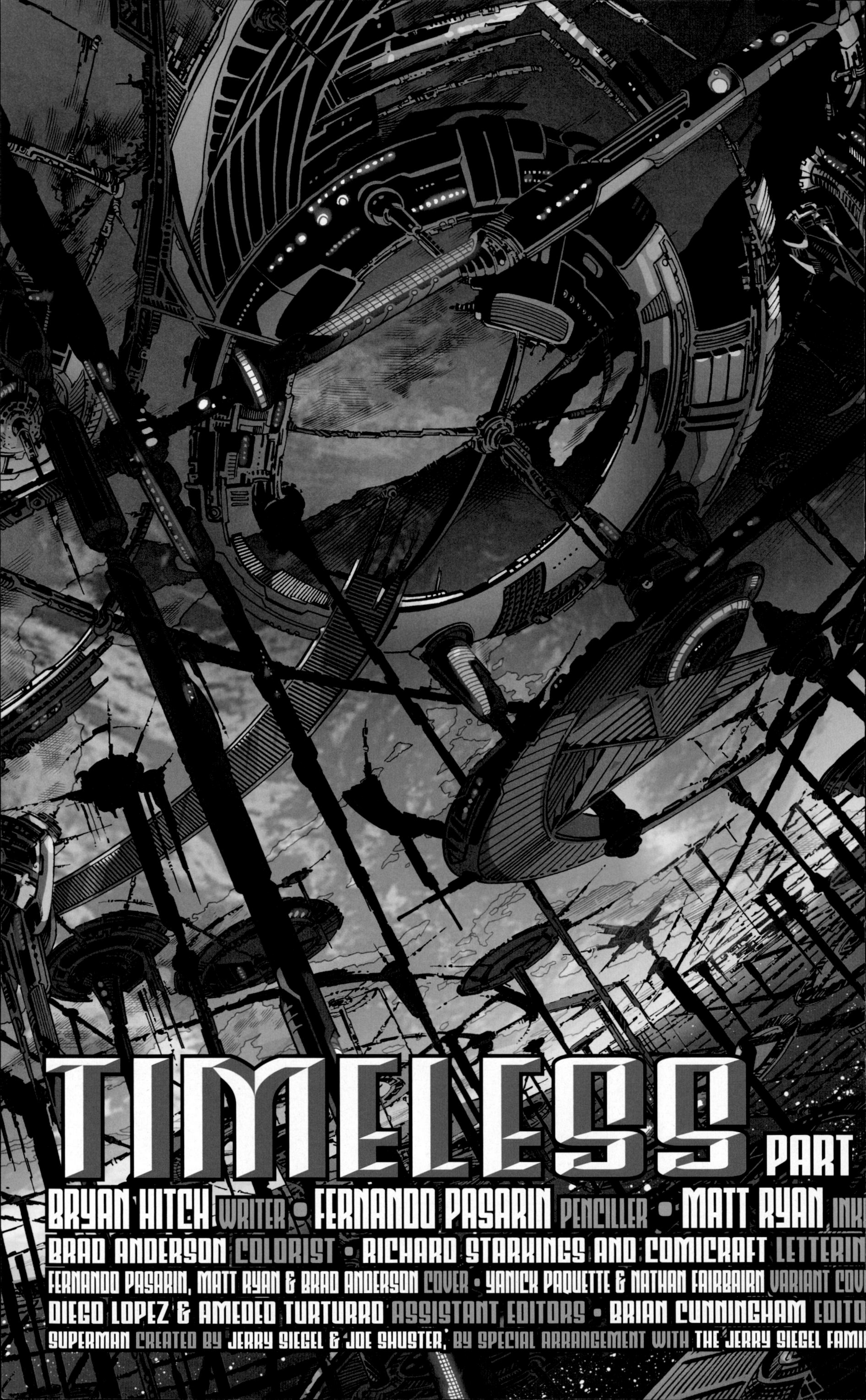
TIMELESS PART
BRYAN HITCH WRITER • FERNANDO PASARIN PENCILLER • MATT RYAN INK
BRAD ANDERSON COLORIST • RICHARD STARKINGS AND COMICRAFT LETTERIN
FERNANDO PASARIN, MATT RYAN & BRAD ANDERSON COVER • YANICK PAQUETTE & NATHAN FAIRBAIRN VARIANT COV
DIEGO LOPEZ & AMEDEO TURTURRO ASSISTANT EDITORS • BRIAN CUNNINGHAM EDITO
SUPERMAN CREATED BY JERRY SIEGEL & JOE SHUSTER, BY SPECIAL ARRANGEMENT WITH THE JERRY SIEGEL FAMI

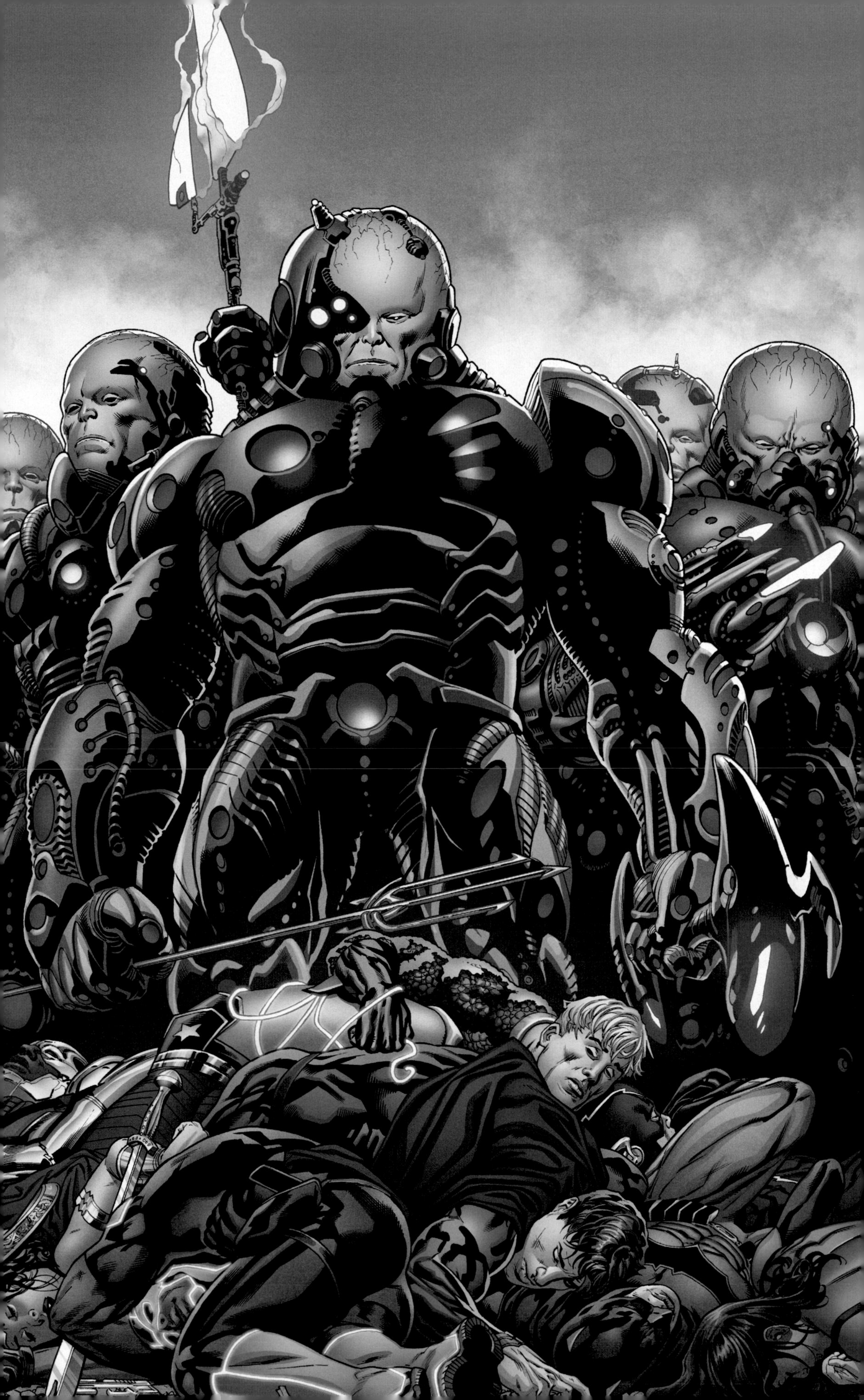

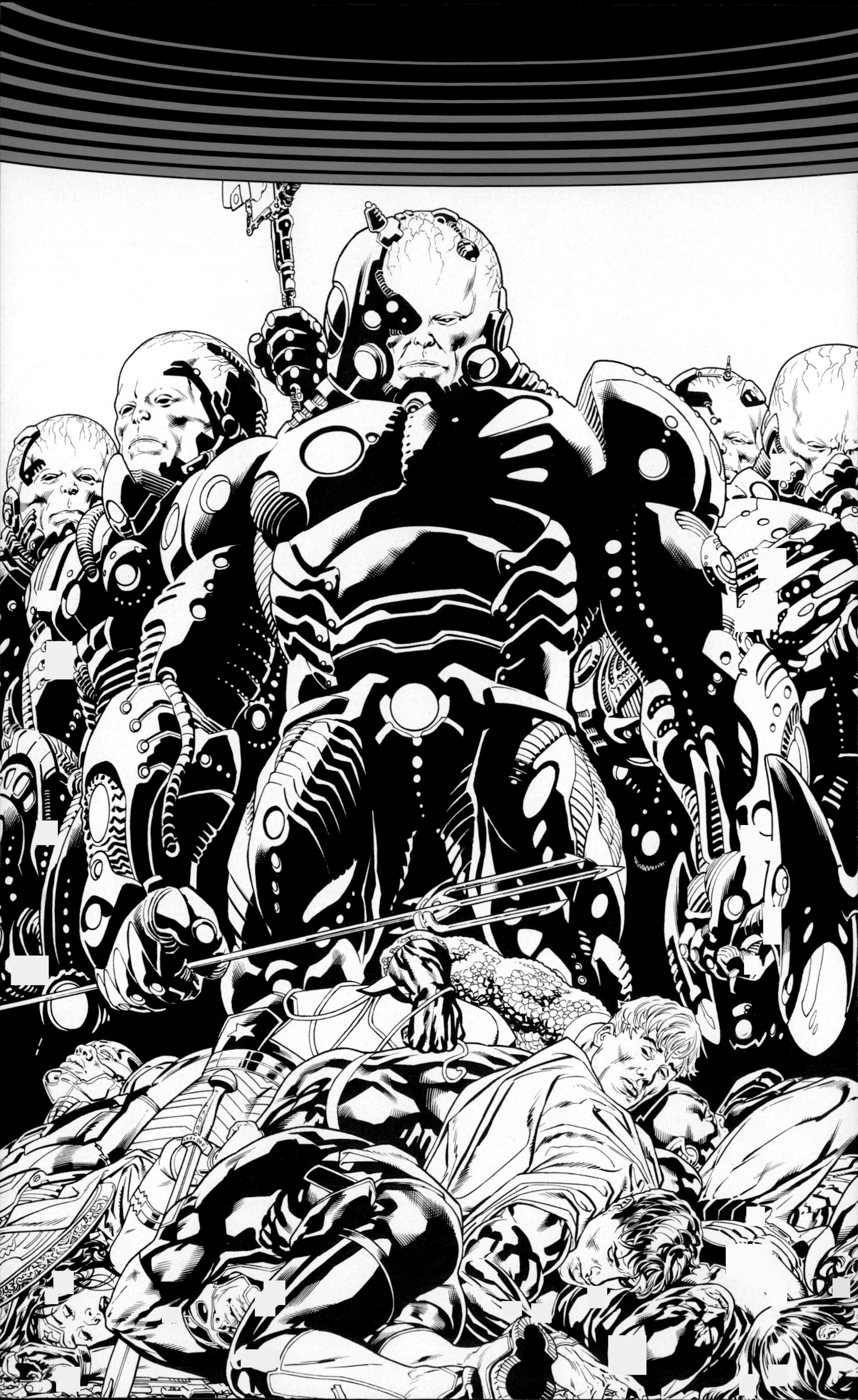

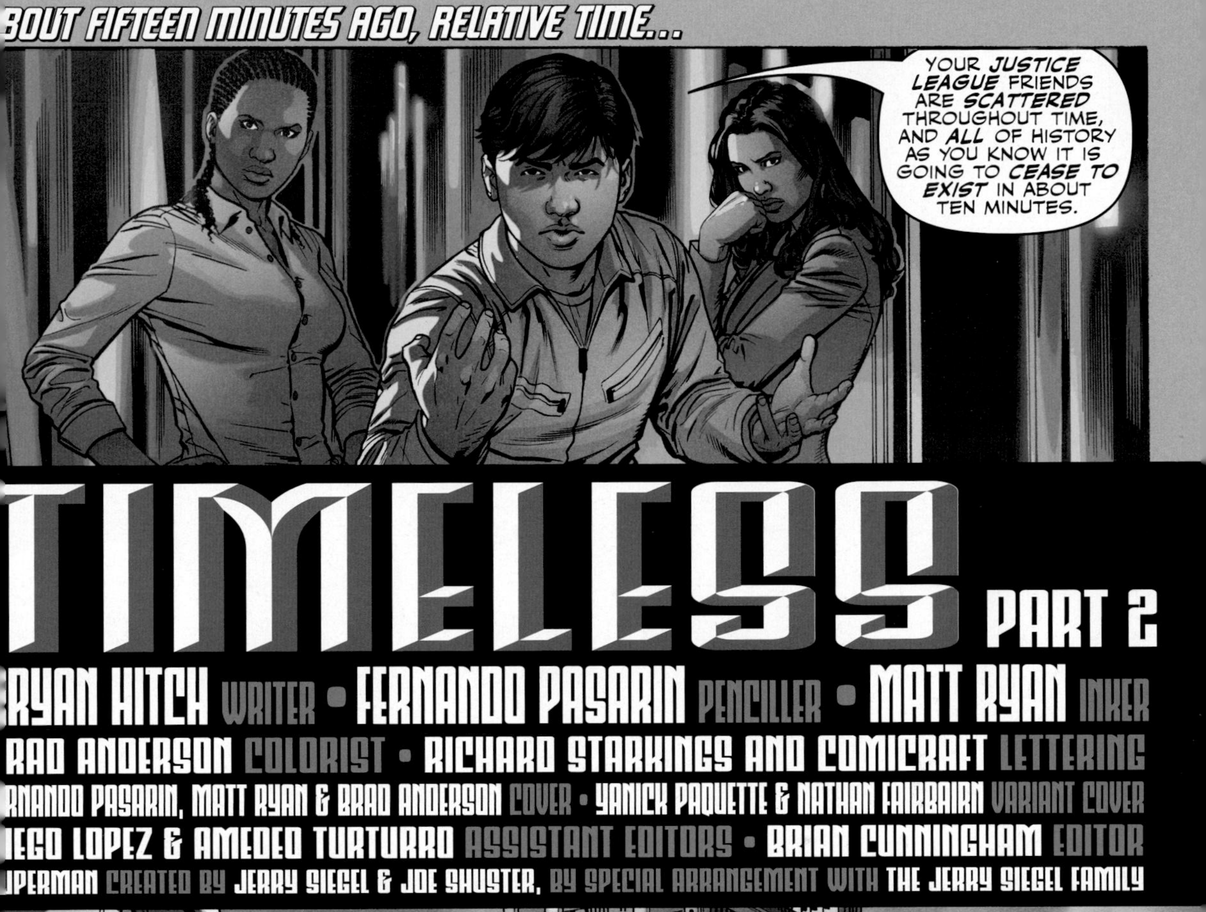
BOUT FIFTEEN MINUTES AGO, RELATIVE TIME...
YOUR JUSTICE LEAGUE FRIENDS ARE SCATTERED THROUGHOUT TIME, AND ALL OF HISTORY AS YOU KNOW IT IS GOING TO CEASE TO EXIST IN ABOUT TEN MINUTES.

TIMELESS PART 2

RYAN HITCH WRITER • FERNANDO PASARIN PENCILLER • MATT RYAN INKER
RAD ANDERSON COLORIST • RICHARD STARKINGS AND COMICRAFT LETTERING
RNANDO PASARIN, MATT RYAN & BRAD ANDERSON COVER • YANICK PAQUETTE & NATHAN FAIRBAIRN VARIANT COVER
IEGO LOPEZ & AMEDEO TURTURRO ASSISTANT EDITORS • BRIAN CUNNINGHAM EDITOR
UPERMAN CREATED BY JERRY SIEGEL & JOE SHUSTER, BY SPECIAL ARRANGEMENT WITH THE JERRY SIEGEL FAMILY

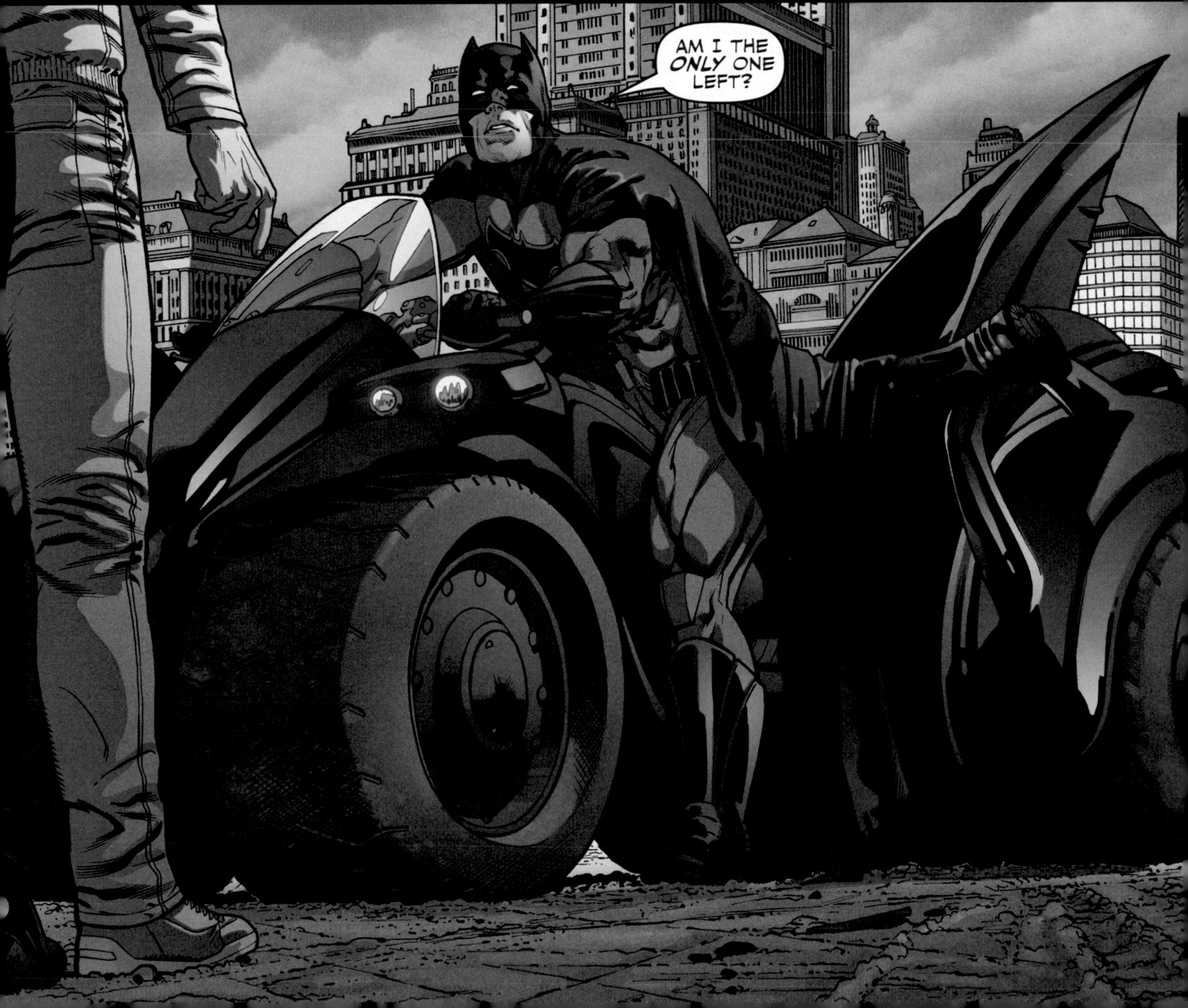
AM I THE ONLY ONE LEFT?

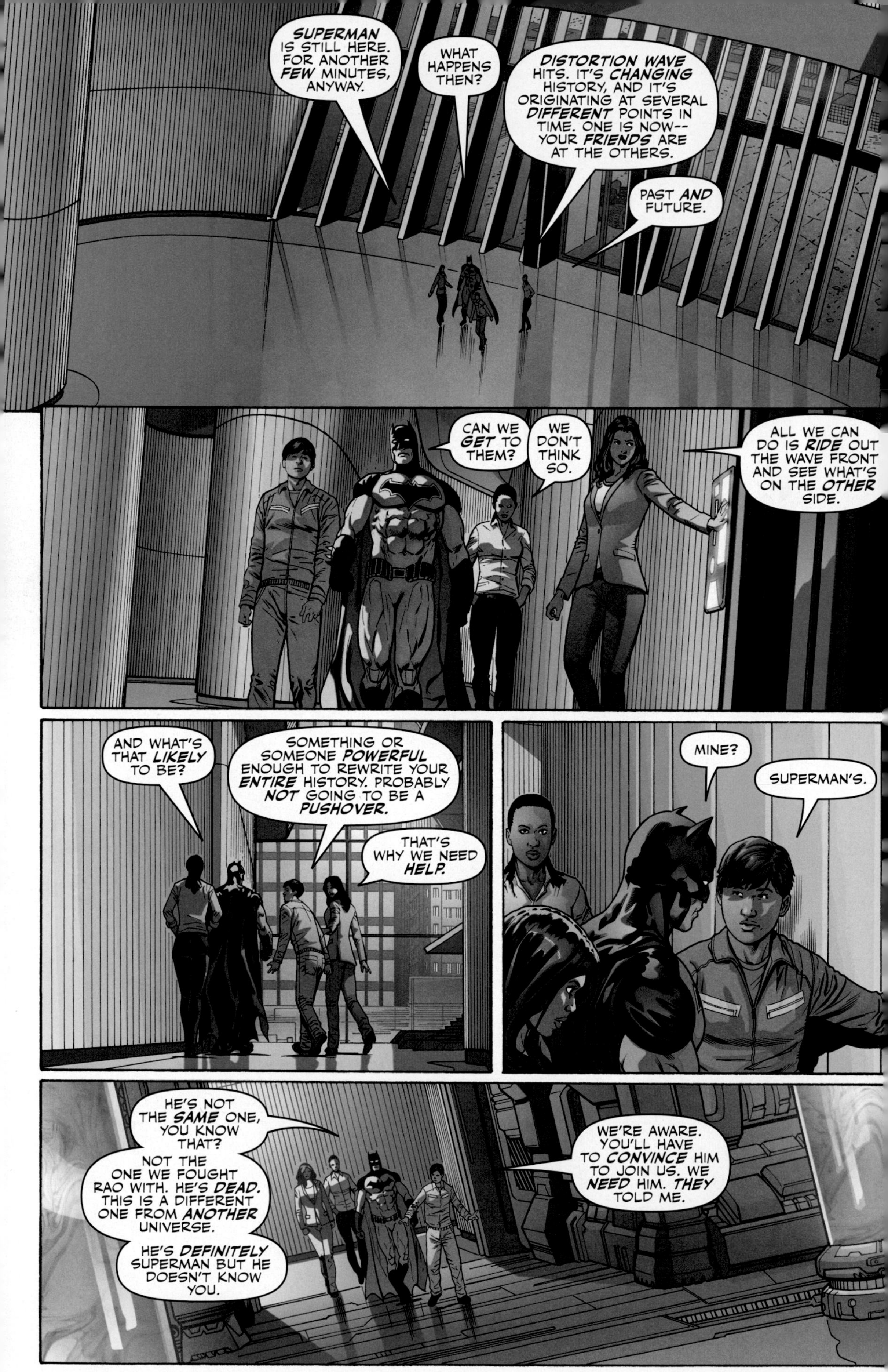
SUPERMAN IS STILL HERE. FOR ANOTHER FEW MINUTES, ANYWAY.
WHAT HAPPENS THEN?
DISTORTION WAVE HITS. IT'S CHANGING HISTORY, AND IT'S ORIGINATING AT SEVERAL DIFFERENT POINTS IN TIME. ONE IS NOW-- YOUR FRIENDS ARE AT THE OTHERS.
PAST AND FUTURE.
CAN WE GET TO THEM?
WE DON'T THINK SO.
ALL WE CAN DO IS RIDE OUT THE WAVE FRONT AND SEE WHAT'S ON THE OTHER SIDE.
AND WHAT'S THAT LIKELY TO BE?
SOMETHING OR SOMEONE POWERFUL ENOUGH TO REWRITE YOUR ENTIRE HISTORY. PROBABLY NOT GOING TO BE A PUSHOVER.
THAT'S WHY WE NEED HELP.
MINE?
SUPERMAN'S.
HE'S NOT THE SAME ONE, YOU KNOW THAT?
NOT THE ONE WE FOUGHT RAO WITH. HE'S DEAD. THIS IS A DIFFERENT ONE FROM ANOTHER UNIVERSE.
HE'S DEFINITELY SUPERMAN BUT HE DOESN'T KNOW YOU.
WE'RE AWARE. YOU'LL HAVE TO CONVINCE HIM TO JOIN US. WE NEED HIM. THEY TOLD ME.

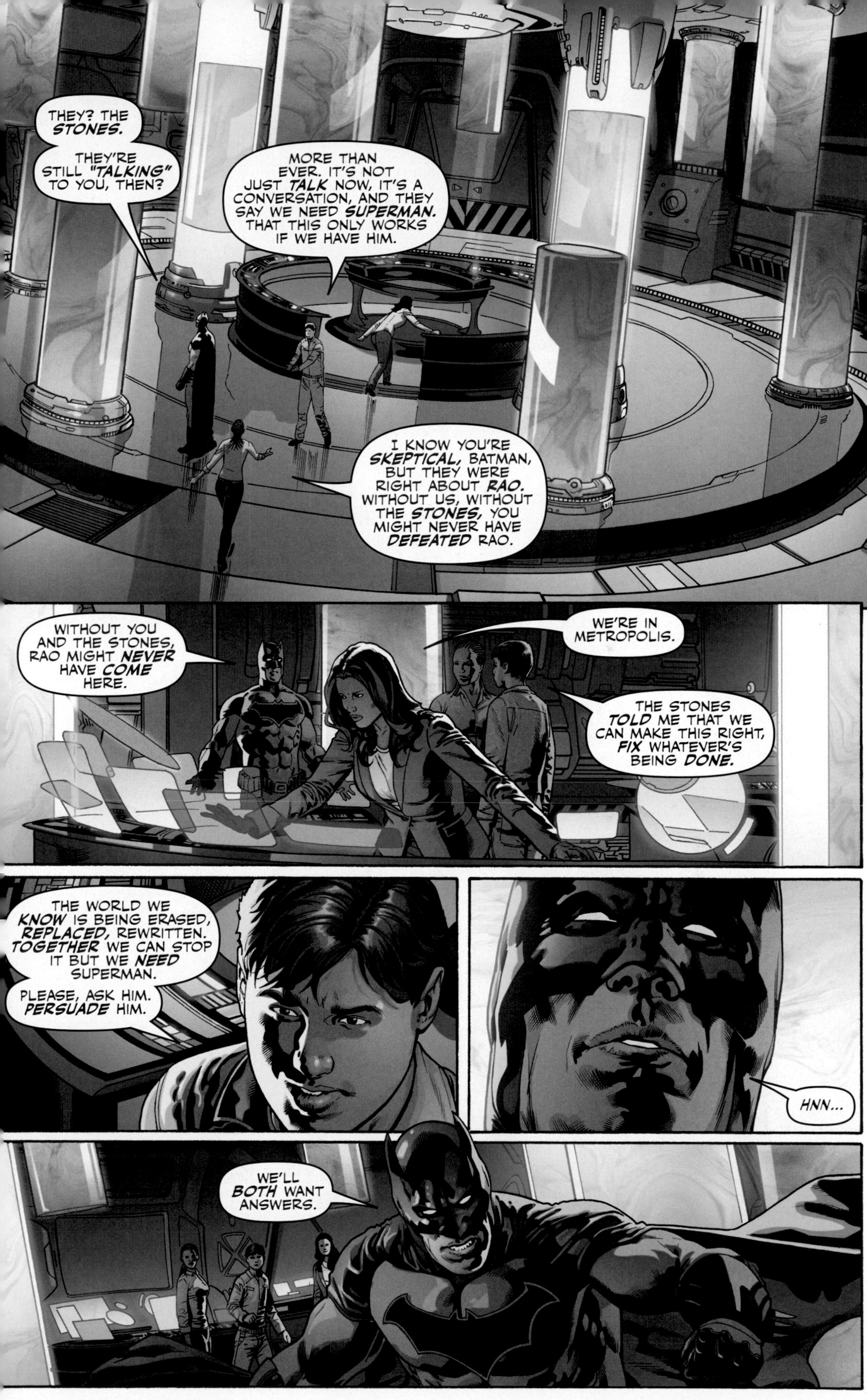
THEY? THE STONES.
THEY'RE STILL "TALKING" TO YOU, THEN?
MORE THAN EVER. IT'S NOT JUST TALK NOW, IT'S A CONVERSATION, AND THEY SAY WE NEED SUPERMAN. THAT THIS ONLY WORKS IF WE HAVE HIM.
I KNOW YOU'RE SKEPTICAL, BATMAN, BUT THEY WERE RIGHT ABOUT RAO. WITHOUT US, WITHOUT THE STONES, YOU MIGHT NEVER HAVE DEFEATED RAO.
WITHOUT YOU AND THE STONES, RAO MIGHT NEVER HAVE COME HERE.
WE'RE IN METROPOLIS.
THE STONES TOLD ME THAT WE CAN MAKE THIS RIGHT, FIX WHATEVER'S BEING DONE.
THE WORLD WE KNOW IS BEING ERASED, REPLACED, REWRITTEN. TOGETHER WE CAN STOP IT BUT WE NEED SUPERMAN.
PLEASE, ASK HIM. PERSUADE HIM.
HNN...
WE'LL BOTH WANT ANSWERS.

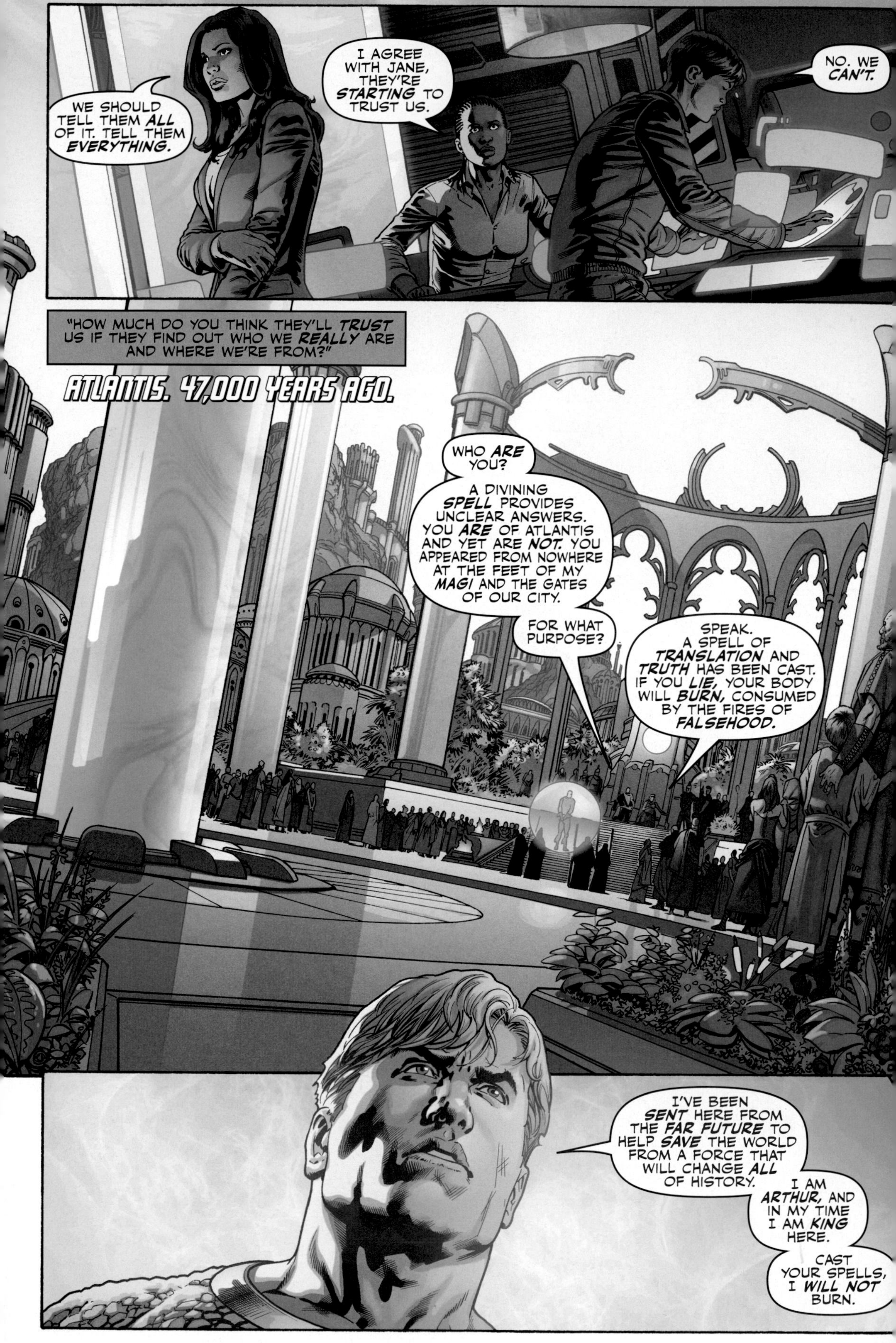
WE SHOULD TELL THEM ALL OF IT. TELL THEM EVERYTHING.
I AGREE WITH JANE, THEY'RE STARTING TO TRUST US.
NO. WE CAN'T.
"HOW MUCH DO YOU THINK THEY'LL TRUST US IF THEY FIND OUT WHO WE REALLY ARE AND WHERE WE'RE FROM?"
ATLANTIS. 47,000 YEARS AGO.
WHO ARE YOU?
A DIVINING SPELL PROVIDES UNCLEAR ANSWERS. YOU ARE OF ATLANTIS AND YET ARE NOT. YOU APPEARED FROM NOWHERE AT THE FEET OF MY MAGI AND THE GATES OF OUR CITY.
FOR WHAT PURPOSE?
SPEAK. A SPELL OF TRANSLATION AND TRUTH HAS BEEN CAST. IF YOU LIE, YOUR BODY WILL BURN, CONSUMED BY THE FIRES OF FALSEHOOD.
I'VE BEEN SENT HERE FROM THE FAR FUTURE TO HELP SAVE THE WORLD FROM A FORCE THAT WILL CHANGE ALL OF HISTORY.
I AM ARTHUR, AND IN MY TIME I AM KING HERE.
CAST YOUR SPELLS, I WILL NOT BURN.

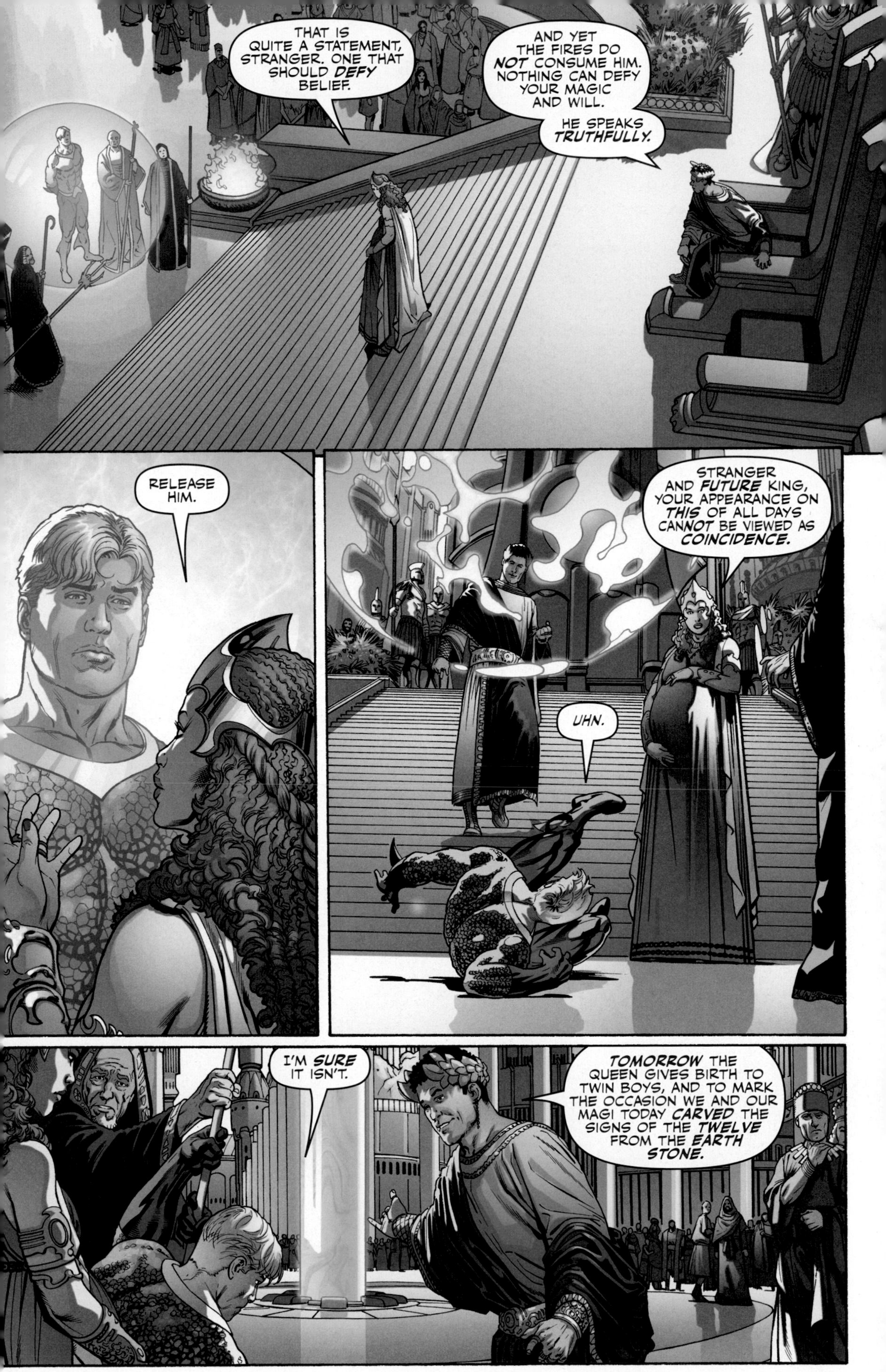

THAT IS QUITE A STATEMENT, STRANGER. ONE THAT SHOULD *DEFY* BELIEF.
AND YET THE FIRES DO *NOT* CONSUME HIM. NOTHING CAN DEFY YOUR MAGIC AND WILL.
HE SPEAKS *TRUTHFULLY.*
RELEASE HIM.
STRANGER AND *FUTURE* KING, YOUR APPEARANCE ON *THIS* OF ALL DAYS CAN*NOT* BE VIEWED AS *COINCIDENCE.*
UHN.
I'M *SURE* IT ISN'T.
TOMORROW THE QUEEN GIVES BIRTH TO TWIN BOYS, AND TO MARK THE OCCASION WE AND OUR MAGI TODAY *CARVED* THE SIGNS OF THE *TWELVE* FROM THE *EARTH STONE.*

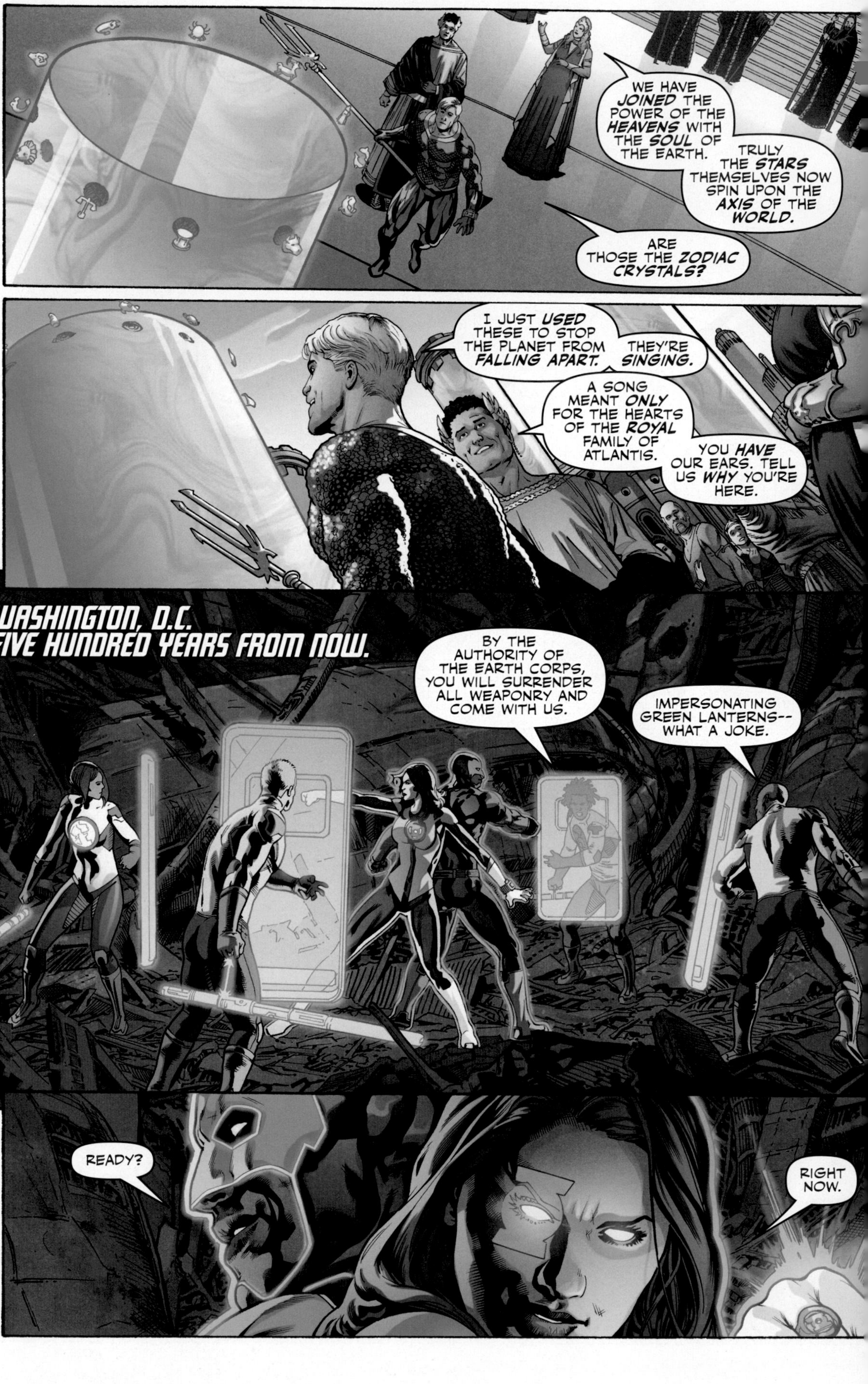

WE HAVE JOINED THE POWER OF THE HEAVENS WITH THE SOUL OF THE EARTH.
TRULY THE STARS THEMSELVES NOW SPIN UPON THE AXIS OF THE WORLD.
ARE THOSE THE ZODIAC CRYSTALS?
I JUST USED THESE TO STOP THE PLANET FROM FALLING APART.
THEY'RE SINGING.
A SONG MEANT ONLY FOR THE HEARTS OF THE ROYAL FAMILY OF ATLANTIS.
YOU HAVE OUR EARS. TELL US WHY YOU'RE HERE.
WASHINGTON, D.C. FIVE HUNDRED YEARS FROM NOW.
BY THE AUTHORITY OF THE EARTH CORPS, YOU WILL SURRENDER ALL WEAPONRY AND COME WITH US.
IMPERSONATING GREEN LANTERNS-- WHAT A JOKE.
READY?
RIGHT NOW.

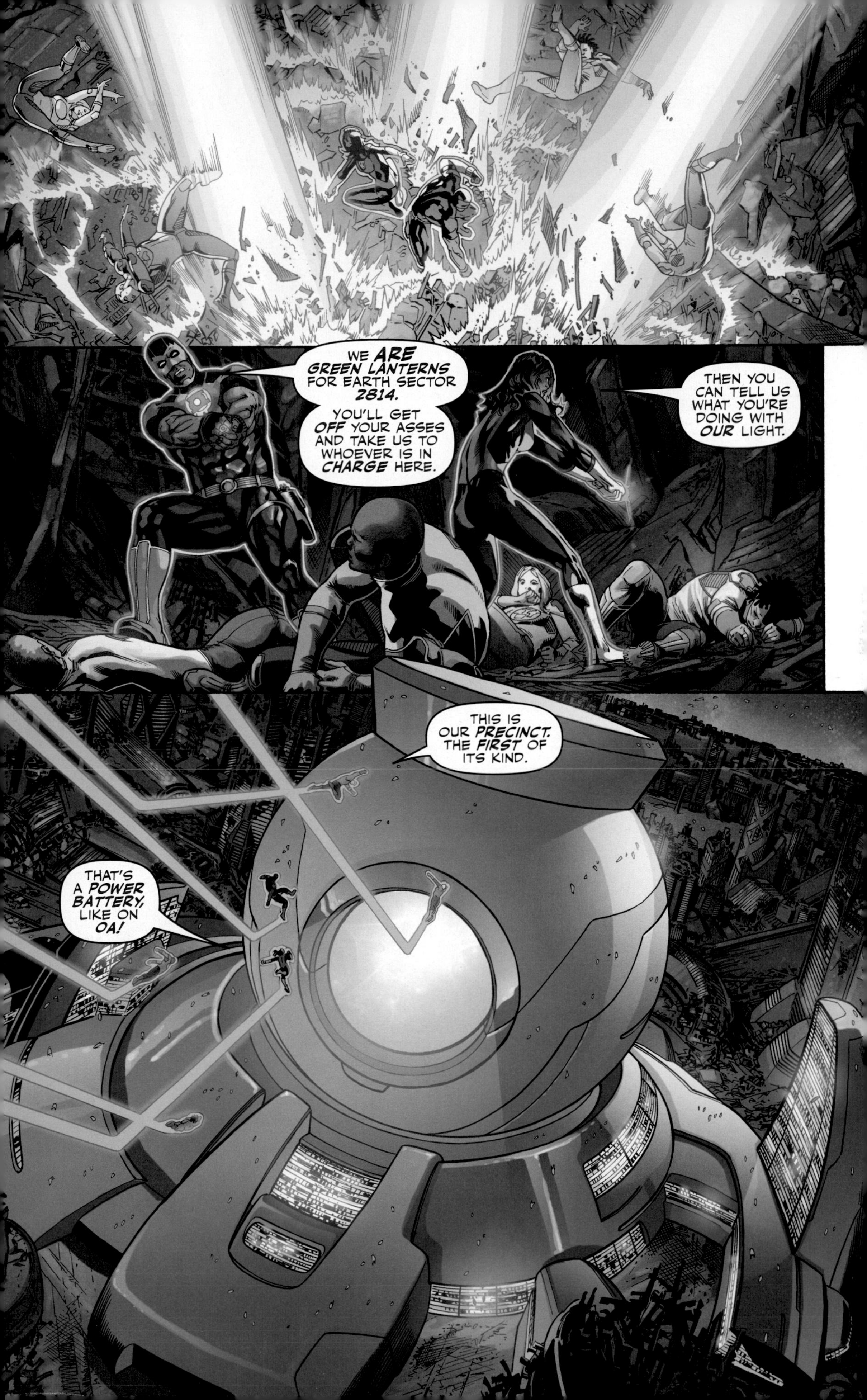
WE ARE GREEN LANTERNS FOR EARTH SECTOR 2814.
YOU'LL GET OFF YOUR ASSES AND TAKE US TO WHOEVER IS IN CHARGE HERE.
THEN YOU CAN TELL US WHAT YOU'RE DOING WITH OUR LIGHT.
THIS IS OUR PRECINCT. THE FIRST OF ITS KIND.
THAT'S A POWER BATTERY, LIKE ON OA!

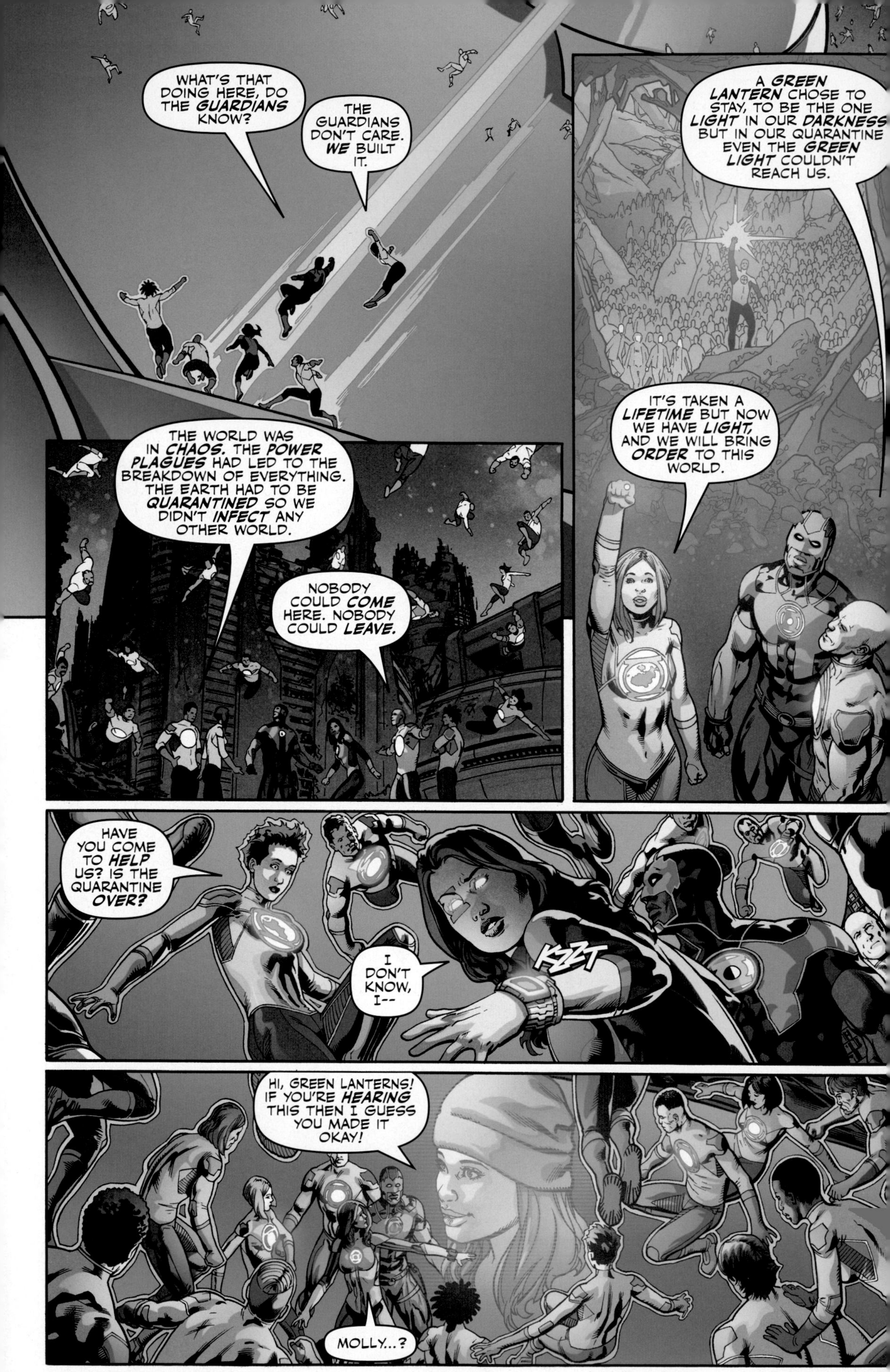
WHAT'S THAT DOING HERE, DO THE GUARDIANS KNOW?
THE GUARDIANS DON'T CARE. WE BUILT IT.
A GREEN LANTERN CHOSE TO STAY, TO BE THE ONE LIGHT IN OUR DARKNESS BUT IN OUR QUARANTINE EVEN THE GREEN LIGHT COULDN'T REACH US.
THE WORLD WAS IN CHAOS. THE POWER PLAGUES HAD LED TO THE BREAKDOWN OF EVERYTHING. THE EARTH HAD TO BE QUARANTINED SO WE DIDN'T INFECT ANY OTHER WORLD.
NOBODY COULD COME HERE. NOBODY COULD LEAVE.
IT'S TAKEN A LIFETIME BUT NOW WE HAVE LIGHT, AND WE WILL BRING ORDER TO THIS WORLD.
HAVE YOU COME TO HELP US? IS THE QUARANTINE OVER?
I DON'T KNOW, I--
KZZT
HI, GREEN LANTERNS! IF YOU'RE HEARING THIS THEN I GUESS YOU MADE IT OKAY!
MOLLY...?

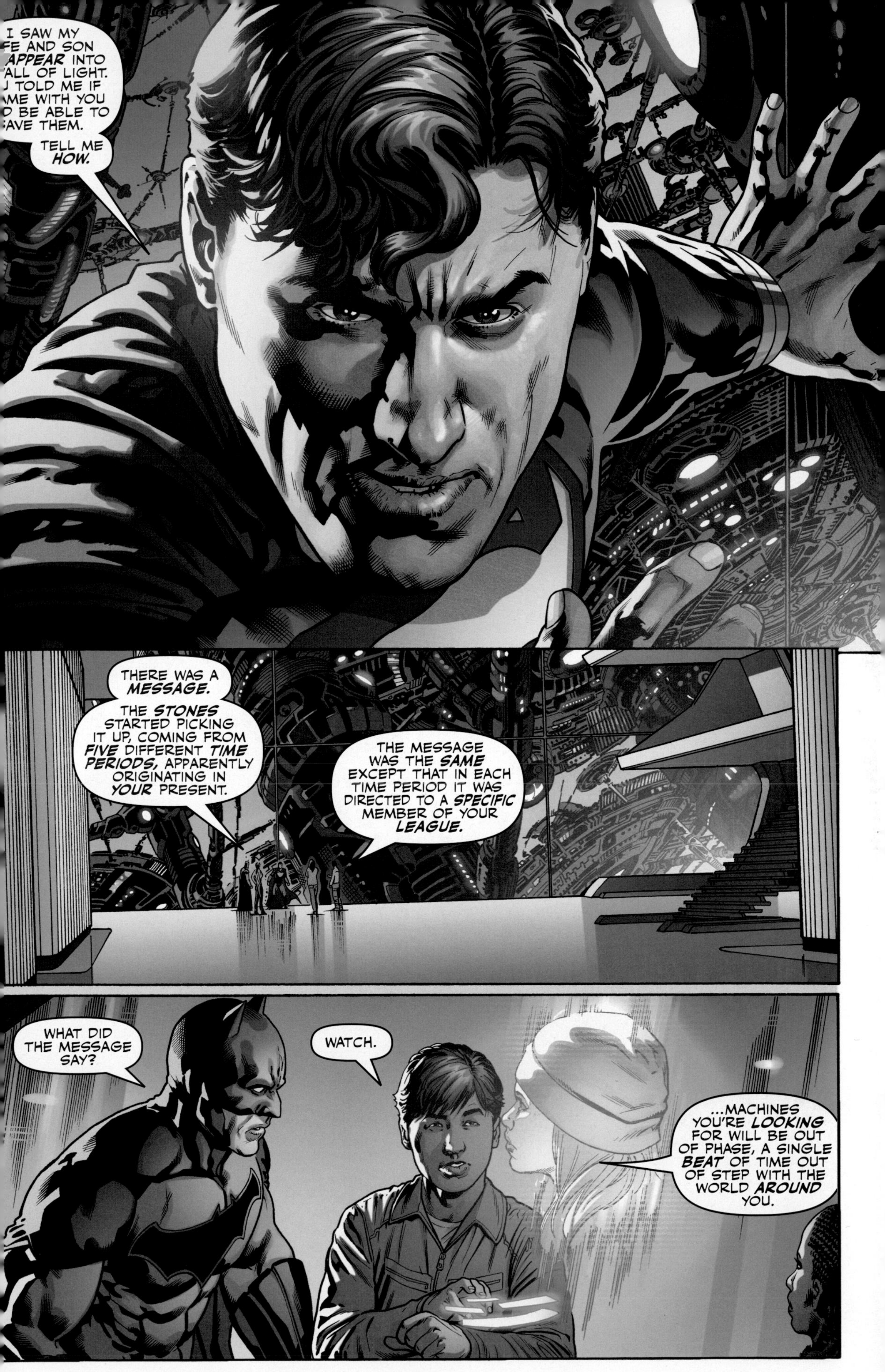
I SAW MY
FE AND SON
APPEAR INTO
ALL OF LIGHT.
U TOLD ME IF
AME WITH YOU
D BE ABLE TO
AVE THEM.
TELL ME HOW.
THERE WAS A MESSAGE.
THE STONES STARTED PICKING IT UP, COMING FROM FIVE DIFFERENT TIME PERIODS, APPARENTLY ORIGINATING IN YOUR PRESENT.
THE MESSAGE WAS THE SAME EXCEPT THAT IN EACH TIME PERIOD IT WAS DIRECTED TO A SPECIFIC MEMBER OF YOUR LEAGUE.
WHAT DID THE MESSAGE SAY?
WATCH.
...MACHINES YOU'RE LOOKING FOR WILL BE OUT OF PHASE, A SINGLE BEAT OF TIME OUT OF STEP WITH THE WORLD AROUND YOU.

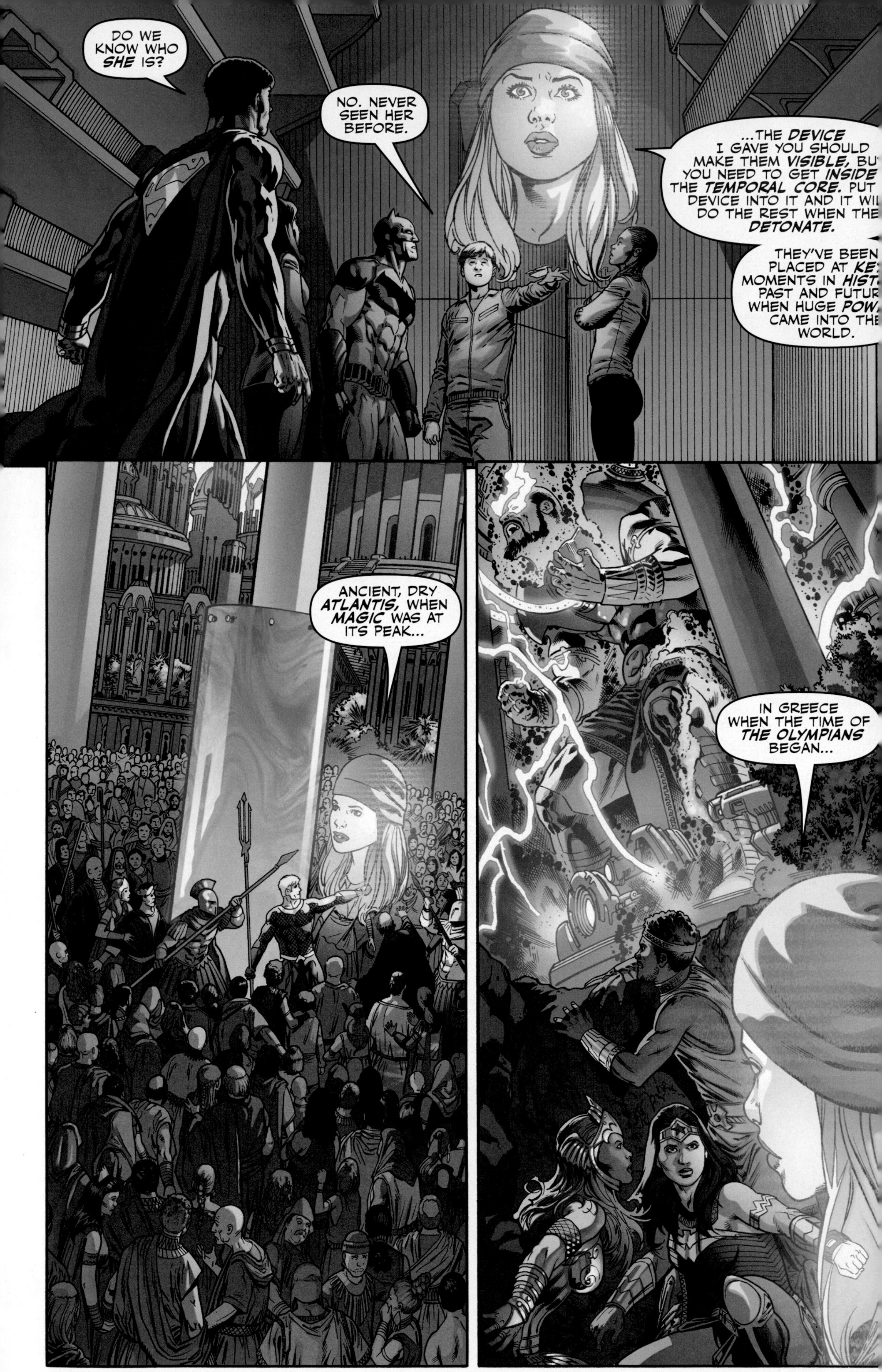
DO WE KNOW WHO SHE IS?
NO. NEVER SEEN HER BEFORE.
...THE DEVICE I GAVE YOU SHOULD MAKE THEM VISIBLE, BU YOU NEED TO GET INSIDE THE TEMPORAL CORE. PUT DEVICE INTO IT AND IT WIL DO THE REST WHEN THE DETONATE.
THEY'VE BEEN PLACED AT KE MOMENTS IN HIST PAST AND FUTUR WHEN HUGE POW CAME INTO THE WORLD.
ANCIENT, DRY ATLANTIS, WHEN MAGIC WAS AT ITS PEAK...
IN GREECE WHEN THE TIME OF THE OLYMPIANS BEGAN...

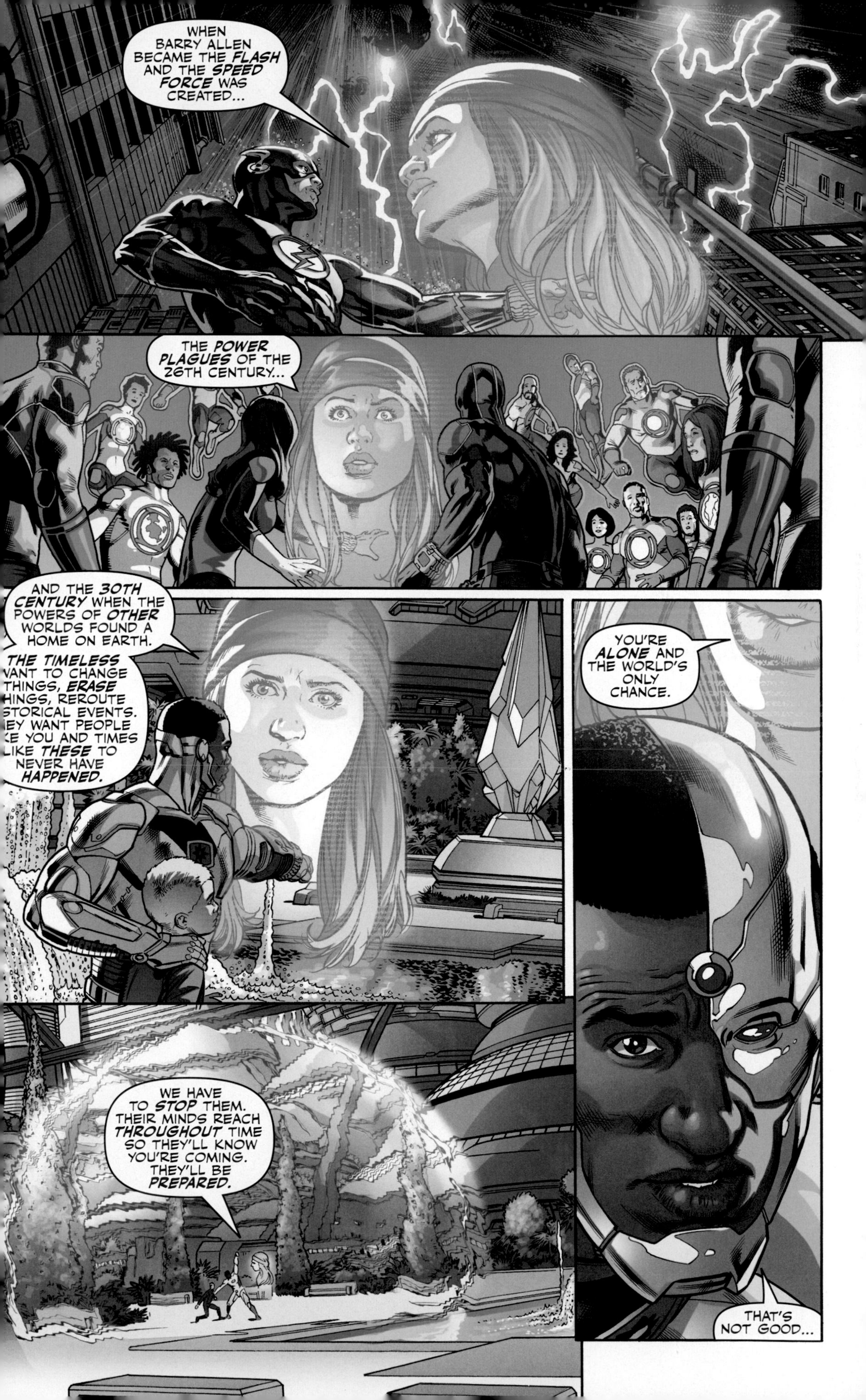
WHEN BARRY ALLEN BECAME THE FLASH AND THE SPEED FORCE WAS CREATED...
THE POWER PLAGUES OF THE 26TH CENTURY...
AND THE 30TH CENTURY WHEN THE POWERS OF OTHER WORLDS FOUND A HOME ON EARTH.
THE TIMELESS WANT TO CHANGE THINGS, ERASE THINGS, REROUTE HISTORICAL EVENTS. THEY WANT PEOPLE LIKE YOU AND TIMES LIKE THESE TO NEVER HAVE HAPPENED.
YOU'RE ALONE AND THE WORLD'S ONLY CHANCE.
WE HAVE TO STOP THEM. THEIR MINDS REACH THROUGHOUT TIME SO THEY'LL KNOW YOU'RE COMING. THEY'LL BE PREPARED.
THAT'S NOT GOOD...

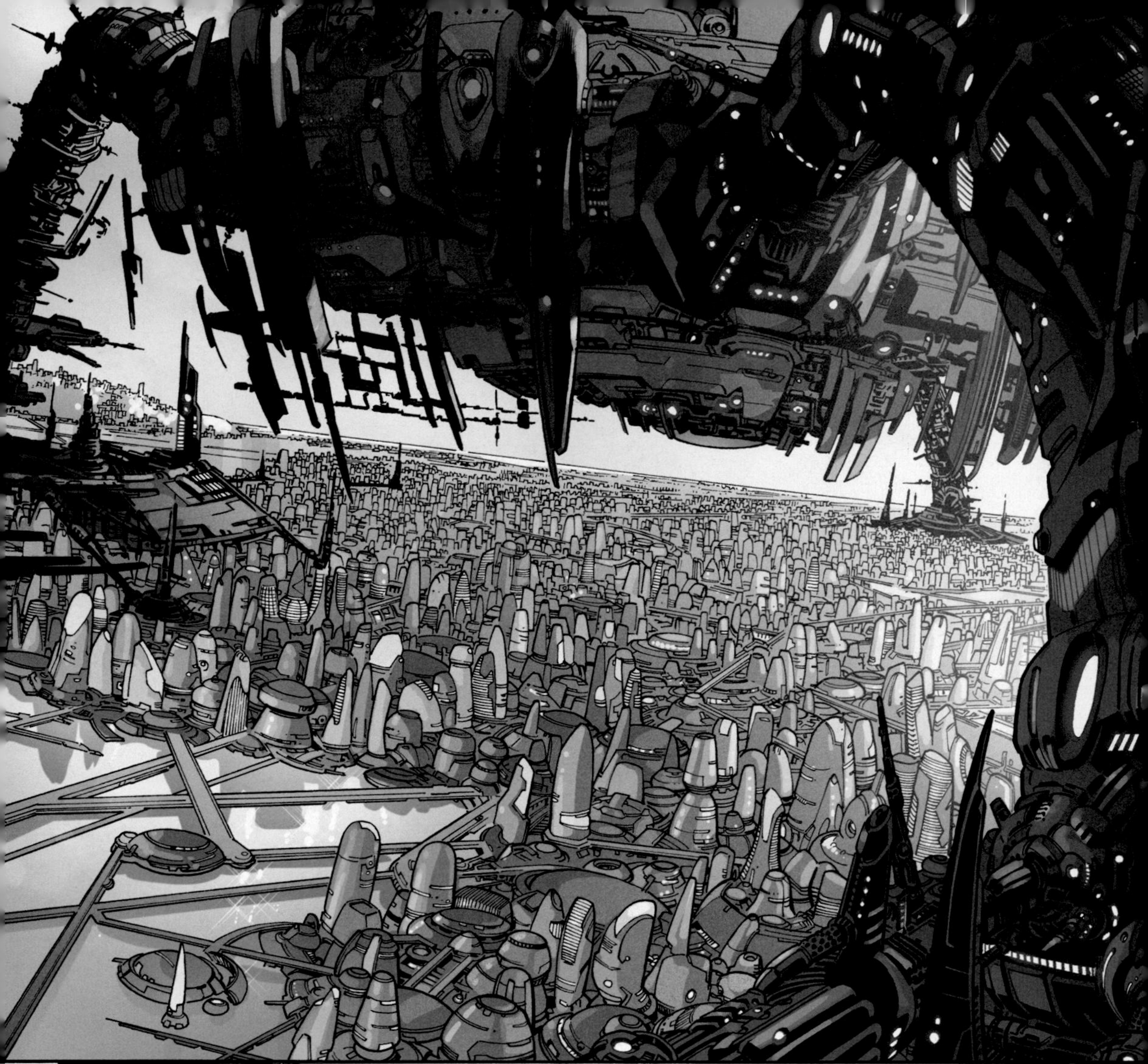

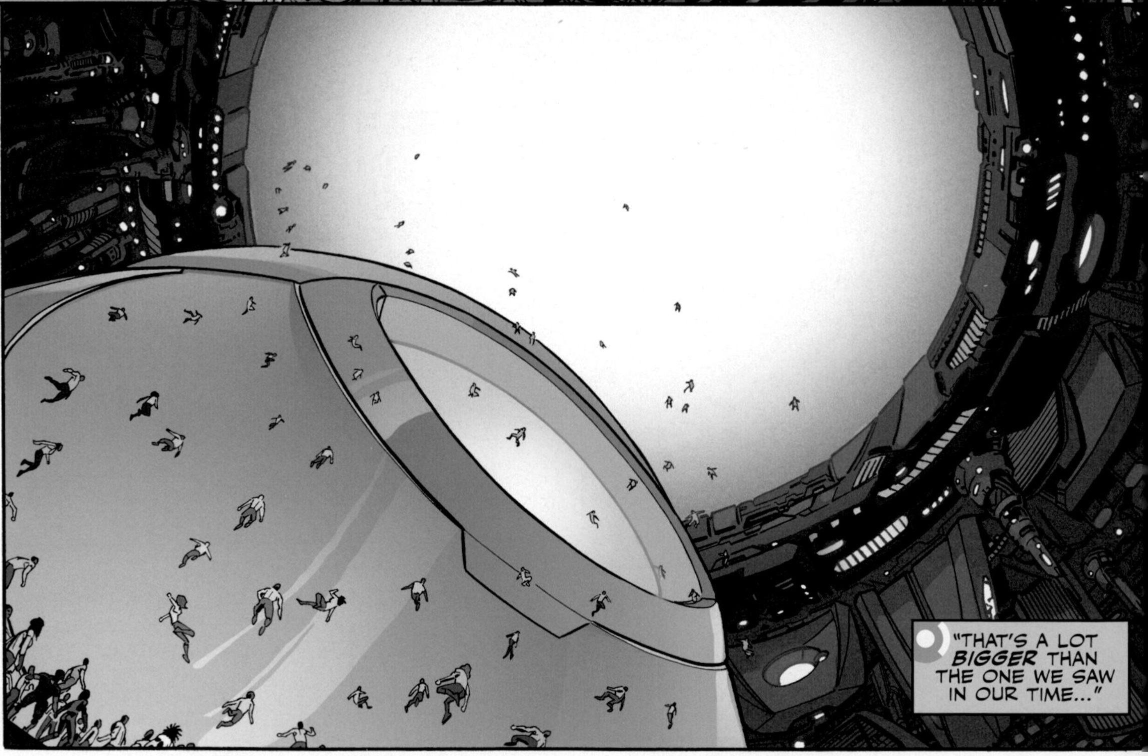
"THAT'S A LOT BIGGER THAN THE ONE WE SAW IN OUR TIME..."

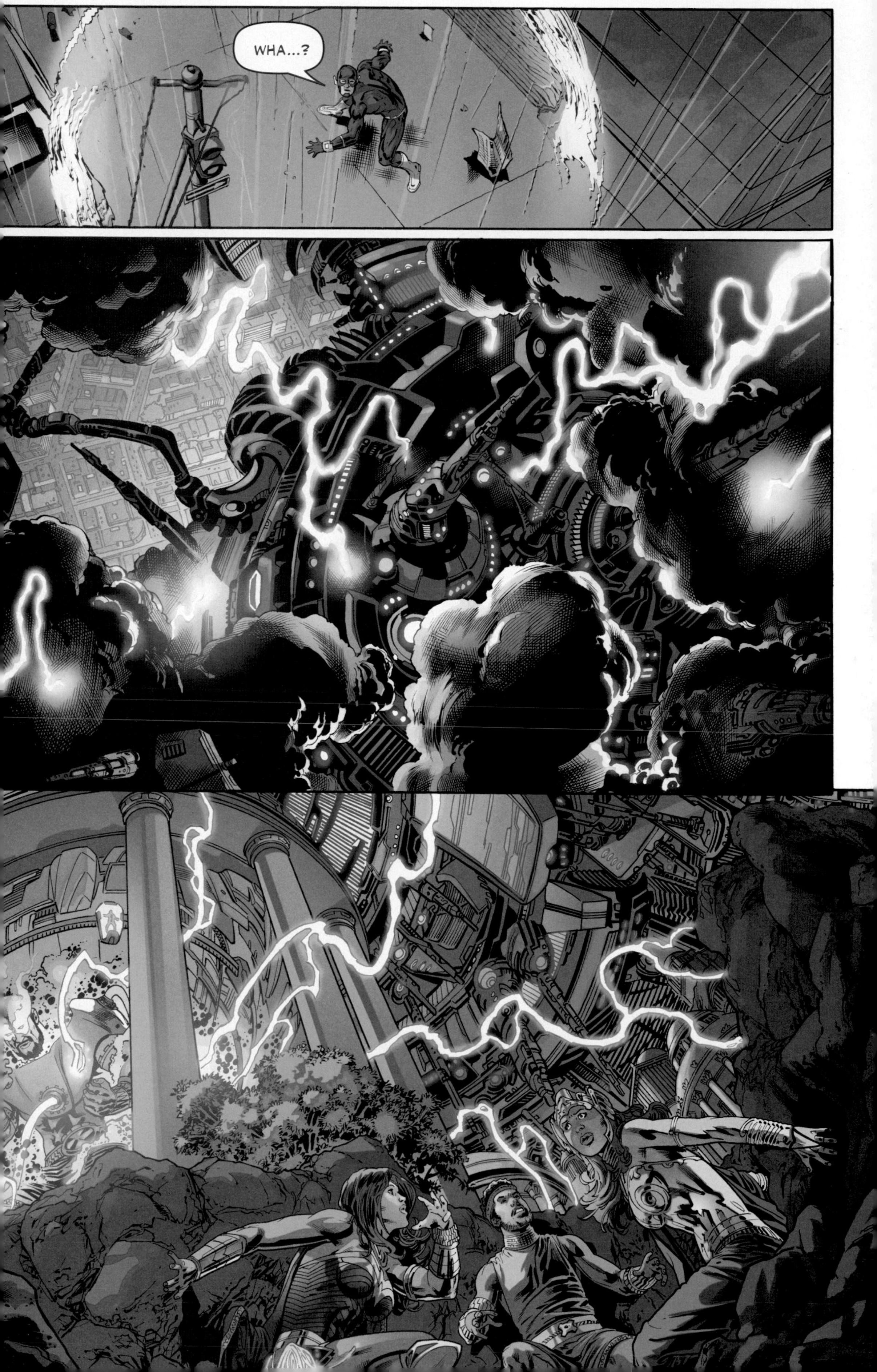
WHA...?

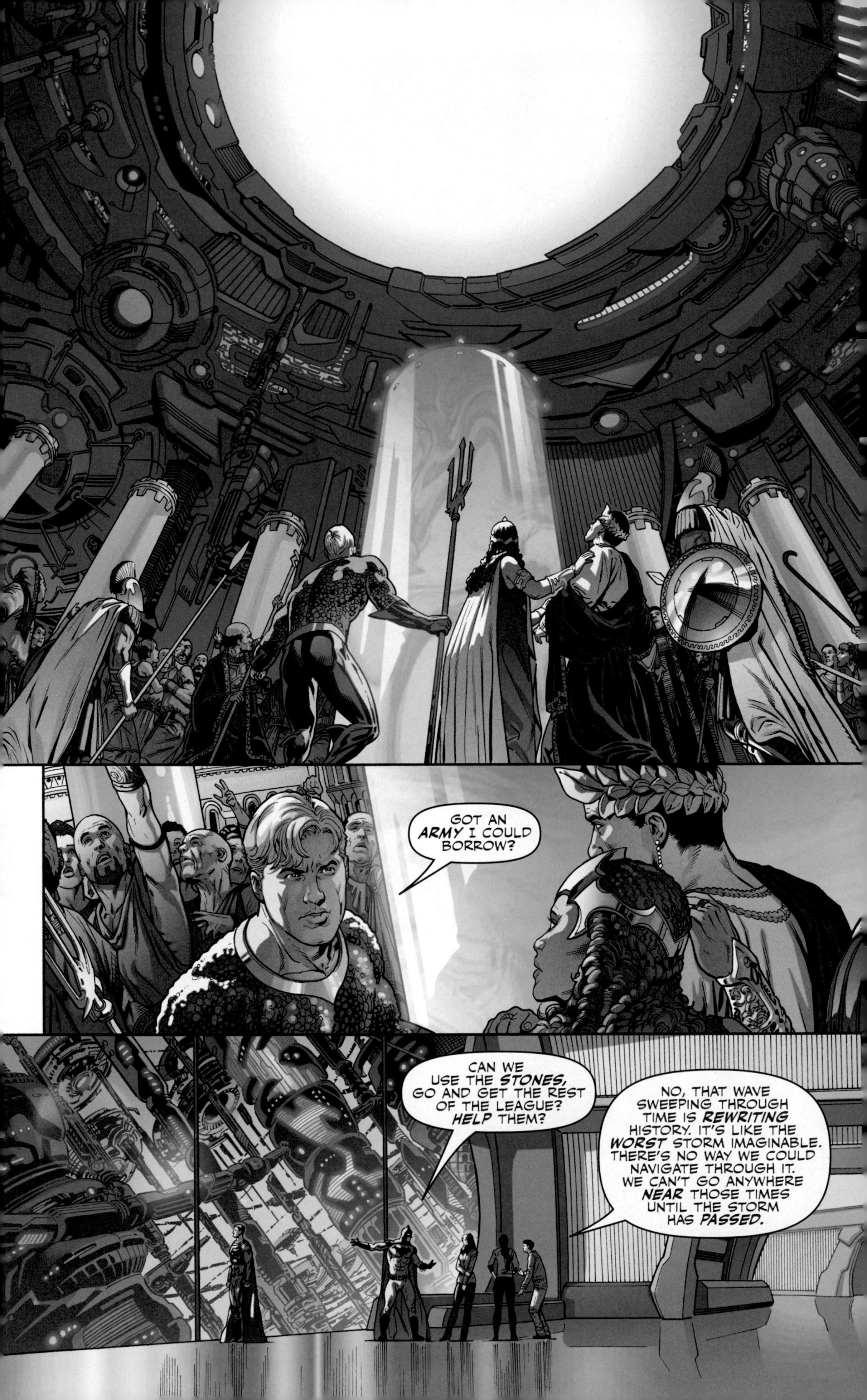

GOT AN ARMY I COULD BORROW?
CAN WE USE THE STONES, GO AND GET THE REST OF THE LEAGUE? HELP THEM?
NO, THAT WAVE SWEEPING THROUGH TIME IS REWRITING HISTORY. IT'S LIKE THE WORST STORM IMAGINABLE. THERE'S NO WAY WE COULD NAVIGATE THROUGH IT. WE CAN'T GO ANYWHERE NEAR THOSE TIMES UNTIL THE STORM HAS PASSED.

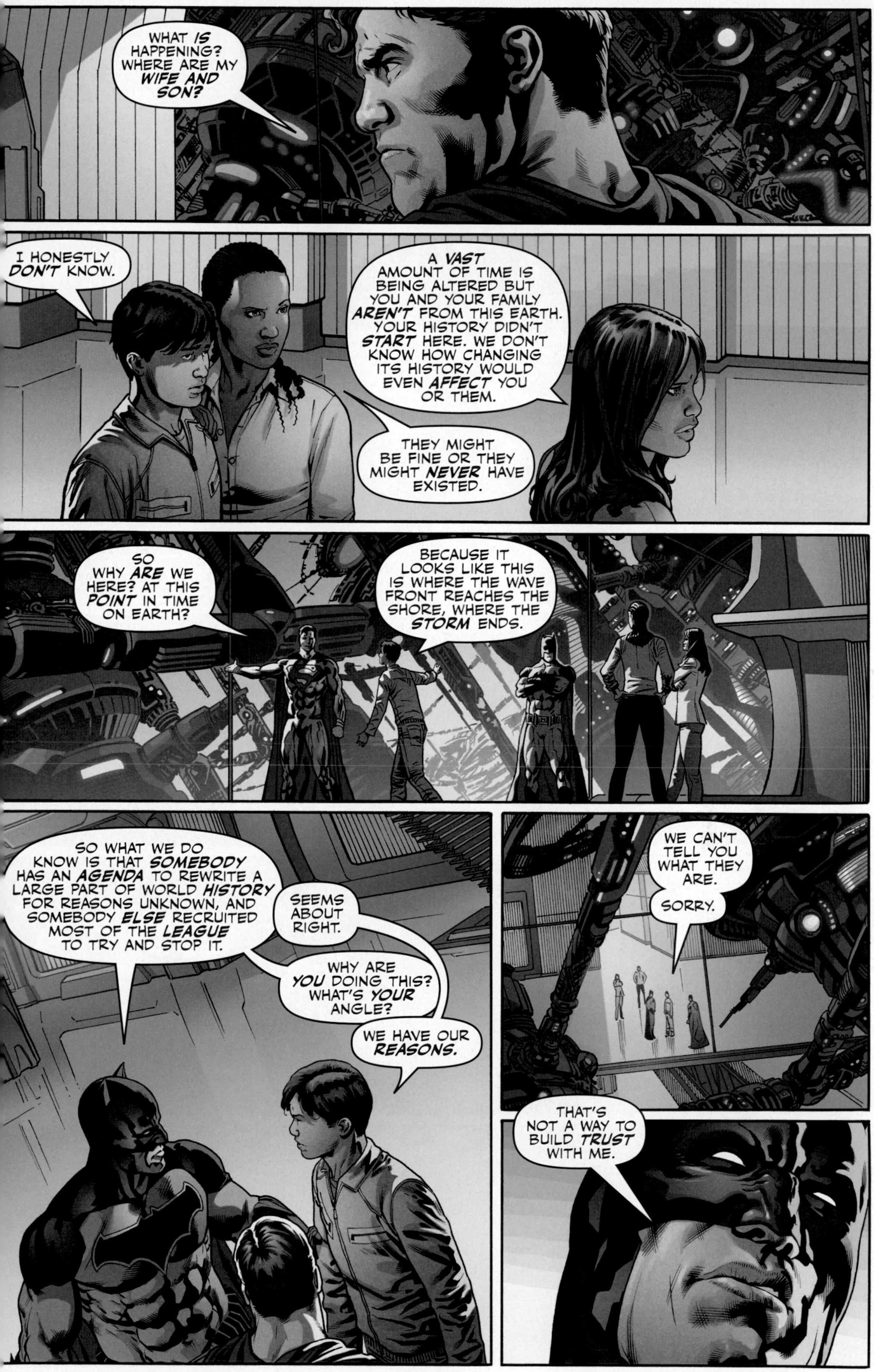
WHAT IS HAPPENING? WHERE ARE MY WIFE AND SON?
I HONESTLY DON'T KNOW.
A VAST AMOUNT OF TIME IS BEING ALTERED BUT YOU AND YOUR FAMILY AREN'T FROM THIS EARTH. YOUR HISTORY DIDN'T START HERE. WE DON'T KNOW HOW CHANGING ITS HISTORY WOULD EVEN AFFECT YOU OR THEM.
THEY MIGHT BE FINE OR THEY MIGHT NEVER HAVE EXISTED.
SO WHY ARE WE HERE? AT THIS POINT IN TIME ON EARTH?
BECAUSE IT LOOKS LIKE THIS IS WHERE THE WAVE FRONT REACHES THE SHORE, WHERE THE STORM ENDS.
SO WHAT WE DO KNOW IS THAT SOMEBODY HAS AN AGENDA TO REWRITE A LARGE PART OF WORLD HISTORY FOR REASONS UNKNOWN, AND SOMEBODY ELSE RECRUITED MOST OF THE LEAGUE TO TRY AND STOP IT.
SEEMS ABOUT RIGHT.
WHY ARE YOU DOING THIS? WHAT'S YOUR ANGLE?
WE HAVE OUR REASONS.
WE CAN'T TELL YOU WHAT THEY ARE.
SORRY.
THAT'S NOT A WAY TO BUILD TRUST WITH ME.

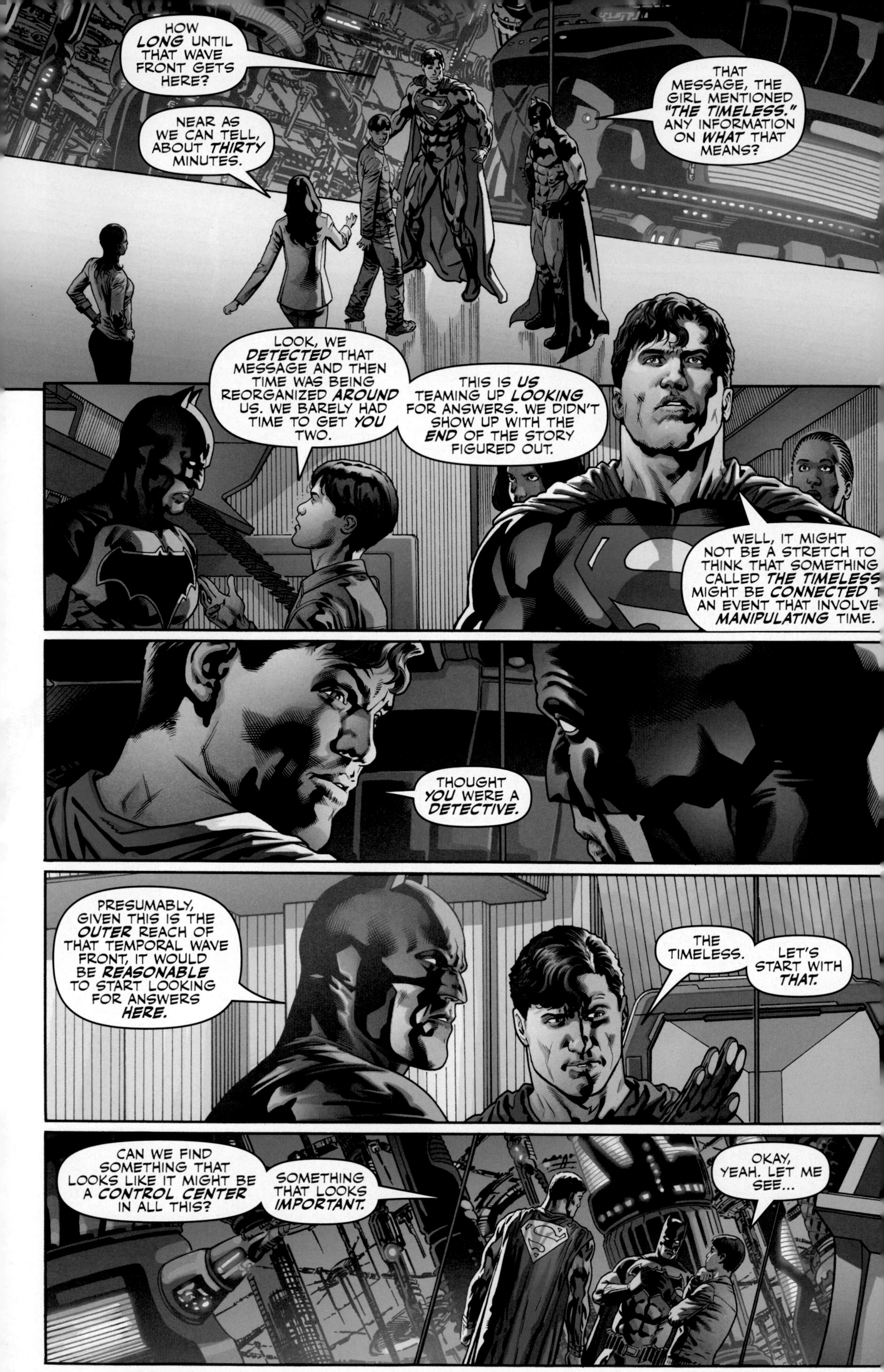
HOW LONG UNTIL THAT WAVE FRONT GETS HERE?
NEAR AS WE CAN TELL, ABOUT THIRTY MINUTES.
THAT MESSAGE, THE GIRL MENTIONED "THE TIMELESS." ANY INFORMATION ON WHAT THAT MEANS?
LOOK, WE DETECTED THAT MESSAGE AND THEN TIME WAS BEING REORGANIZED AROUND US. WE BARELY HAD TIME TO GET YOU TWO.
THIS IS US TEAMING UP LOOKING FOR ANSWERS. WE DIDN'T SHOW UP WITH THE END OF THE STORY FIGURED OUT.
WELL, IT MIGHT NOT BE A STRETCH TO THINK THAT SOMETHING CALLED THE TIMELESS MIGHT BE CONNECTED TO AN EVENT THAT INVOLVES MANIPULATING TIME.
THOUGHT YOU WERE A DETECTIVE.
PRESUMABLY, GIVEN THIS IS THE OUTER REACH OF THAT TEMPORAL WAVE FRONT, IT WOULD BE REASONABLE TO START LOOKING FOR ANSWERS HERE.
THE TIMELESS.
LET'S START WITH THAT.
CAN WE FIND SOMETHING THAT LOOKS LIKE IT MIGHT BE A CONTROL CENTER IN ALL THIS?
SOMETHING THAT LOOKS IMPORTANT.
OKAY, YEAH. LET ME SEE...

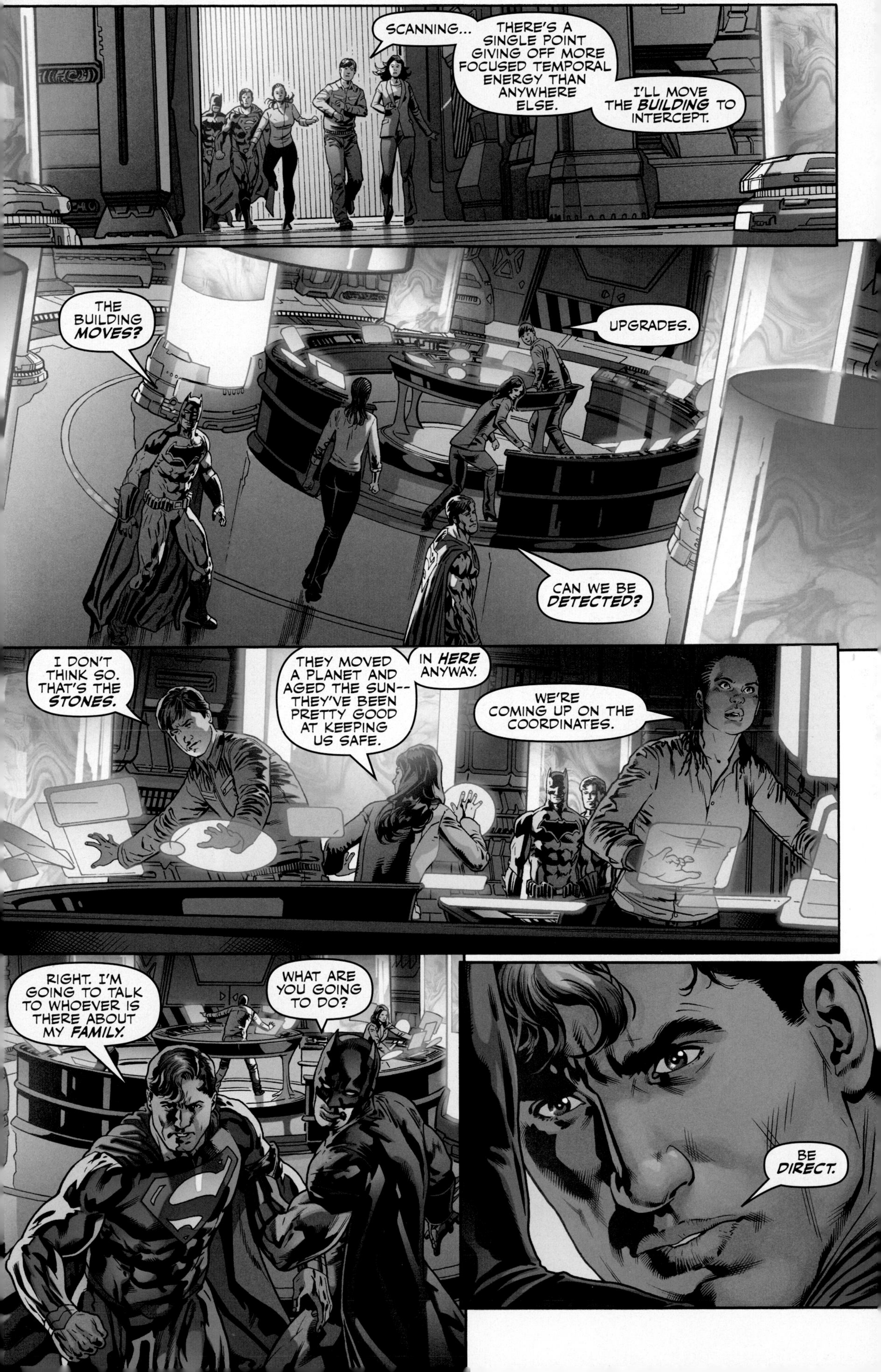
SCANNING... THERE'S A SINGLE POINT GIVING OFF MORE FOCUSED TEMPORAL ENERGY THAN ANYWHERE ELSE.
I'LL MOVE THE BUILDING TO INTERCEPT.
THE BUILDING MOVES?
UPGRADES.
CAN WE BE DETECTED?
I DON'T THINK SO. THAT'S THE STONES.
THEY MOVED A PLANET AND AGED THE SUN-- THEY'VE BEEN PRETTY GOOD AT KEEPING US SAFE.
IN HERE ANYWAY.
WE'RE COMING UP ON THE COORDINATES.
RIGHT. I'M GOING TO TALK TO WHOEVER IS THERE ABOUT MY FAMILY.
WHAT ARE YOU GOING TO DO?
BE DIRECT.

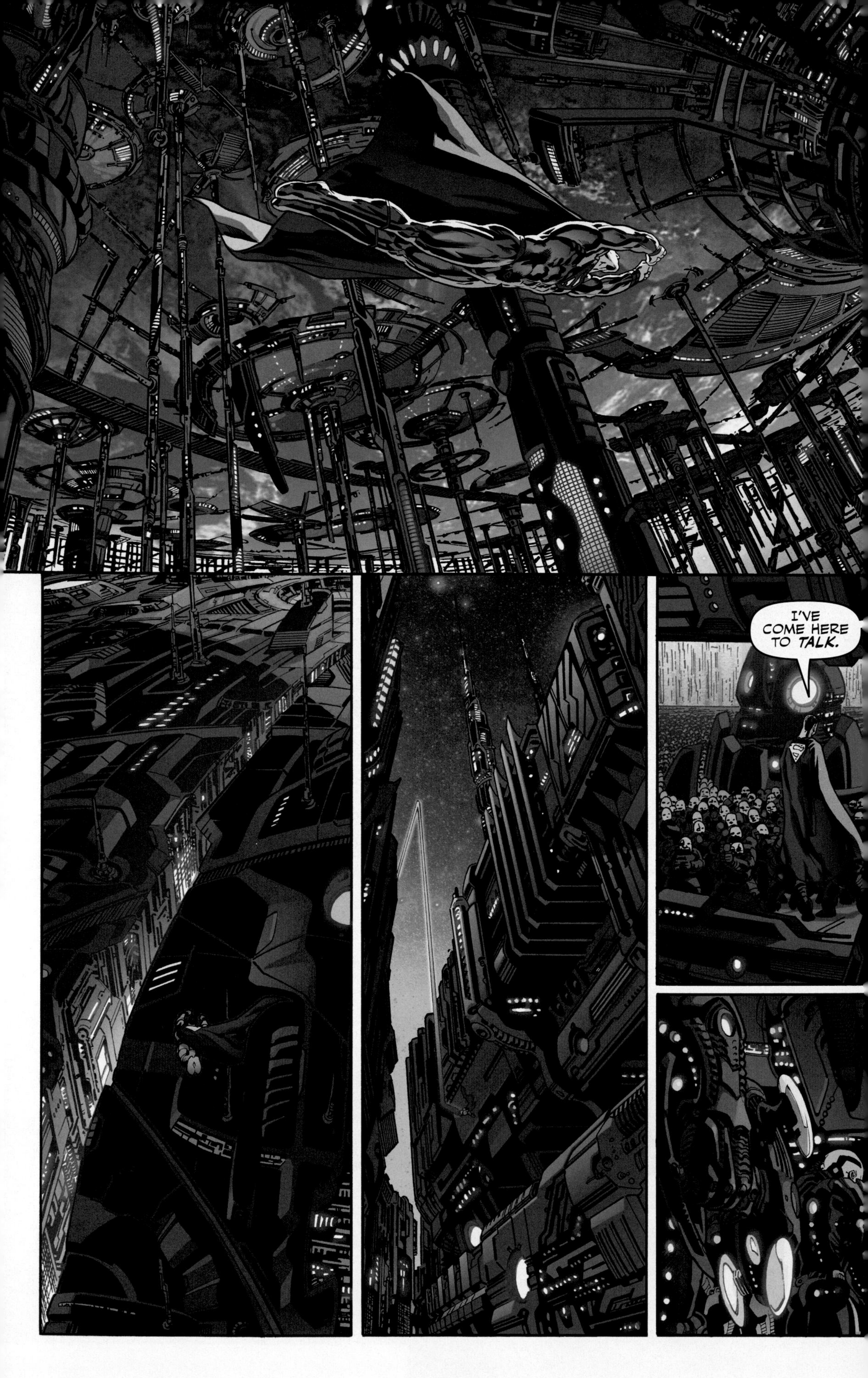
I'VE COME HERE TO TALK.

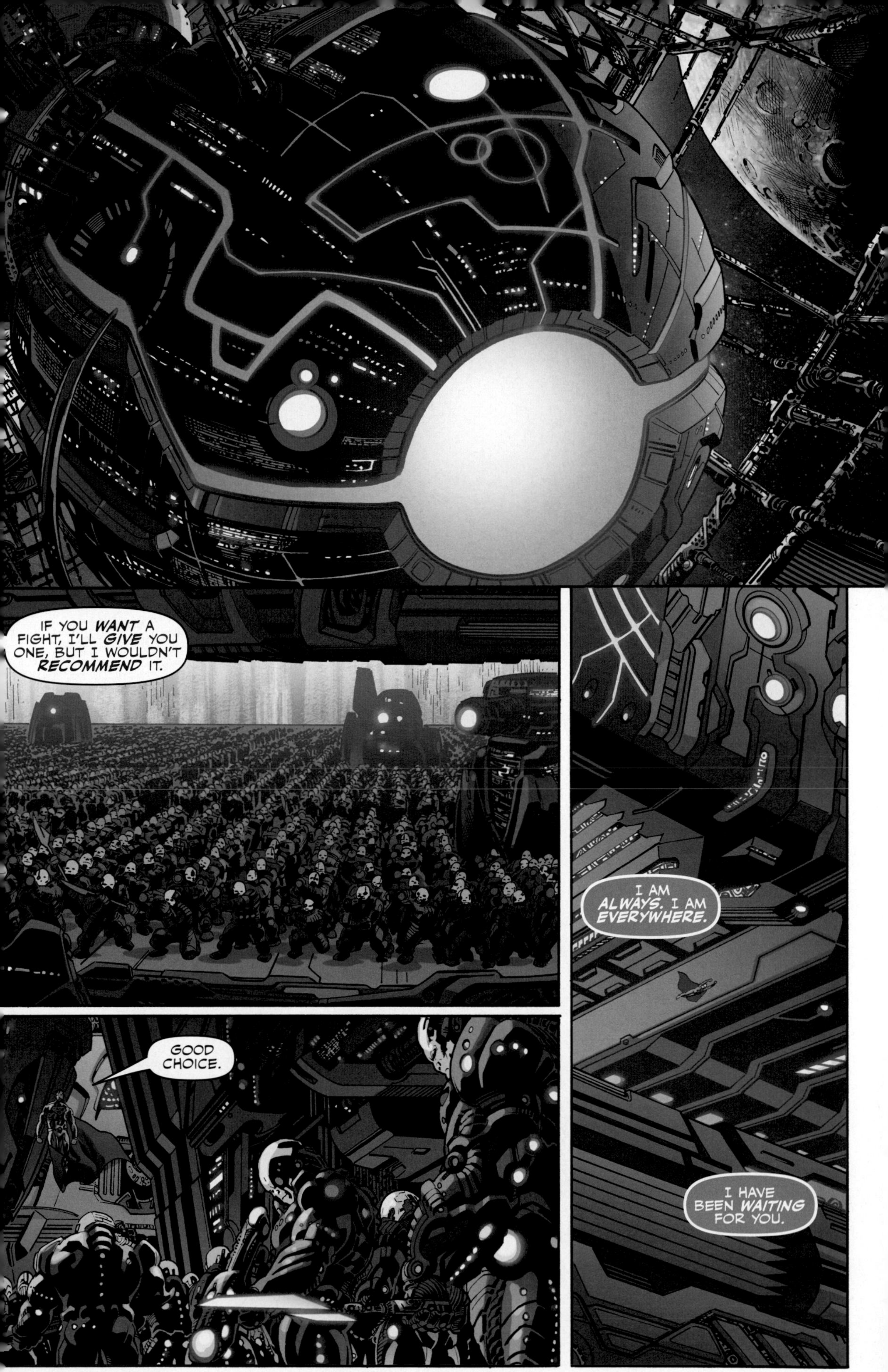
IF YOU WANT A FIGHT, I'LL GIVE YOU ONE, BUT I WOULDN'T RECOMMEND IT.
I AM ALWAYS. I AM EVERYWHERE.
I HAVE BEEN WAITING FOR YOU.
GOOD CHOICE.

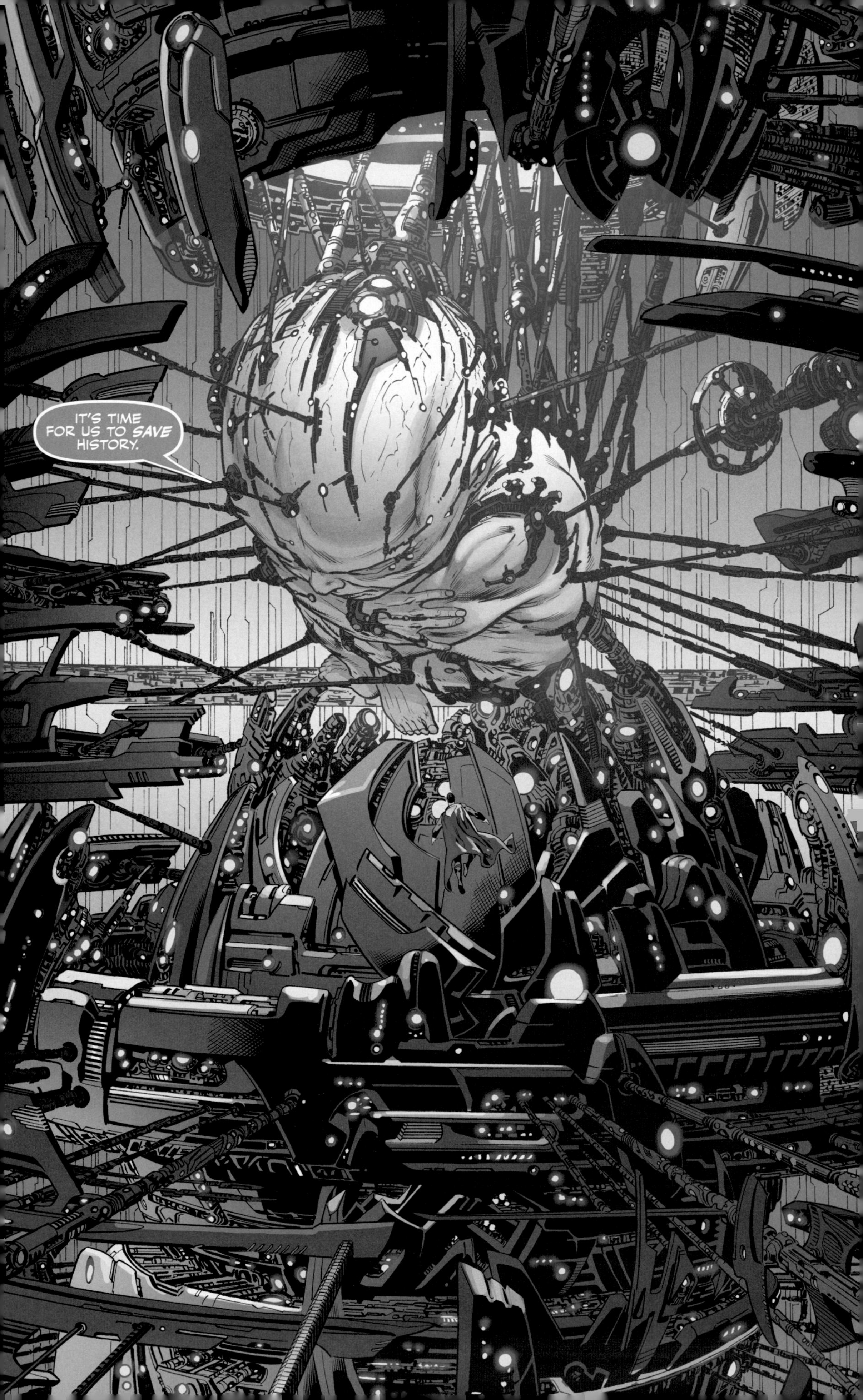
IT'S TIME FOR US TO *SAVE* HISTORY.

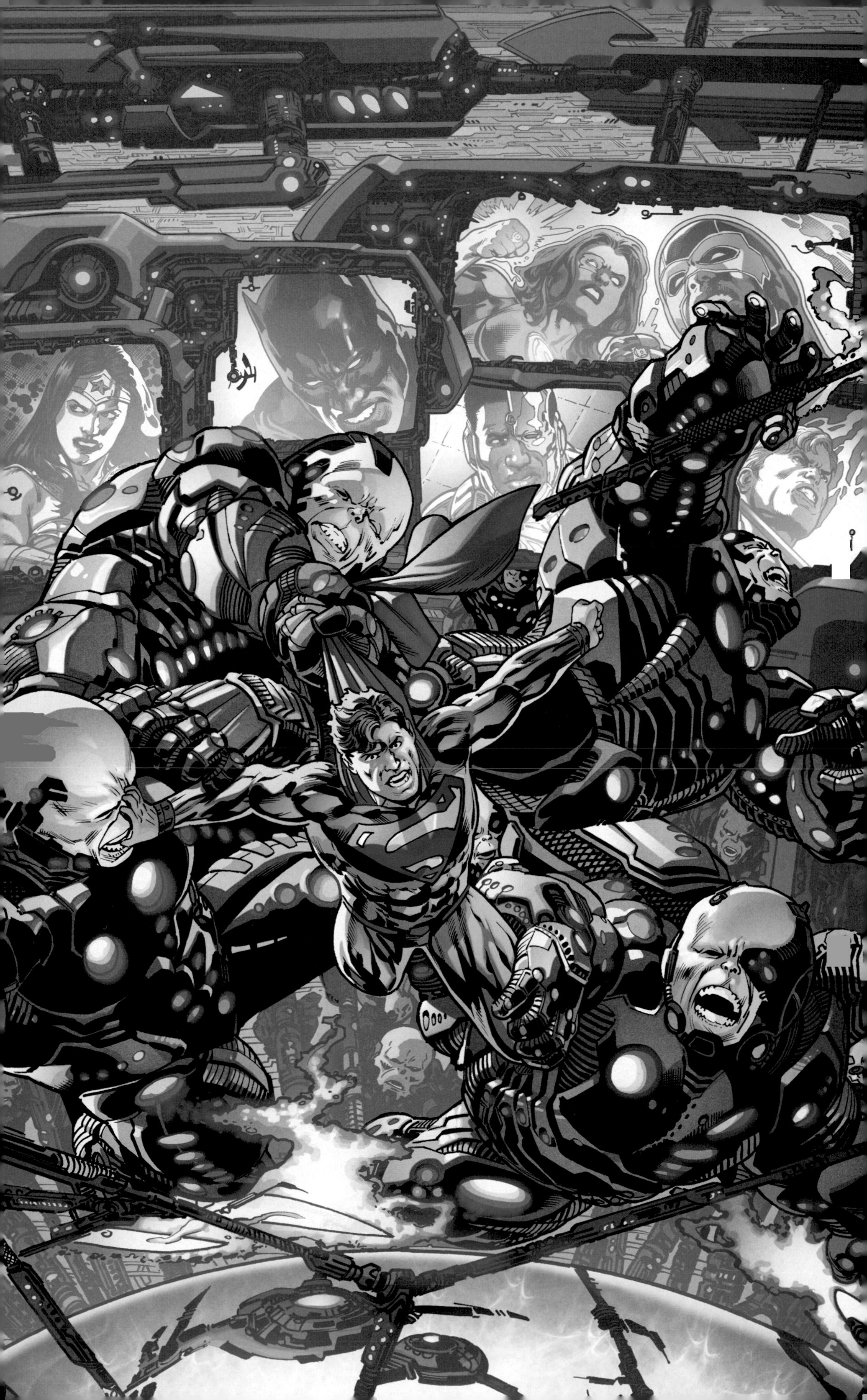

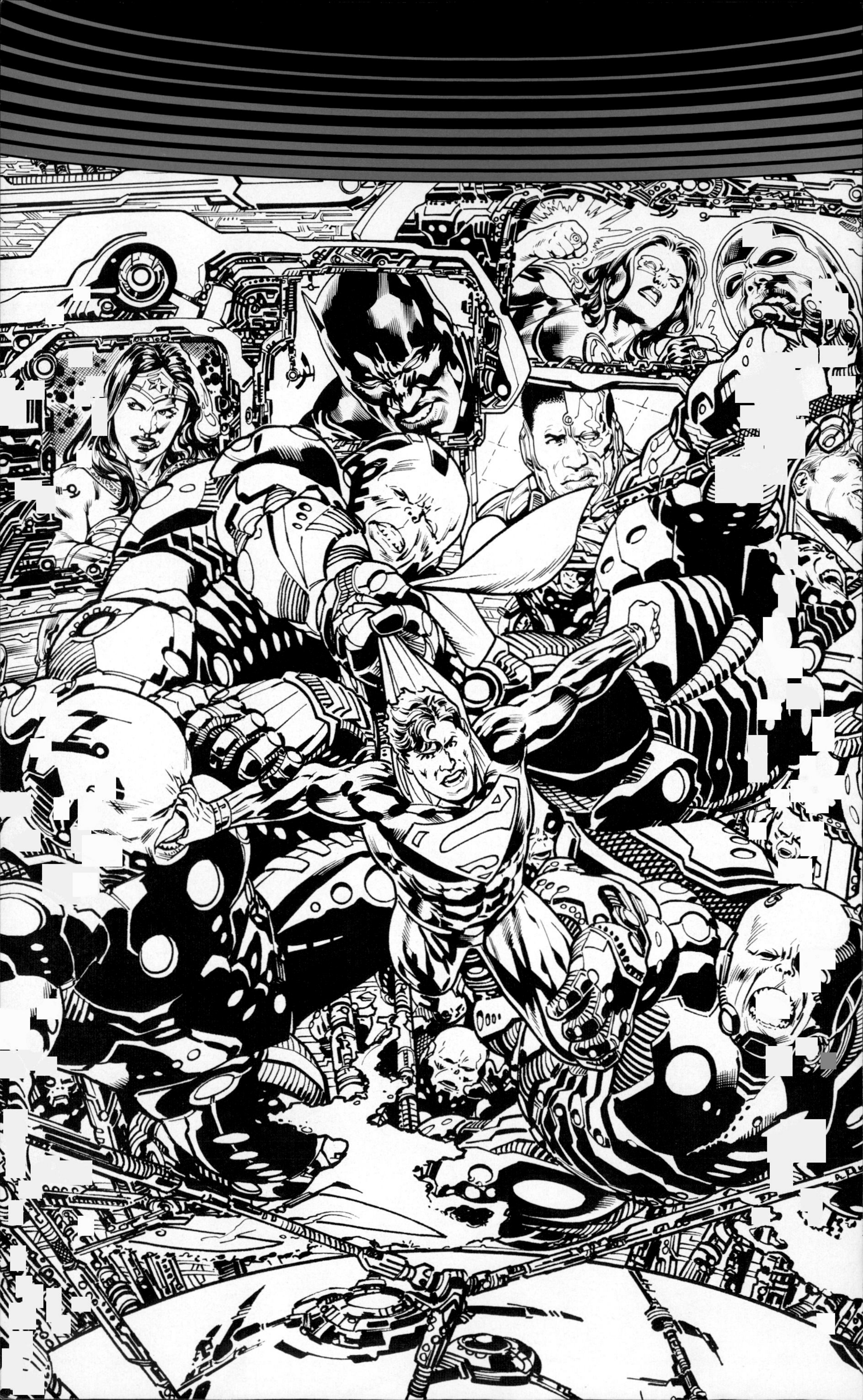

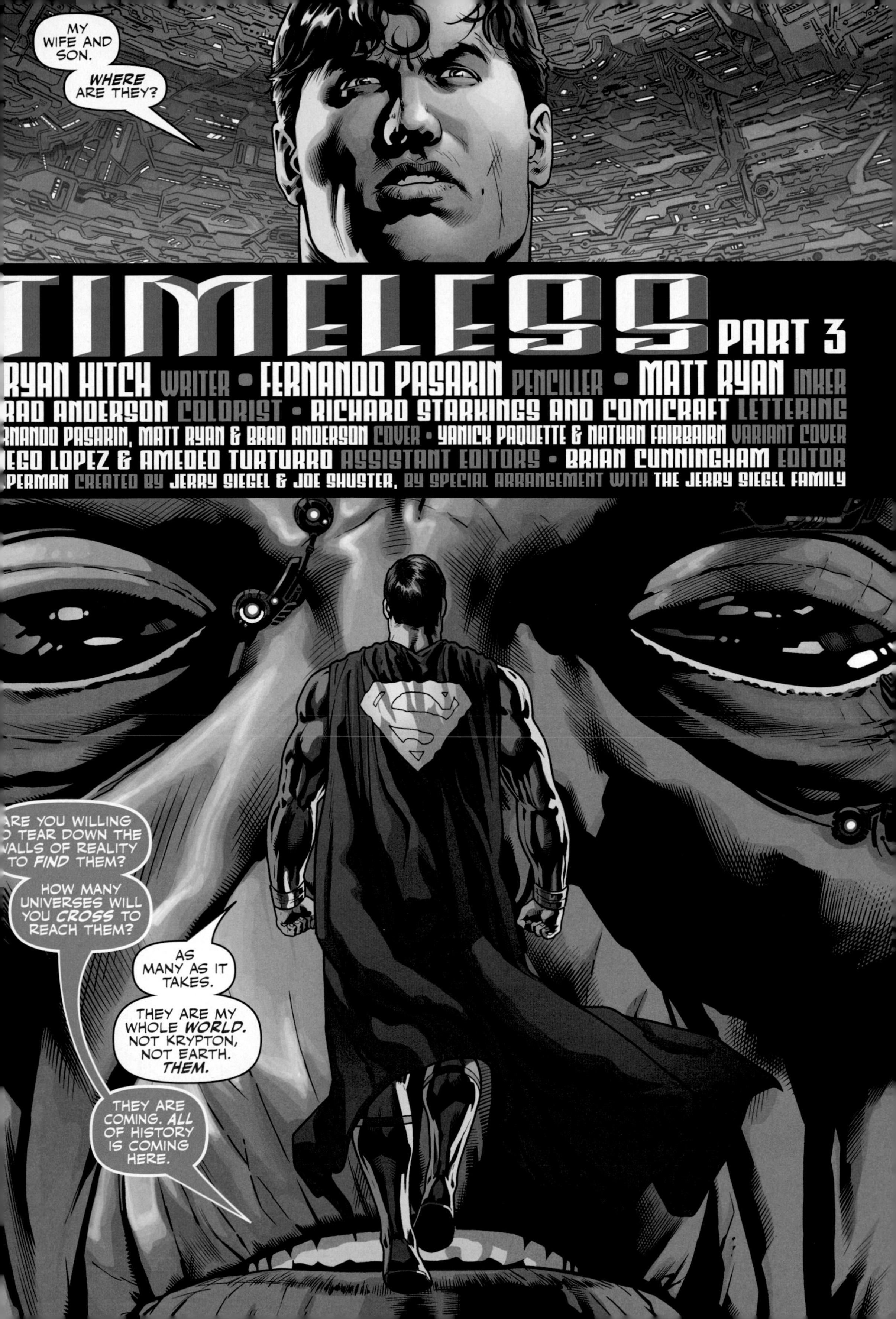
MY WIFE AND SON. WHERE ARE THEY?
TIMELESS PART 3
RYAN HITCH WRITER • FERNANDO PASARIN PENCILLER • MATT RYAN INKER
RAD ANDERSON COLORIST • RICHARD STARKINGS AND COMICRAFT LETTERING
RNANDO PASARIN, MATT RYAN & BRAD ANDERSON COVER • YANICK PAQUETTE & NATHAN FAIRBAIRN VARIANT COVER
EGO LOPEZ & AMEDEO TURTURRO ASSISTANT EDITORS • BRIAN CUNNINGHAM EDITOR
PERMAN CREATED BY JERRY SIEGEL & JOE SHUSTER, BY SPECIAL ARRANGEMENT WITH THE JERRY SIEGEL FAMILY
ARE YOU WILLING O TEAR DOWN THE VALLS OF REALITY TO FIND THEM?
HOW MANY UNIVERSES WILL YOU CROSS TO REACH THEM?
AS MANY AS IT TAKES.
THEY ARE MY WHOLE WORLD. NOT KRYPTON, NOT EARTH. THEM.
THEY ARE COMING. ALL OF HISTORY IS COMING HERE.

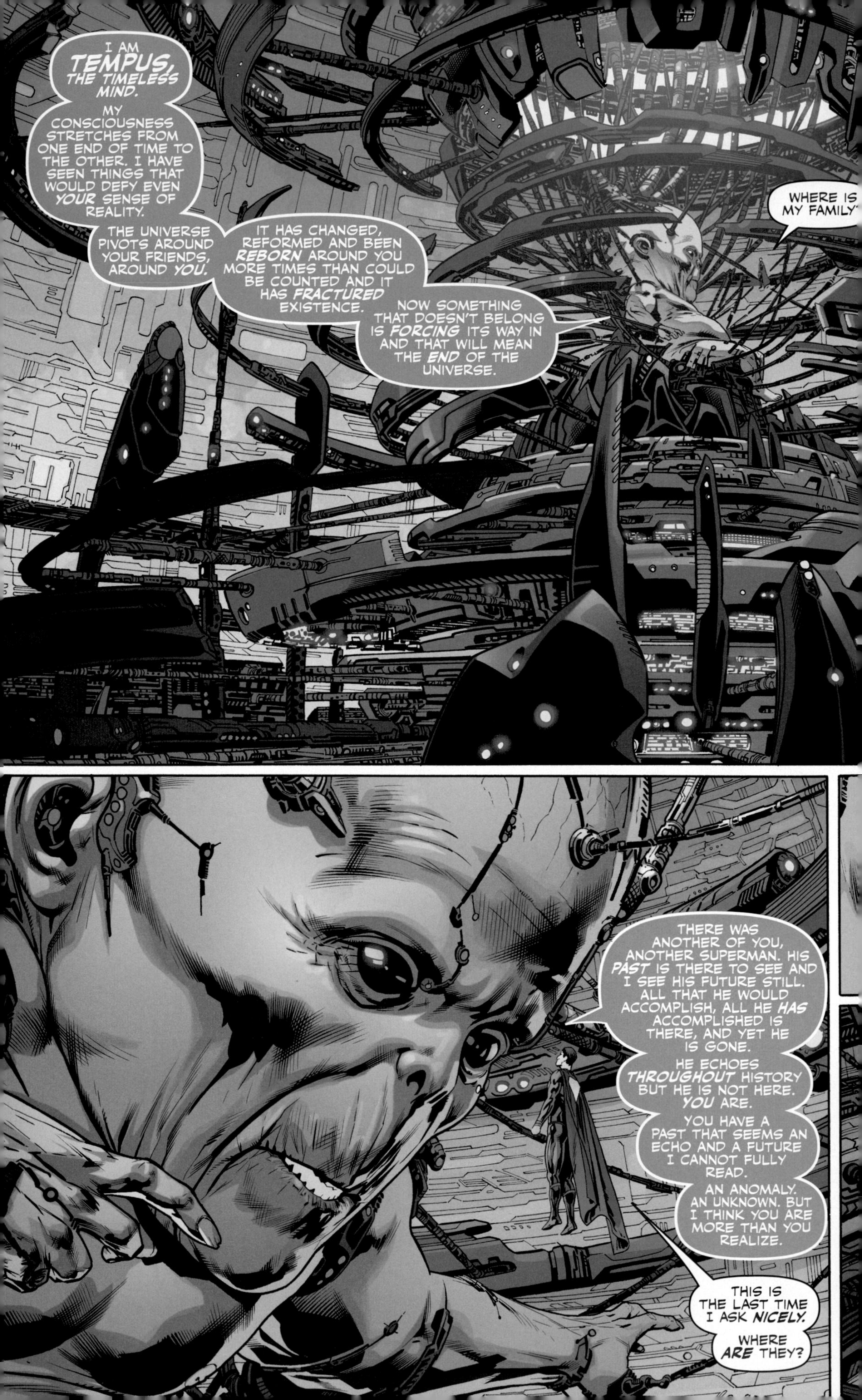
I AM TEMPUS, THE TIMELESS MIND.
MY CONSCIOUSNESS STRETCHES FROM ONE END OF TIME TO THE OTHER. I HAVE SEEN THINGS THAT WOULD DEFY EVEN YOUR SENSE OF REALITY.
THE UNIVERSE PIVOTS AROUND YOUR FRIENDS, AROUND YOU.
IT HAS CHANGED, REFORMED AND BEEN REBORN AROUND YOU MORE TIMES THAN COULD BE COUNTED AND IT HAS FRACTURED EXISTENCE.
NOW SOMETHING THAT DOESN'T BELONG IS FORCING ITS WAY IN AND THAT WILL MEAN THE END OF THE UNIVERSE.
WHERE IS MY FAMILY
THERE WAS ANOTHER OF YOU, ANOTHER SUPERMAN. HIS PAST IS THERE TO SEE AND I SEE HIS FUTURE STILL. ALL THAT HE WOULD ACCOMPLISH, ALL HE HAS ACCOMPLISHED IS THERE, AND YET HE IS GONE.
HE ECHOES THROUGHOUT HISTORY BUT HE IS NOT HERE. YOU ARE.
YOU HAVE A PAST THAT SEEMS AN ECHO AND A FUTURE I CANNOT FULLY READ.
AN ANOMALY. AN UNKNOWN. BUT I THINK YOU ARE MORE THAN YOU REALIZE.
THIS IS THE LAST TIME I ASK NICELY.
WHERE ARE THEY?

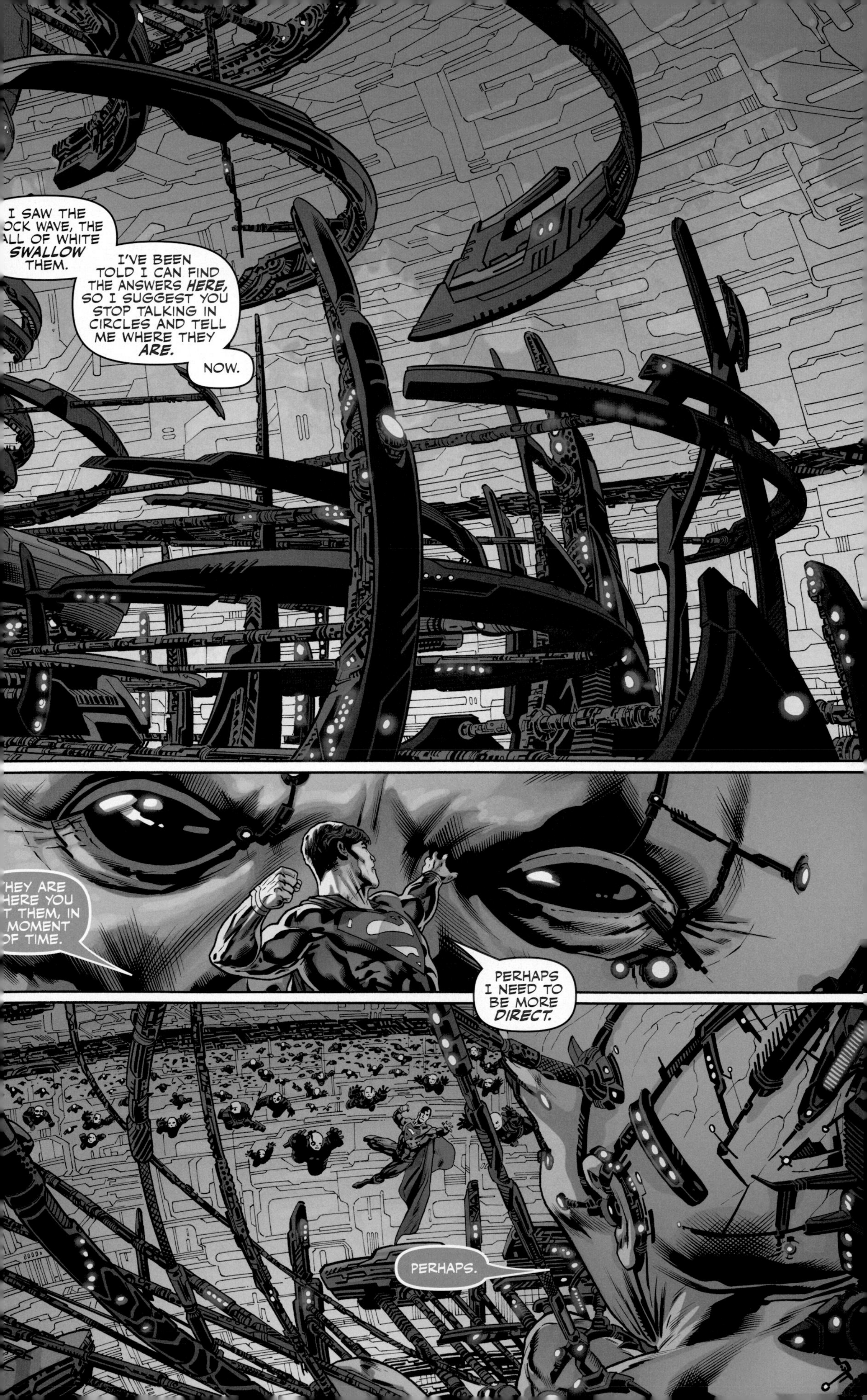
I SAW THE OCK WAVE, THE ALL OF WHITE SWALLOW THEM.
I'VE BEEN TOLD I CAN FIND THE ANSWERS HERE, SO I SUGGEST YOU STOP TALKING IN CIRCLES AND TELL ME WHERE THEY ARE.
NOW.
HEY ARE HERE YOU T THEM, IN MOMENT OF TIME.
PERHAPS I NEED TO BE MORE DIRECT.
PERHAPS.

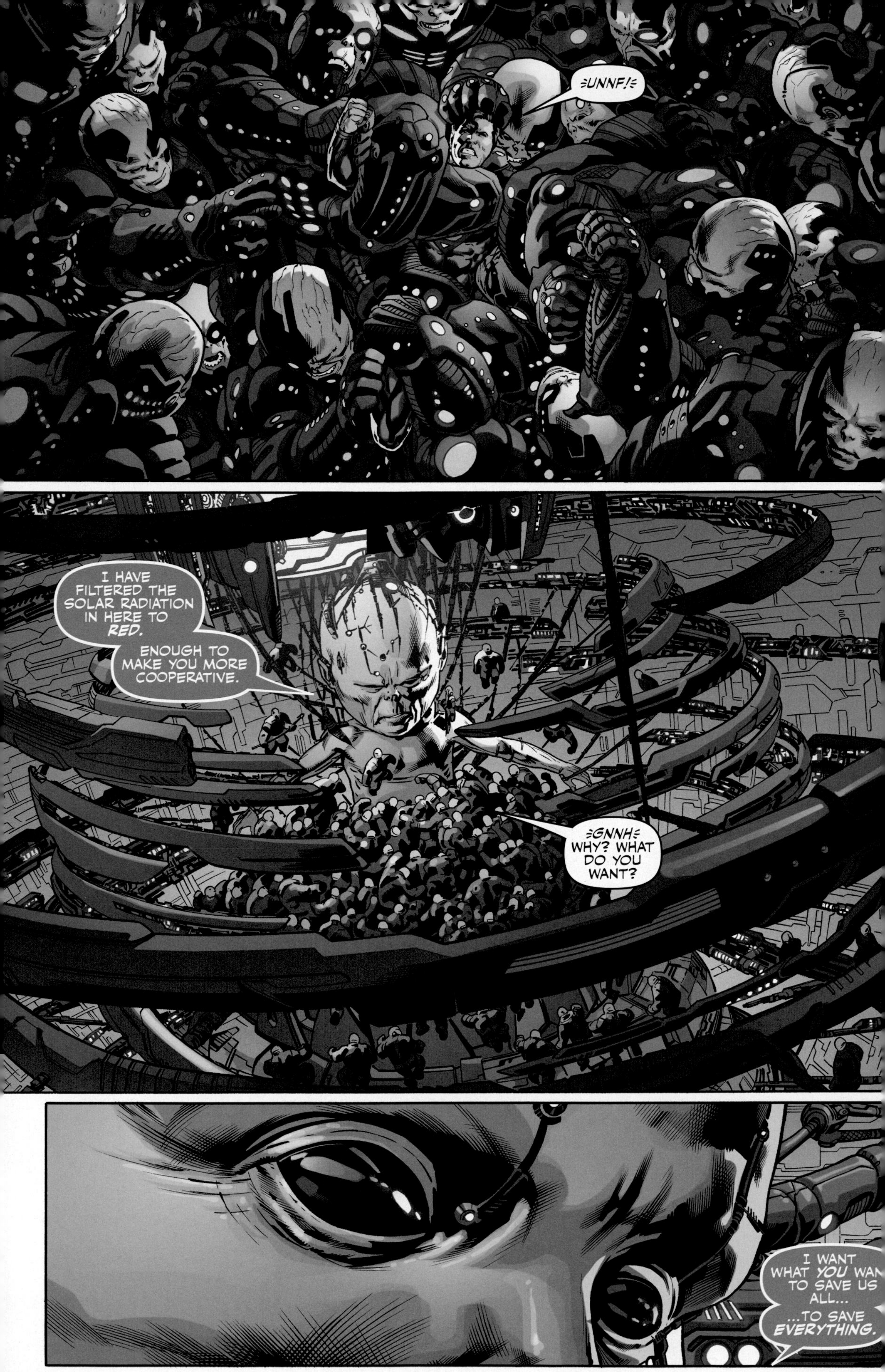
UNNF!
I HAVE FILTERED THE SOLAR RADIATION IN HERE TO *RED*.
ENOUGH TO MAKE YOU MORE COOPERATIVE.
GNNH WHY? WHAT DO YOU WANT?
I WANT WHAT *YOU* WAN
TO SAVE US ALL...
...TO SAVE *EVERYTHING*.

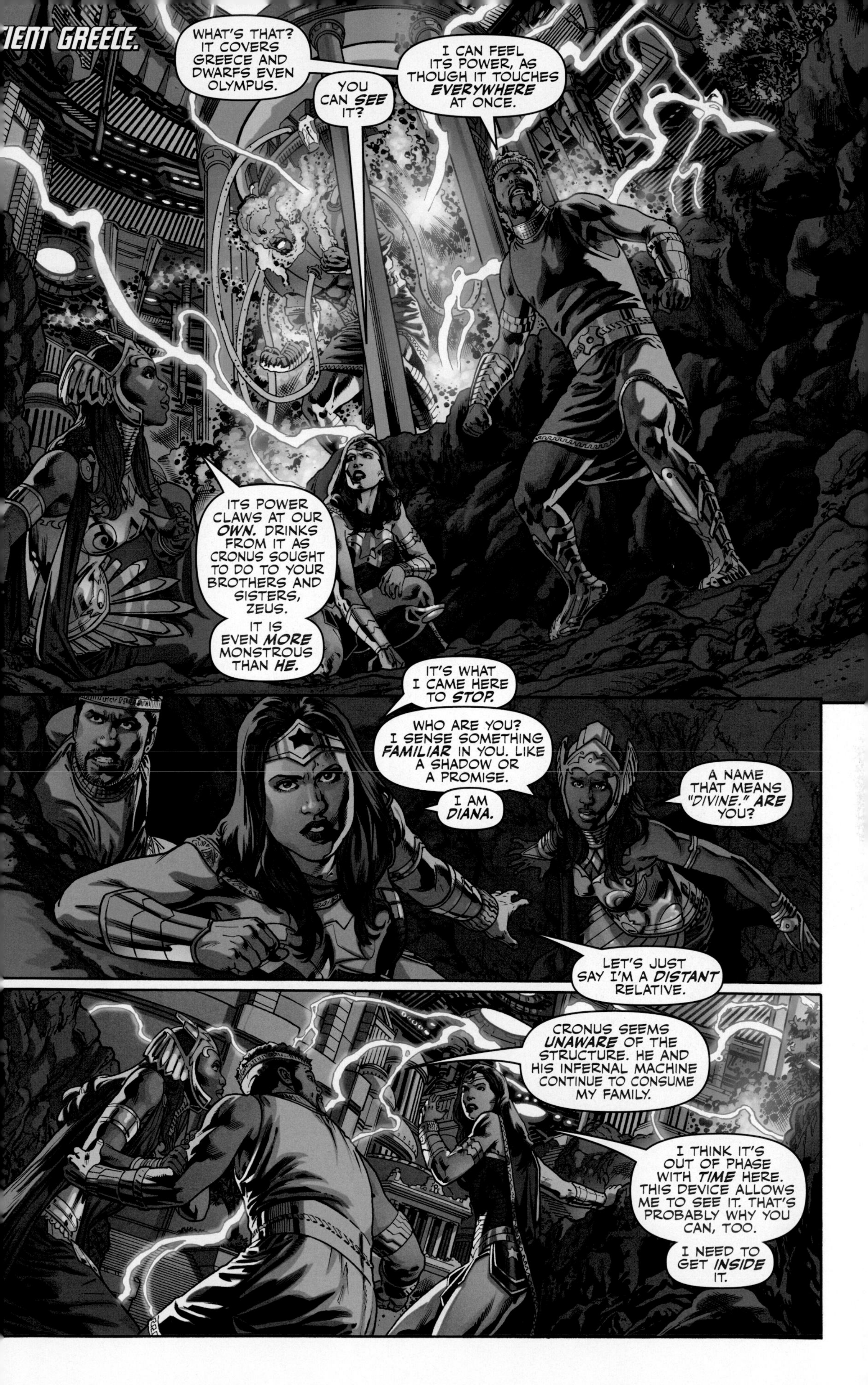
IENT GREECE.
WHAT'S THAT? IT COVERS GREECE AND DWARFS EVEN OLYMPUS.
YOU CAN SEE IT?
I CAN FEEL ITS POWER, AS THOUGH IT TOUCHES EVERYWHERE AT ONCE.
ITS POWER CLAWS AT OUR OWN. DRINKS FROM IT AS CRONUS SOUGHT TO DO TO YOUR BROTHERS AND SISTERS, ZEUS.
IT IS EVEN MORE MONSTROUS THAN HE.
IT'S WHAT I CAME HERE TO STOP.
WHO ARE YOU? I SENSE SOMETHING FAMILIAR IN YOU. LIKE A SHADOW OR A PROMISE.
I AM DIANA.
A NAME THAT MEANS "DIVINE." ARE YOU?
LET'S JUST SAY I'M A DISTANT RELATIVE.
CRONUS SEEMS UNAWARE OF THE STRUCTURE. HE AND HIS INFERNAL MACHINE CONTINUE TO CONSUME MY FAMILY.
I THINK IT'S OUT OF PHASE WITH TIME HERE. THIS DEVICE ALLOWS ME TO SEE IT. THAT'S PROBABLY WHY YOU CAN, TOO.
I NEED TO GET INSIDE IT.

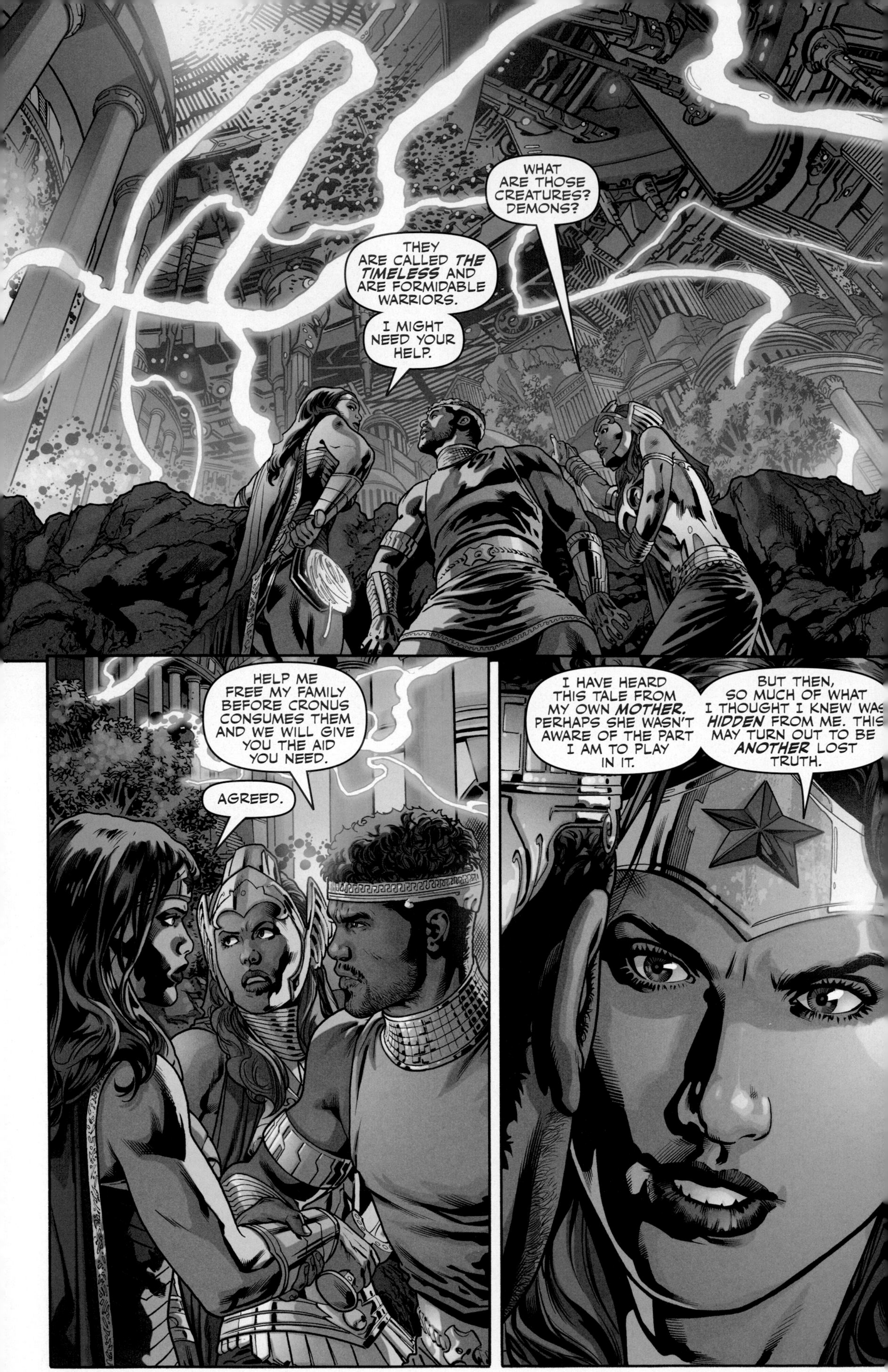
WHAT ARE THOSE CREATURES? DEMONS?
THEY ARE CALLED *THE TIMELESS* AND ARE FORMIDABLE WARRIORS.
I MIGHT NEED YOUR HELP.
HELP ME FREE MY FAMILY BEFORE CRONUS CONSUMES THEM AND WE WILL GIVE YOU THE AID YOU NEED.
AGREED.
I HAVE HEARD THIS TALE FROM MY OWN *MOTHER.* PERHAPS SHE WASN'T AWARE OF THE PART I AM TO PLAY IN IT.
BUT THEN, SO MUCH OF WHAT I THOUGHT I KNEW WAS *HIDDEN* FROM ME. THIS MAY TURN OUT TO BE *ANOTHER* LOST TRUTH.

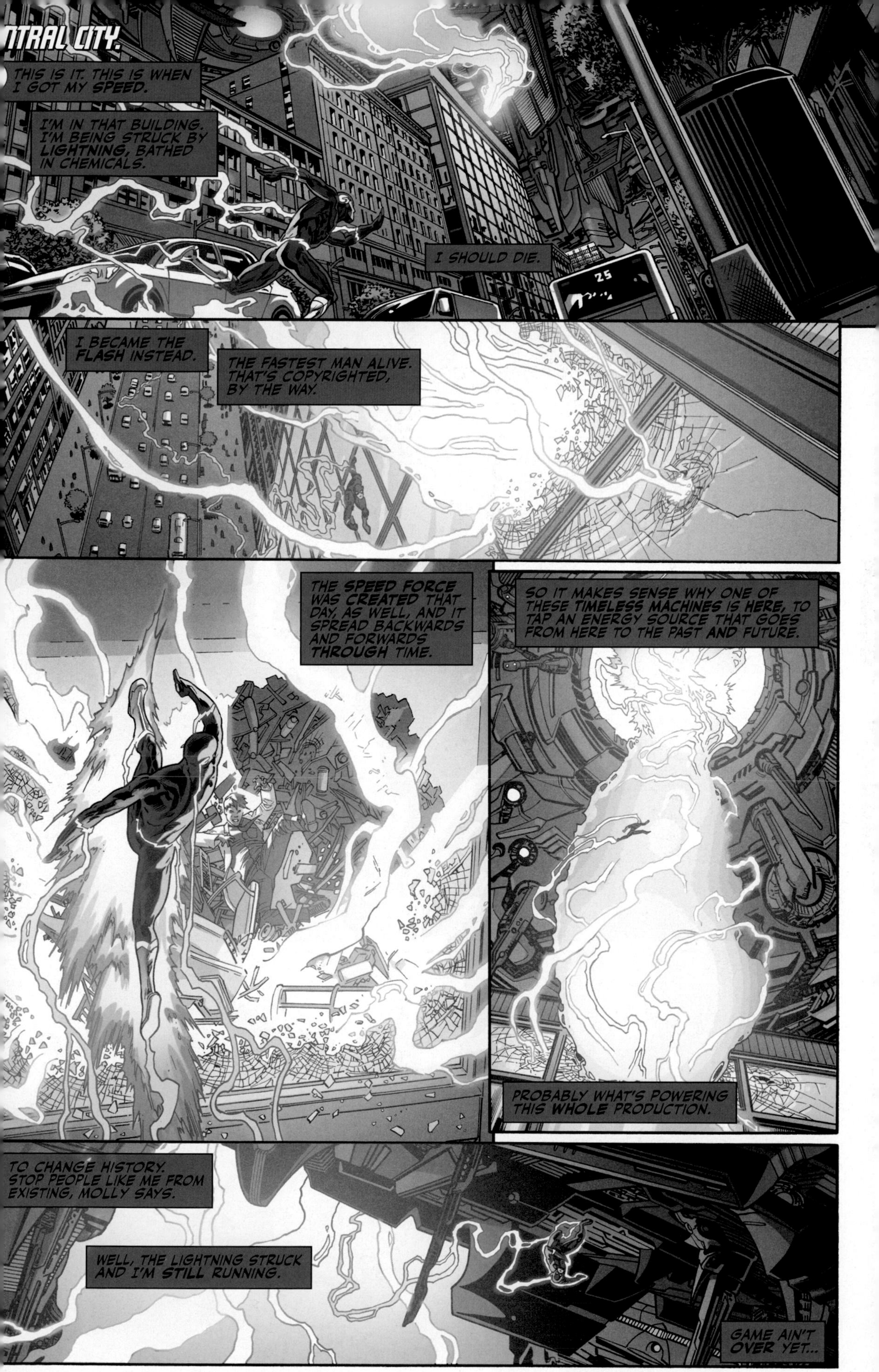
NTRAL CITY.
THIS IS IT. THIS IS WHEN I GOT MY SPEED.
I'M IN THAT BUILDING. I'M BEING STRUCK BY LIGHTNING, BATHED IN CHEMICALS.
I SHOULD DIE.
25
I BECAME THE FLASH INSTEAD.
THE FASTEST MAN ALIVE. THAT'S COPYRIGHTED, BY THE WAY.
THE SPEED FORCE WAS CREATED THAT DAY, AS WELL, AND IT SPREAD BACKWARDS AND FORWARDS THROUGH TIME.
SO IT MAKES SENSE WHY ONE OF THESE TIMELESS MACHINES IS HERE, TO TAP AN ENERGY SOURCE THAT GOES FROM HERE TO THE PAST AND FUTURE.
PROBABLY WHAT'S POWERING THIS WHOLE PRODUCTION.
TO CHANGE HISTORY. STOP PEOPLE LIKE ME FROM EXISTING, MOLLY SAYS.
WELL, THE LIGHTNING STRUCK AND I'M STILL RUNNING.
GAME AIN'T OVER YET...

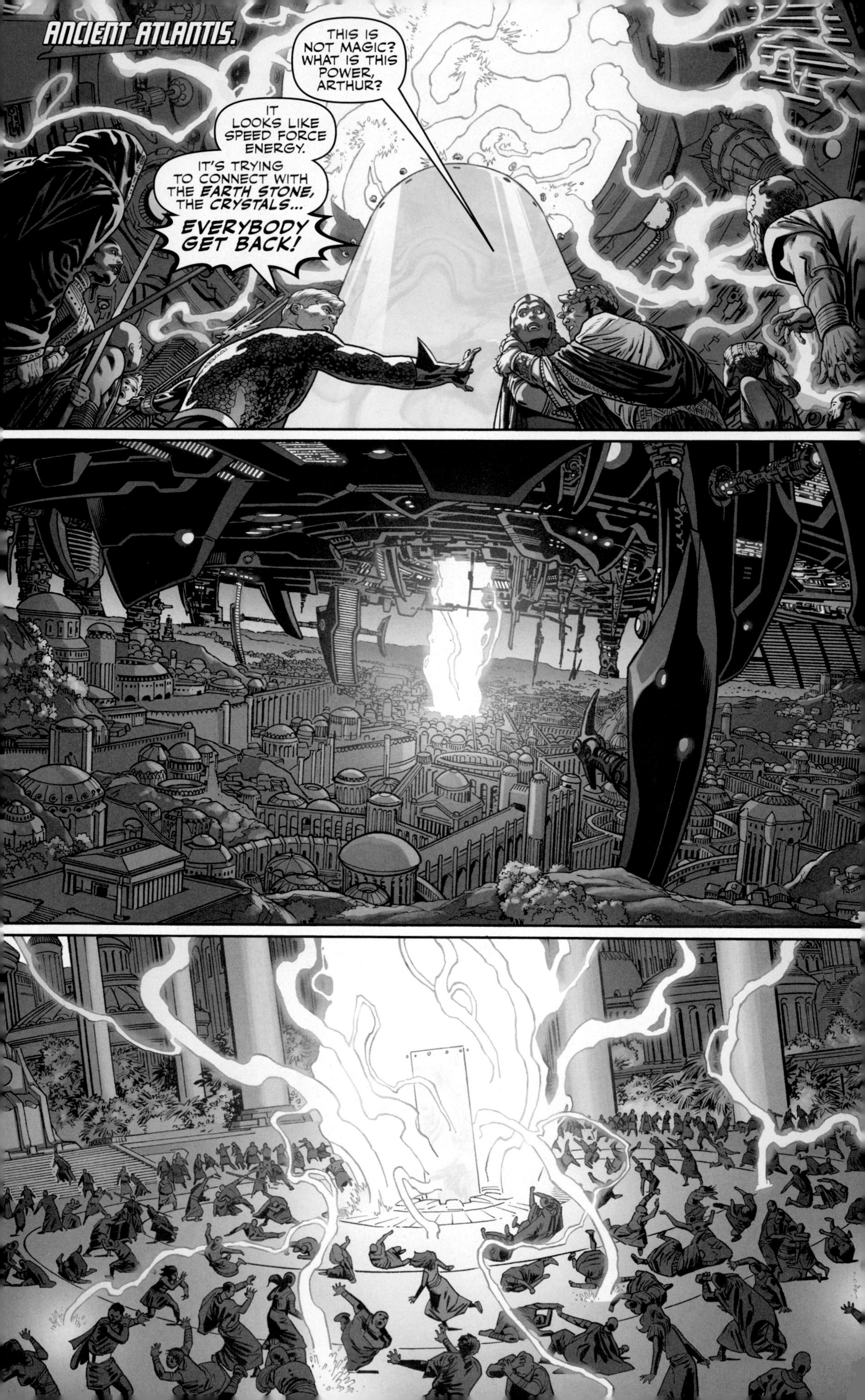
ANCIENT ATLANTIS.
THIS IS NOT MAGIC? WHAT IS THIS POWER, ARTHUR?
IT LOOKS LIKE SPEED FORCE ENERGY.
IT'S TRYING TO CONNECT WITH THE EARTH STONE, THE CRYSTALS...
EVERYBODY GET BACK!

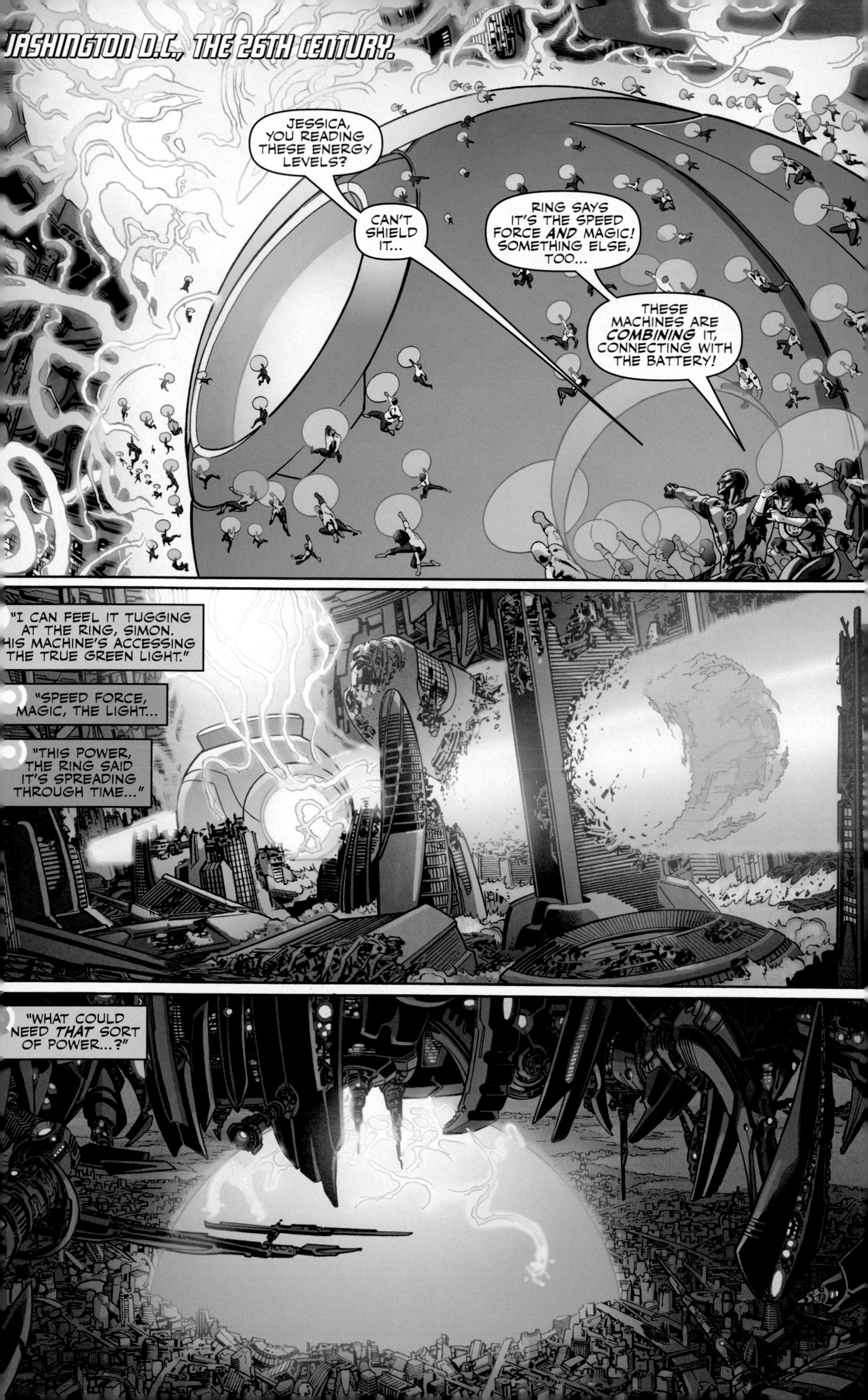
JASHINGTON D.C., THE 26TH CENTURY.
JESSICA, YOU READING THESE ENERGY LEVELS?
CAN'T SHIELD IT...
RING SAYS IT'S THE SPEED FORCE *AND* MAGIC! SOMETHING ELSE, TOO...
THESE MACHINES ARE *COMBINING* IT, CONNECTING WITH THE BATTERY!
"I CAN FEEL IT TUGGING AT THE RING, SIMON. HIS MACHINE'S ACCESSING THE TRUE GREEN LIGHT."
"SPEED FORCE, MAGIC, THE LIGHT...
"THIS POWER, THE RING SAID IT'S SPREADING THROUGH TIME..."
"WHAT COULD NEED *THAT* SORT OF POWER...?"

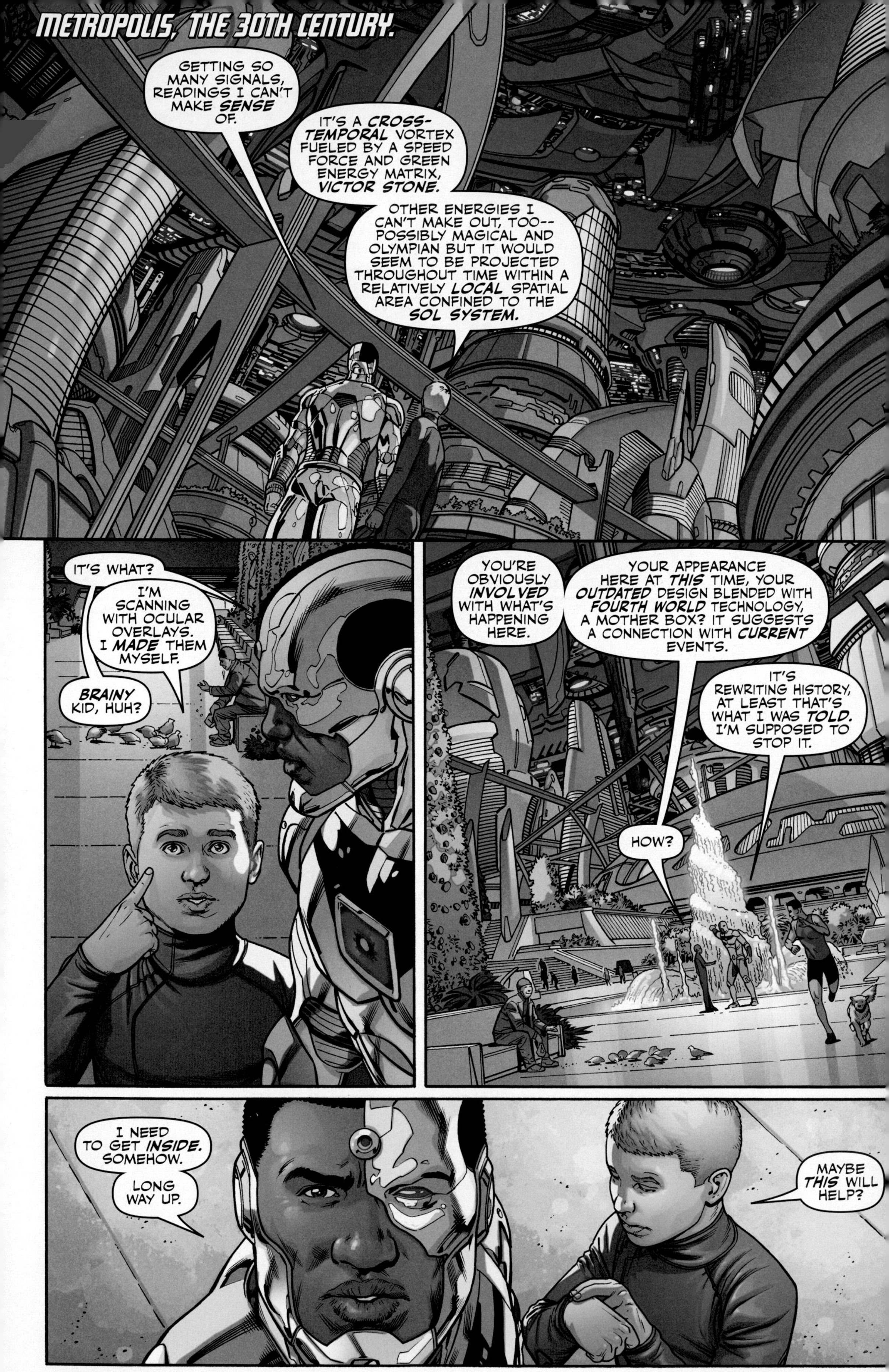
METROPOLIS, THE 30TH CENTURY.
GETTING SO MANY SIGNALS, READINGS I CAN'T MAKE SENSE OF.
IT'S A CROSS-TEMPORAL VORTEX FUELED BY A SPEED FORCE AND GREEN ENERGY MATRIX, VICTOR STONE.
OTHER ENERGIES I CAN'T MAKE OUT, TOO-- POSSIBLY MAGICAL AND OLYMPIAN BUT IT WOULD SEEM TO BE PROJECTED THROUGHOUT TIME WITHIN A RELATIVELY LOCAL SPATIAL AREA CONFINED TO THE SOL SYSTEM.
IT'S WHAT?
I'M SCANNING WITH OCULAR OVERLAYS. I MADE THEM MYSELF.
BRAINY KID, HUH?
YOU'RE OBVIOUSLY INVOLVED WITH WHAT'S HAPPENING HERE.
YOUR APPEARANCE HERE AT THIS TIME, YOUR OUTDATED DESIGN BLENDED WITH FOURTH WORLD TECHNOLOGY, A MOTHER BOX? IT SUGGESTS A CONNECTION WITH CURRENT EVENTS.
HOW?
IT'S REWRITING HISTORY, AT LEAST THAT'S WHAT I WAS TOLD. I'M SUPPOSED TO STOP IT.
I NEED TO GET INSIDE. SOMEHOW.
LONG WAY UP.
MAYBE THIS WILL HELP?

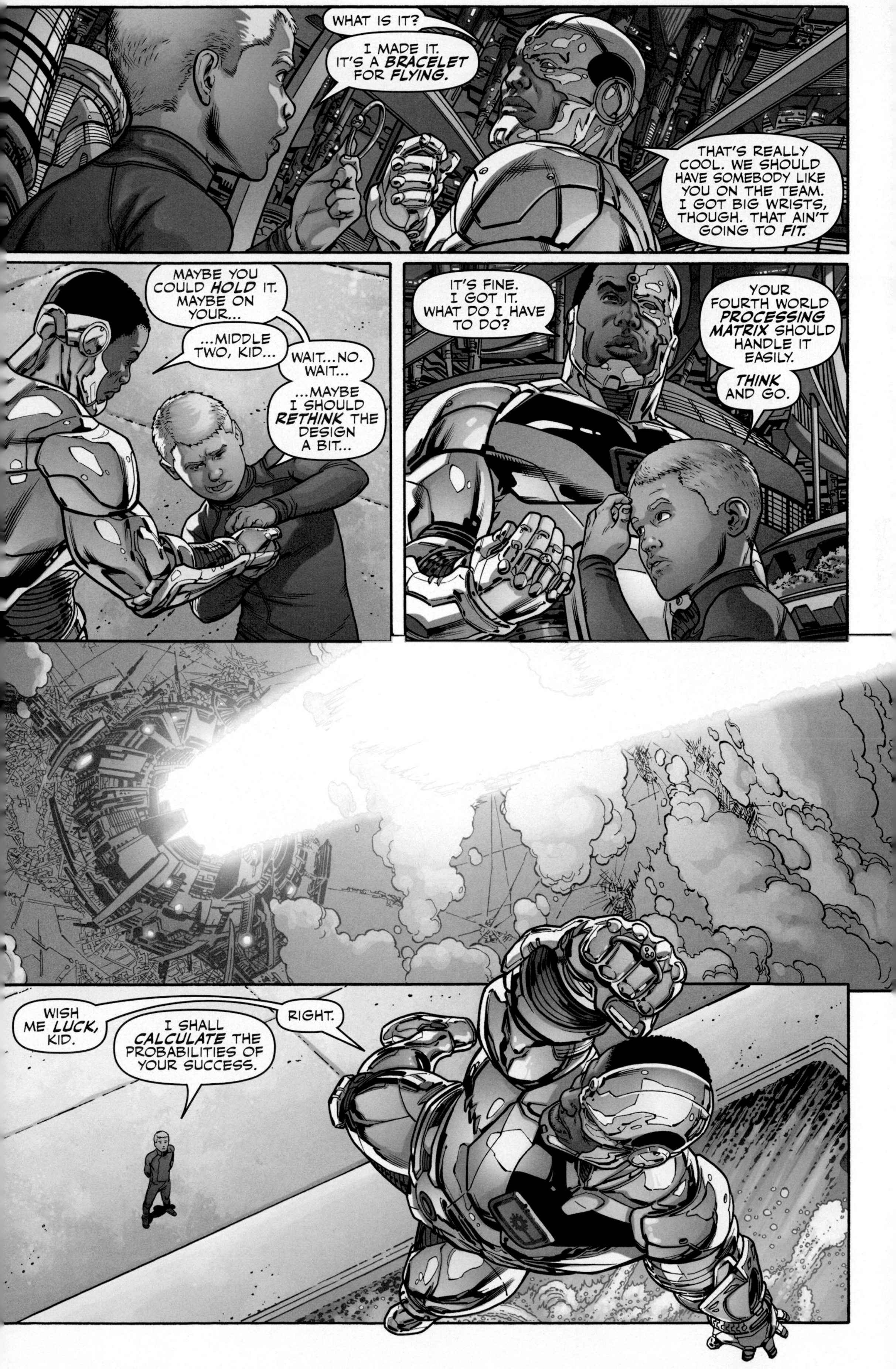
WHAT IS IT?
I MADE IT. IT'S A BRACELET FOR FLYING.
THAT'S REALLY COOL. WE SHOULD HAVE SOMEBODY LIKE YOU ON THE TEAM. I GOT BIG WRISTS, THOUGH. THAT AIN'T GOING TO FIT.
MAYBE YOU COULD HOLD IT. MAYBE ON YOUR...
...MIDDLE TWO, KID...
WAIT...NO. WAIT...
...MAYBE I SHOULD RETHINK THE DESIGN A BIT...
IT'S FINE. I GOT IT. WHAT DO I HAVE TO DO?
YOUR FOURTH WORLD PROCESSING MATRIX SHOULD HANDLE IT EASILY.
THINK AND GO.
WISH ME LUCK, KID.
I SHALL CALCULATE THE PROBABILITIES OF YOUR SUCCESS.
RIGHT.

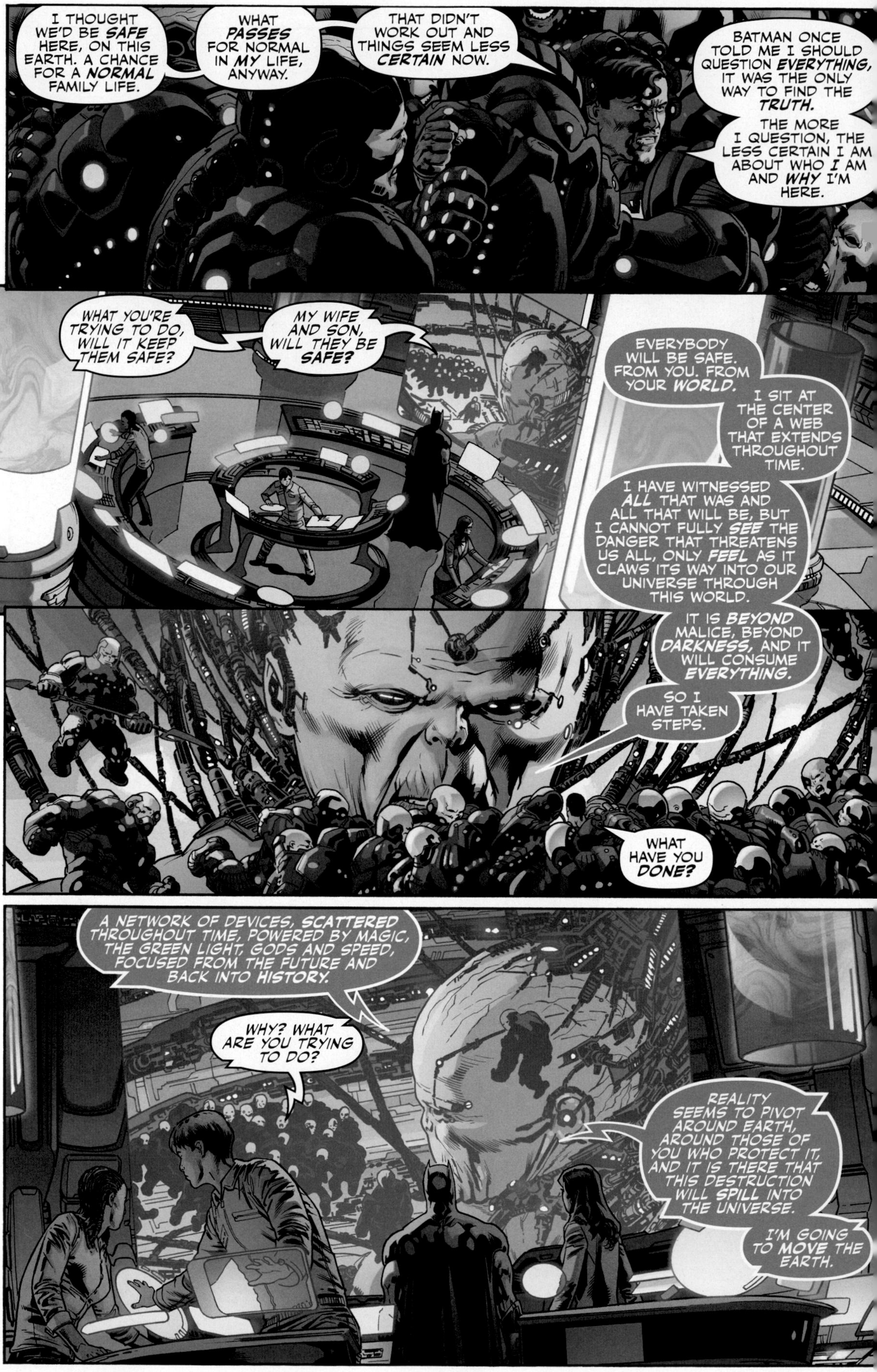
I THOUGHT WE'D BE SAFE HERE, ON THIS EARTH. A CHANCE FOR A NORMAL FAMILY LIFE.
WHAT PASSES FOR NORMAL IN MY LIFE, ANYWAY.
THAT DIDN'T WORK OUT AND THINGS SEEM LESS CERTAIN NOW.
BATMAN ONCE TOLD ME I SHOULD QUESTION EVERYTHING, IT WAS THE ONLY WAY TO FIND THE TRUTH.
THE MORE I QUESTION, THE LESS CERTAIN I AM ABOUT WHO I AM AND WHY I'M HERE.
WHAT YOU'RE TRYING TO DO, WILL IT KEEP THEM SAFE?
MY WIFE AND SON, WILL THEY BE SAFE?
EVERYBODY WILL BE SAFE. FROM YOU. FROM YOUR WORLD.
I SIT AT THE CENTER OF A WEB THAT EXTENDS THROUGHOUT TIME.
I HAVE WITNESSED ALL THAT WAS AND ALL THAT WILL BE, BUT I CANNOT FULLY SEE THE DANGER THAT THREATENS US ALL, ONLY FEEL AS IT CLAWS ITS WAY INTO OUR UNIVERSE THROUGH THIS WORLD.
IT IS BEYOND MALICE, BEYOND DARKNESS, AND IT WILL CONSUME EVERYTHING.
SO I HAVE TAKEN STEPS.
WHAT HAVE YOU DONE?
A NETWORK OF DEVICES, SCATTERED THROUGHOUT TIME, POWERED BY MAGIC, THE GREEN LIGHT, GODS AND SPEED, FOCUSED FROM THE FUTURE AND BACK INTO HISTORY.
WHY? WHAT ARE YOU TRYING TO DO?
REALITY SEEMS TO PIVOT AROUND EARTH, AROUND THOSE OF YOU WHO PROTECT IT, AND IT IS THERE THAT THIS DESTRUCTION WILL SPILL INTO THE UNIVERSE.
I'M GOING TO MOVE THE EARTH.

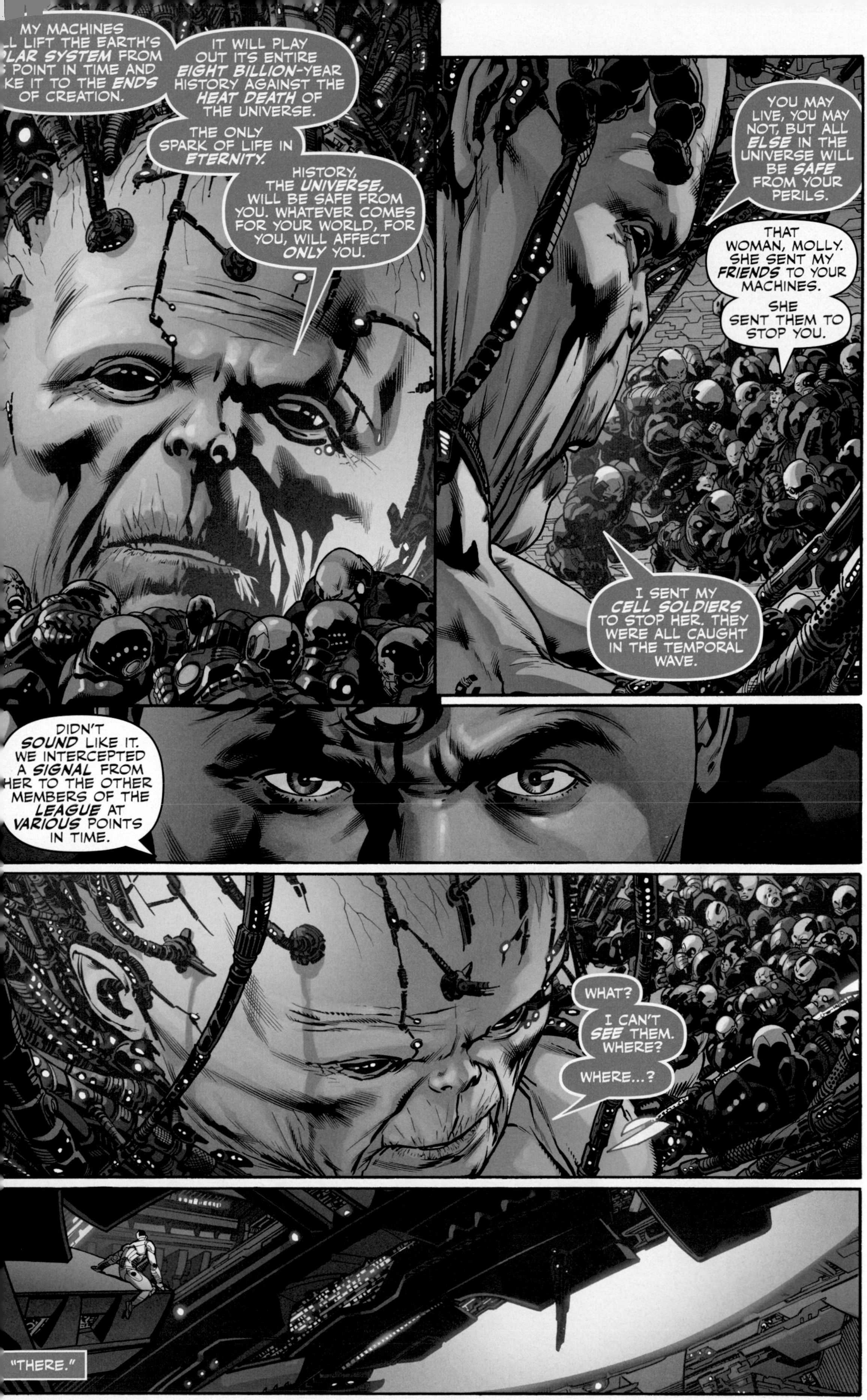
MY MACHINES L LIFT THE EARTH'S LAR SYSTEM FROM POINT IN TIME AND KE IT TO THE ENDS OF CREATION.
IT WILL PLAY OUT ITS ENTIRE EIGHT BILLION-YEAR HISTORY AGAINST THE HEAT DEATH OF THE UNIVERSE.
THE ONLY SPARK OF LIFE IN ETERNITY.
HISTORY, THE UNIVERSE, WILL BE SAFE FROM YOU. WHATEVER COMES FOR YOUR WORLD, FOR YOU, WILL AFFECT ONLY YOU.
YOU MAY LIVE, YOU MAY NOT, BUT ALL ELSE IN THE UNIVERSE WILL BE SAFE FROM YOUR PERILS.
THAT WOMAN, MOLLY. SHE SENT MY FRIENDS TO YOUR MACHINES.
SHE SENT THEM TO STOP YOU.
I SENT MY CELL SOLDIERS TO STOP HER. THEY WERE ALL CAUGHT IN THE TEMPORAL WAVE.
DIDN'T SOUND LIKE IT. WE INTERCEPTED A SIGNAL FROM HER TO THE OTHER MEMBERS OF THE LEAGUE AT VARIOUS POINTS IN TIME.
WHAT?
I CAN'T SEE THEM. WHERE?
WHERE...?
"THERE."

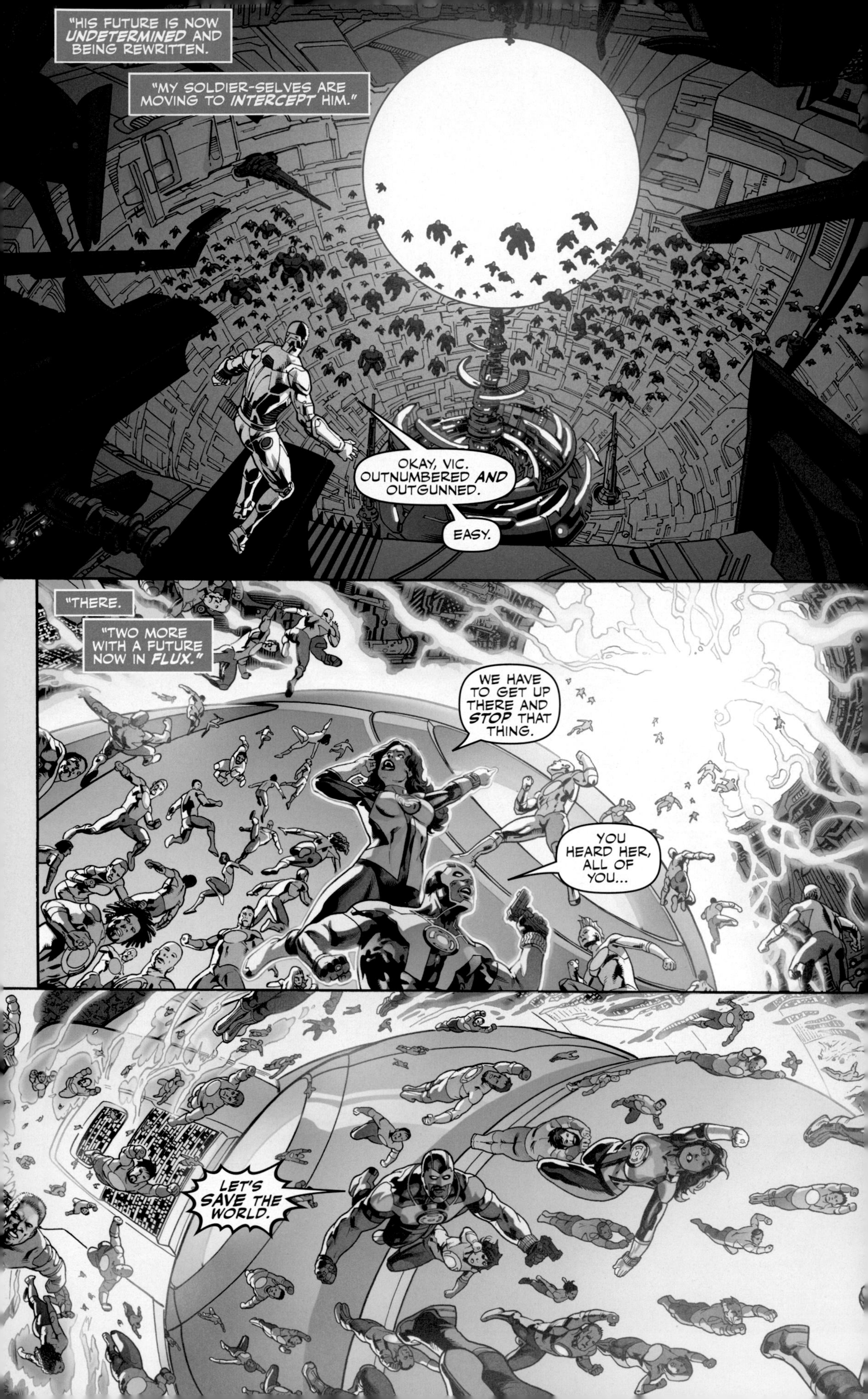
"HIS FUTURE IS NOW *UNDETERMINED* AND BEING REWRITTEN.
"MY SOLDIER-SELVES ARE MOVING TO *INTERCEPT* HIM."
OKAY, VIC. OUTNUMBERED *AND* OUTGUNNED.
EASY.
"THERE.
"TWO MORE WITH A FUTURE NOW IN *FLUX*."
WE HAVE TO GET UP THERE AND *STOP* THAT THING.
YOU HEARD HER, ALL OF YOU...
LET'S *SAVE* THE WORLD.

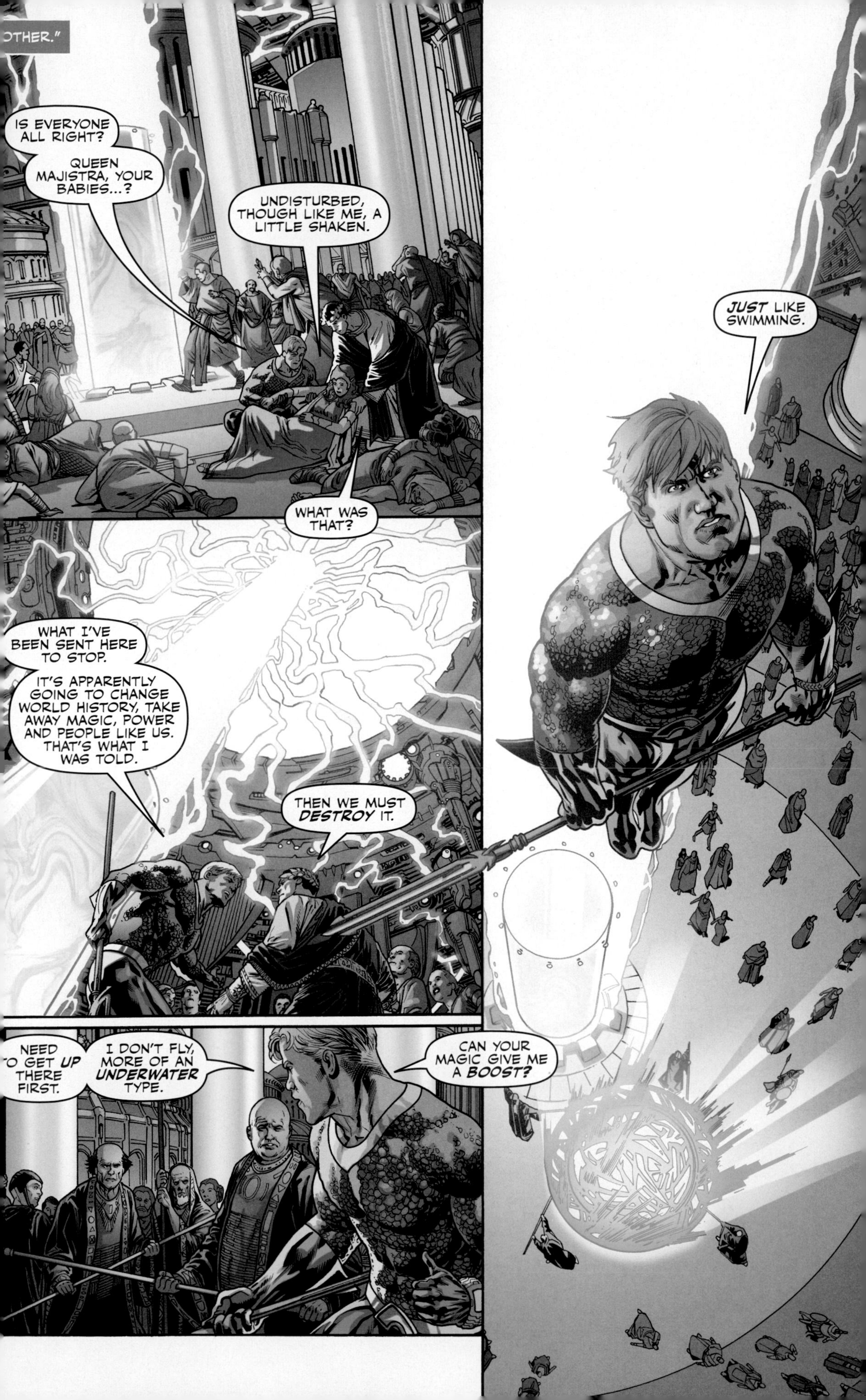
OTHER."
IS EVERYONE ALL RIGHT?
QUEEN MAJISTRA, YOUR BABIES...?
UNDISTURBED, THOUGH LIKE ME, A LITTLE SHAKEN.
WHAT WAS THAT?
WHAT I'VE BEEN SENT HERE TO STOP.
IT'S APPARENTLY GOING TO CHANGE WORLD HISTORY, TAKE AWAY MAGIC, POWER AND PEOPLE LIKE US. THAT'S WHAT I WAS TOLD.
THEN WE MUST DESTROY IT.
NEED TO GET UP THERE FIRST.
I DON'T FLY, MORE OF AN UNDERWATER TYPE.
CAN YOUR MAGIC GIVE ME A BOOST?
JUST LIKE SWIMMING.

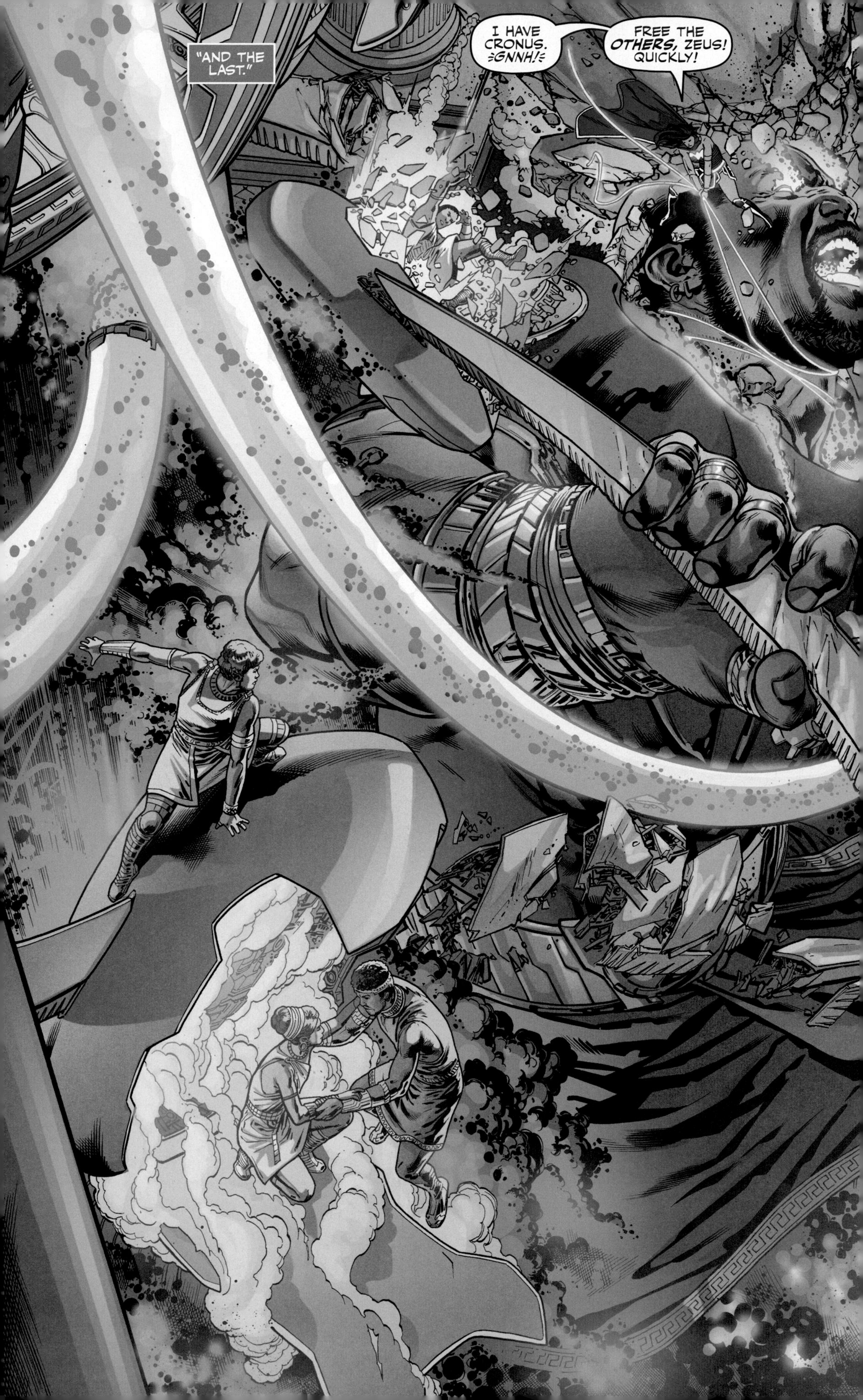
"AND THE LAST."
I HAVE CRONUS. GNNH!
FREE THE OTHERS, ZEUS! QUICKLY!

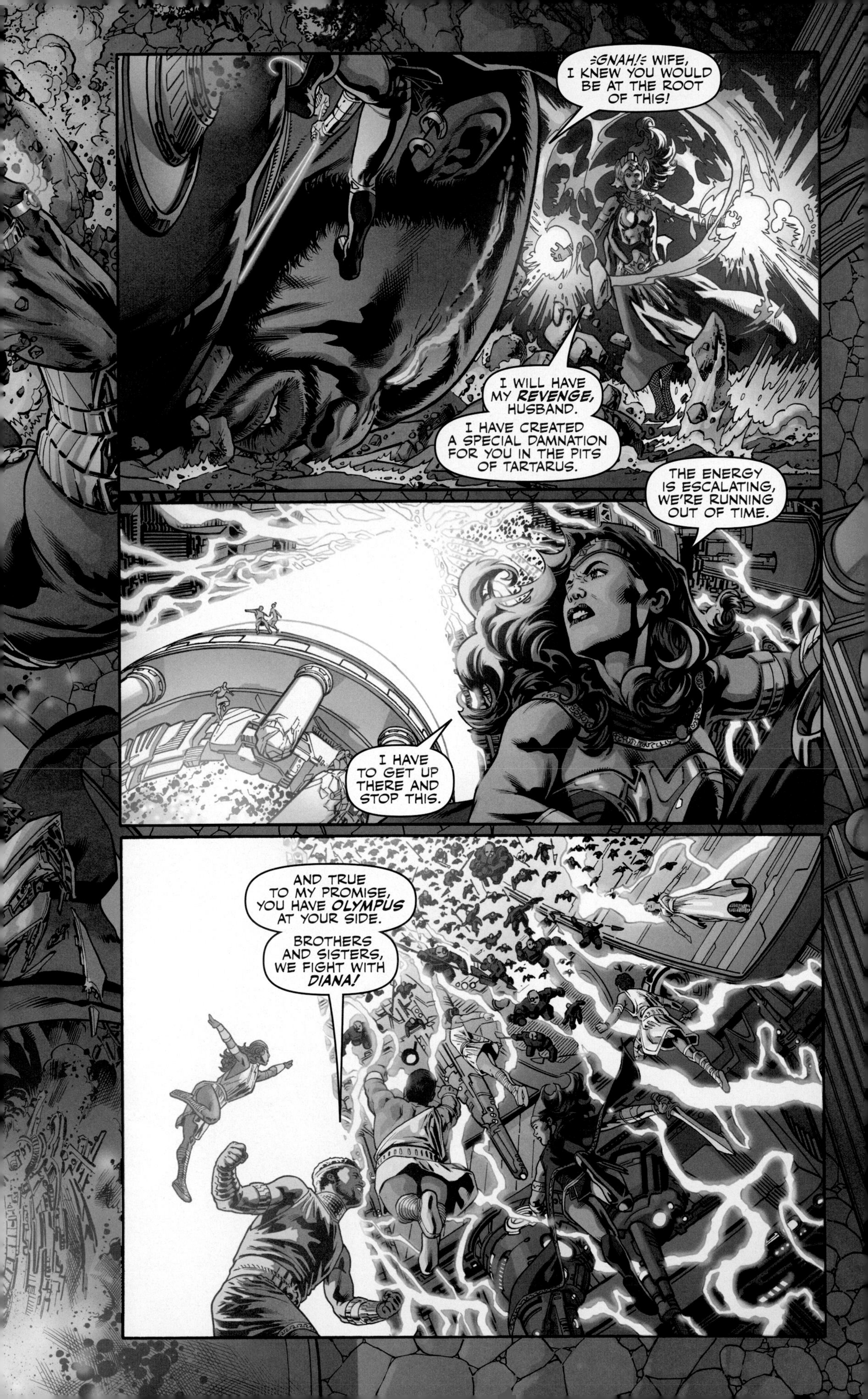

GNAH! WIFE, I KNEW YOU WOULD BE AT THE ROOT OF THIS!
I WILL HAVE MY ***REVENGE,*** HUSBAND.
I HAVE CREATED A SPECIAL DAMNATION FOR YOU IN THE PITS OF TARTARUS.
THE ENERGY IS ESCALATING, WE'RE RUNNING OUT OF TIME.
I HAVE TO GET UP THERE AND STOP THIS.
AND TRUE TO MY PROMISE, YOU HAVE ***OLYMPUS*** AT YOUR SIDE.
BROTHERS AND SISTERS, WE FIGHT WITH ***DIANA!***

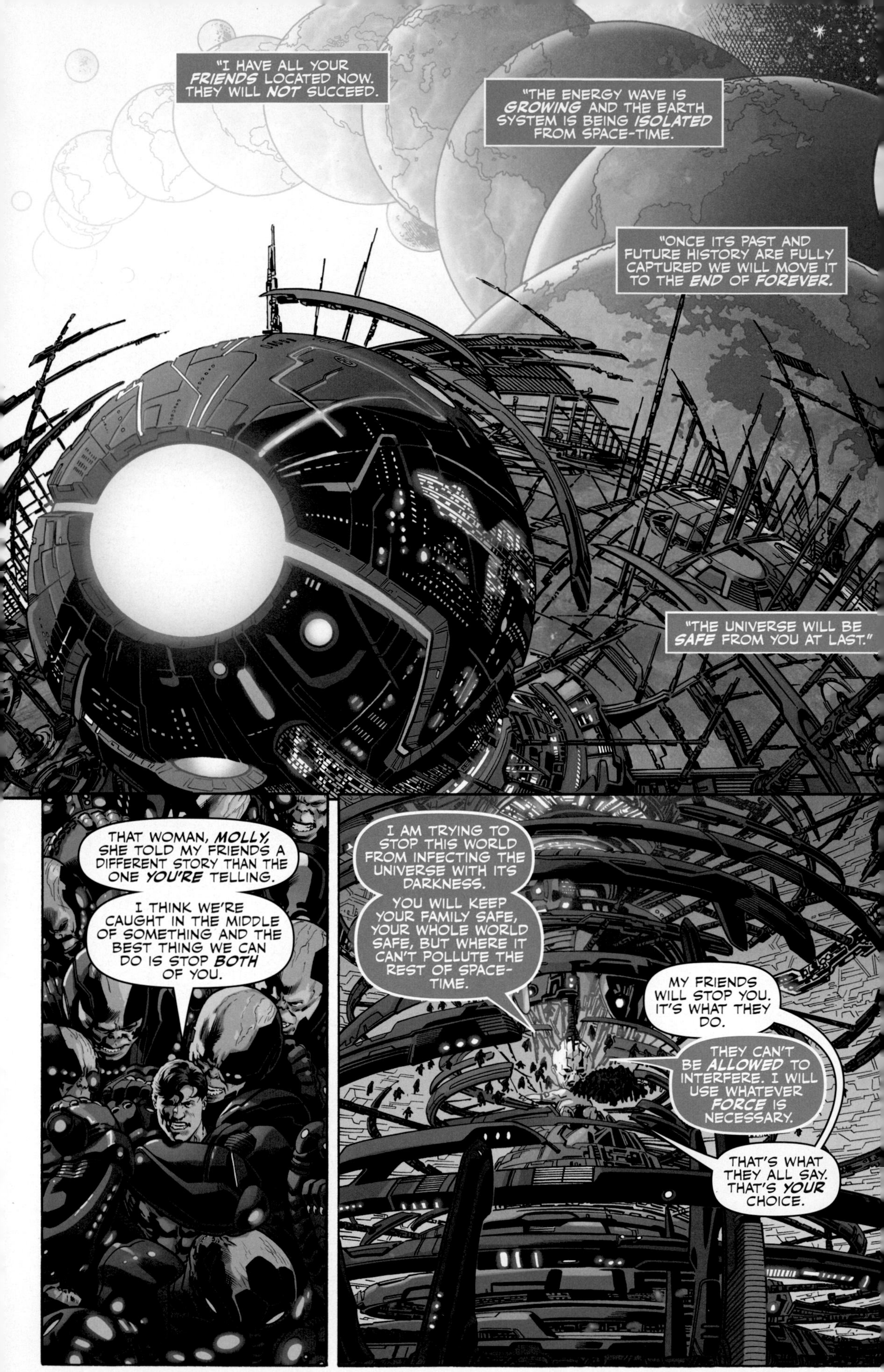
"I HAVE ALL YOUR FRIENDS LOCATED NOW. THEY WILL NOT SUCCEED.
"THE ENERGY WAVE IS GROWING AND THE EARTH SYSTEM IS BEING ISOLATED FROM SPACE-TIME.
"ONCE ITS PAST AND FUTURE HISTORY ARE FULLY CAPTURED WE WILL MOVE IT TO THE END OF FOREVER.
"THE UNIVERSE WILL BE SAFE FROM YOU AT LAST."
THAT WOMAN, MOLLY, SHE TOLD MY FRIENDS A DIFFERENT STORY THAN THE ONE YOU'RE TELLING.
I THINK WE'RE CAUGHT IN THE MIDDLE OF SOMETHING AND THE BEST THING WE CAN DO IS STOP BOTH OF YOU.
I AM TRYING TO STOP THIS WORLD FROM INFECTING THE UNIVERSE WITH ITS DARKNESS.
YOU WILL KEEP YOUR FAMILY SAFE, YOUR WHOLE WORLD SAFE, BUT WHERE IT CAN'T POLLUTE THE REST OF SPACE-TIME.
MY FRIENDS WILL STOP YOU. IT'S WHAT THEY DO.
THEY CAN'T BE ALLOWED TO INTERFERE. I WILL USE WHATEVER FORCE IS NECESSARY.
THAT'S WHAT THEY ALL SAY. THAT'S YOUR CHOICE.

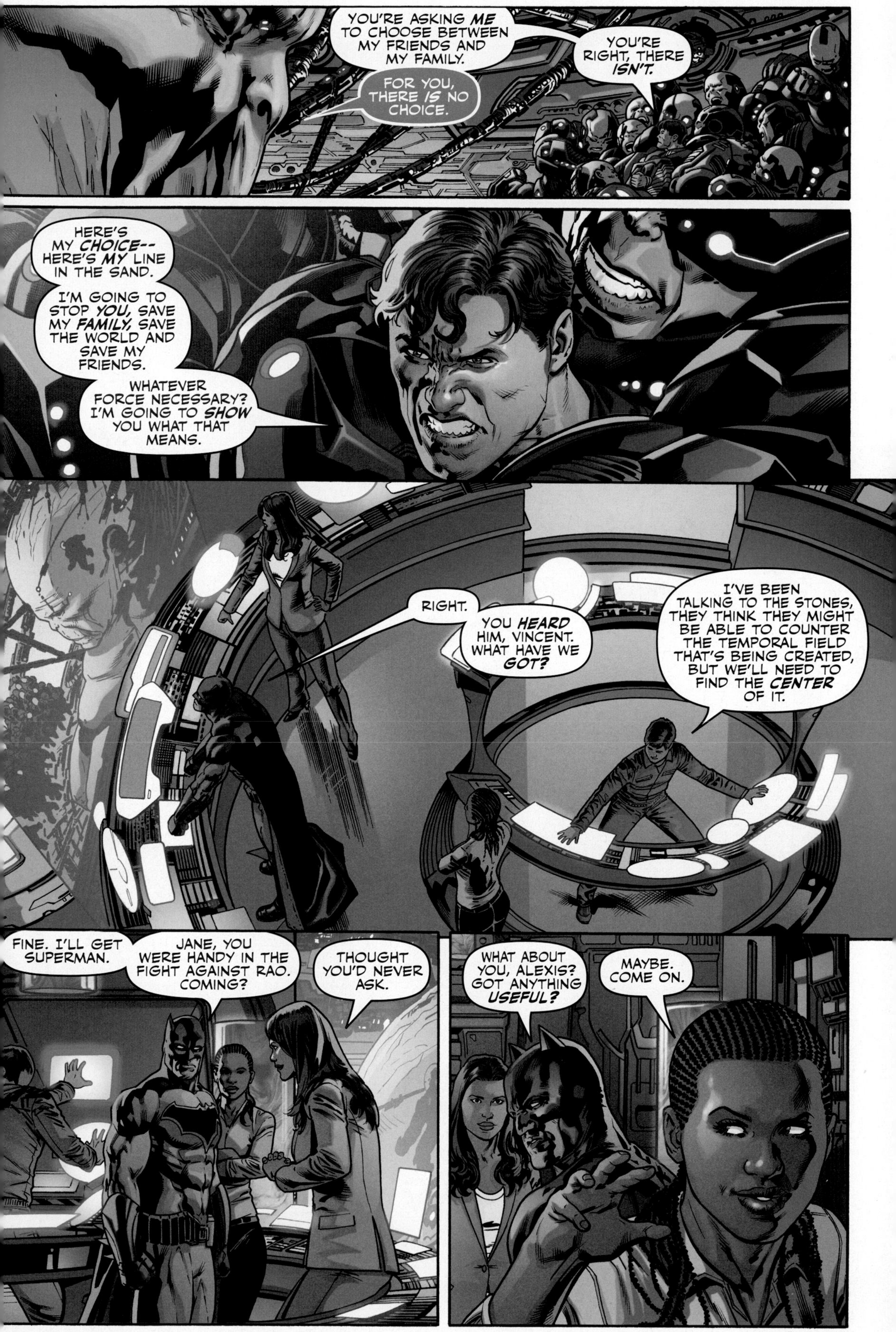
YOU'RE ASKING ME TO CHOOSE BETWEEN MY FRIENDS AND MY FAMILY.
FOR YOU, THERE IS NO CHOICE.
YOU'RE RIGHT, THERE ISN'T.
HERE'S MY CHOICE-- HERE'S MY LINE IN THE SAND.
I'M GOING TO STOP YOU, SAVE MY FAMILY, SAVE THE WORLD AND SAVE MY FRIENDS.
WHATEVER FORCE NECESSARY? I'M GOING TO SHOW YOU WHAT THAT MEANS.
RIGHT.
YOU HEARD HIM, VINCENT. WHAT HAVE WE GOT?
I'VE BEEN TALKING TO THE STONES, THEY THINK THEY MIGHT BE ABLE TO COUNTER THE TEMPORAL FIELD THAT'S BEING CREATED, BUT WE'LL NEED TO FIND THE CENTER OF IT.
FINE. I'LL GET SUPERMAN.
JANE, YOU WERE HANDY IN THE FIGHT AGAINST RAO. COMING?
THOUGHT YOU'D NEVER ASK.
WHAT ABOUT YOU, ALEXIS? GOT ANYTHING USEFUL?
MAYBE. COME ON.

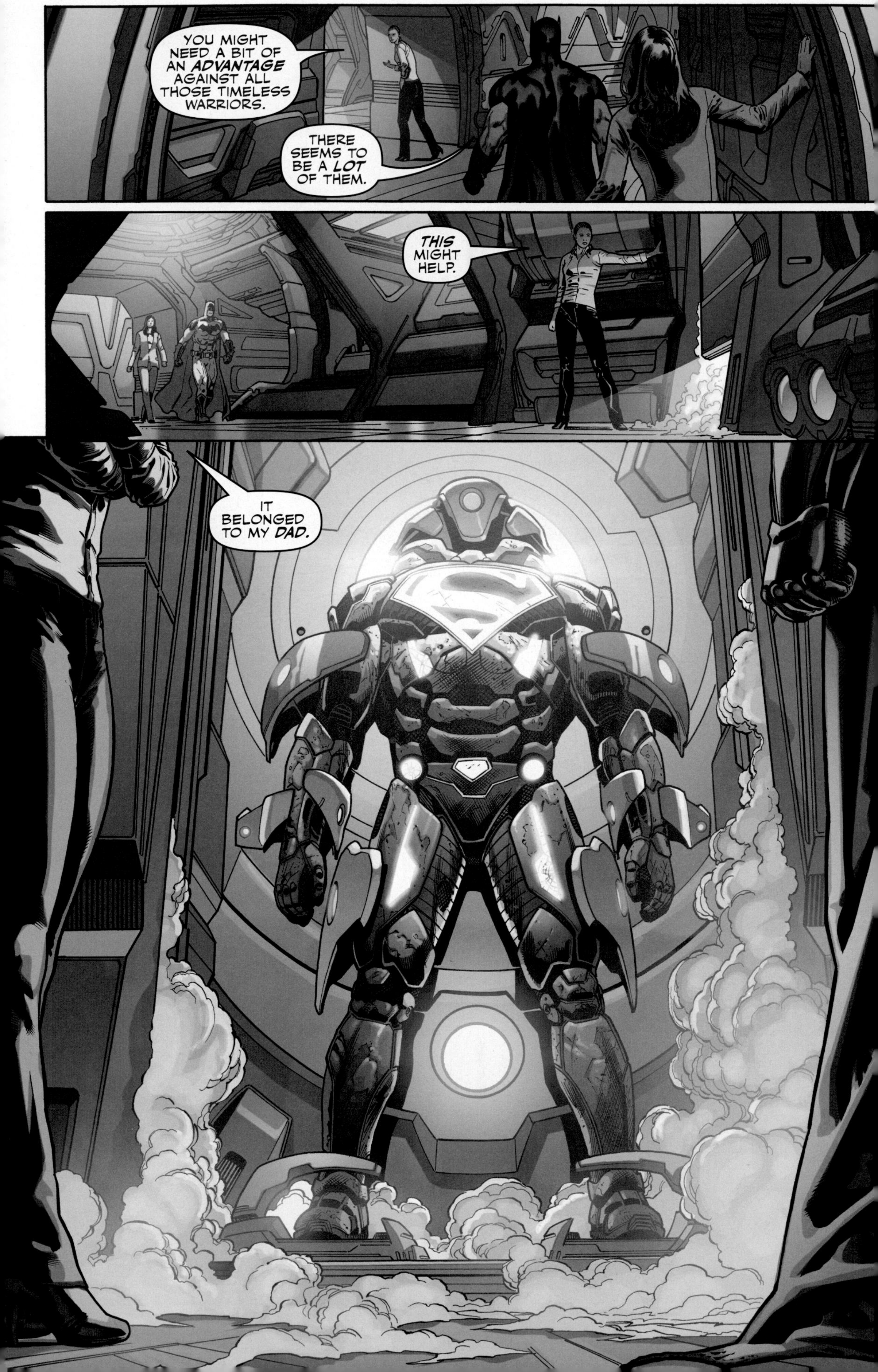
YOU MIGHT NEED A BIT OF AN ADVANTAGE AGAINST ALL THOSE TIMELESS WARRIORS.
THERE SEEMS TO BE A LOT OF THEM.
THIS MIGHT HELP.
IT BELONGED TO MY DAD.

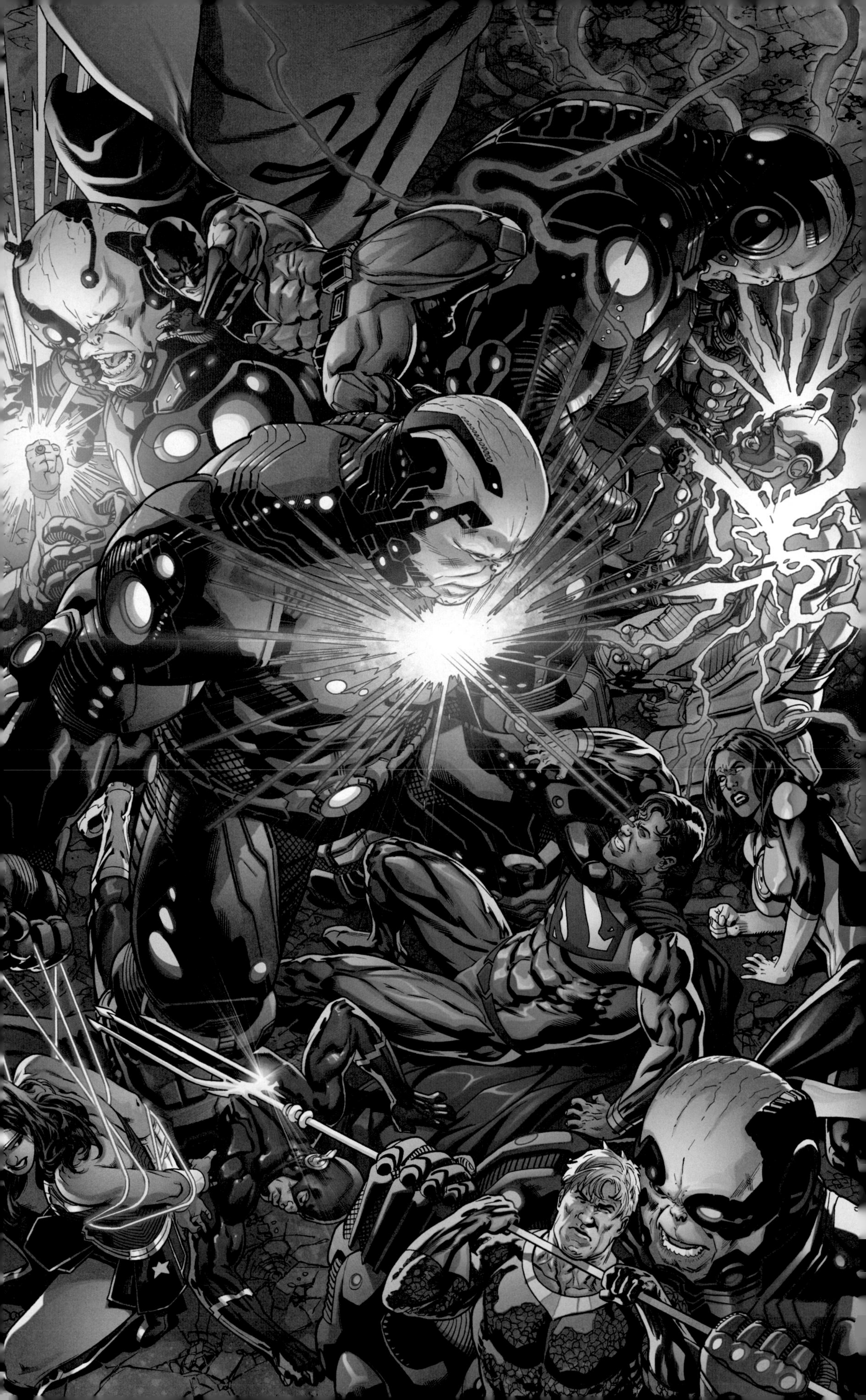

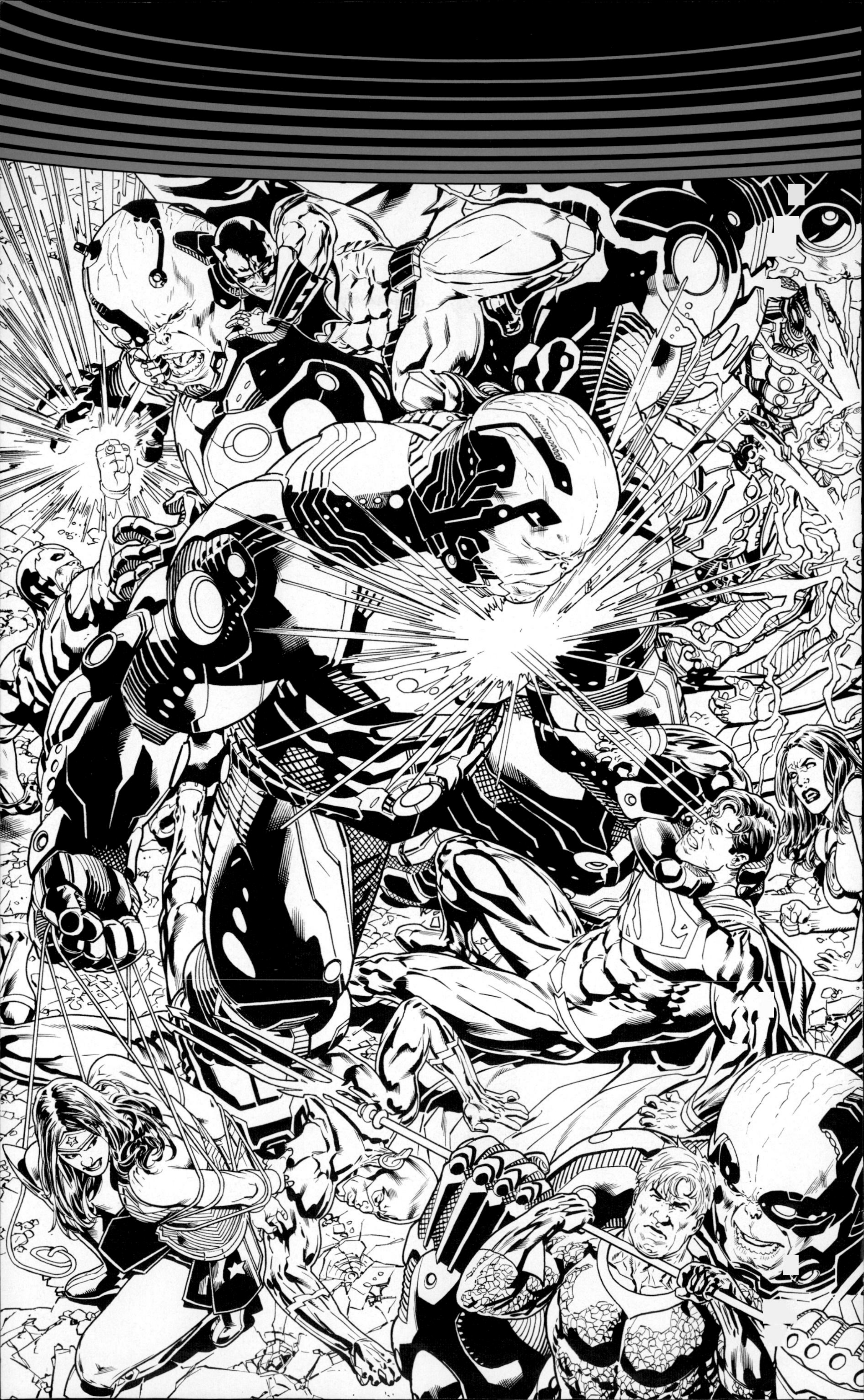

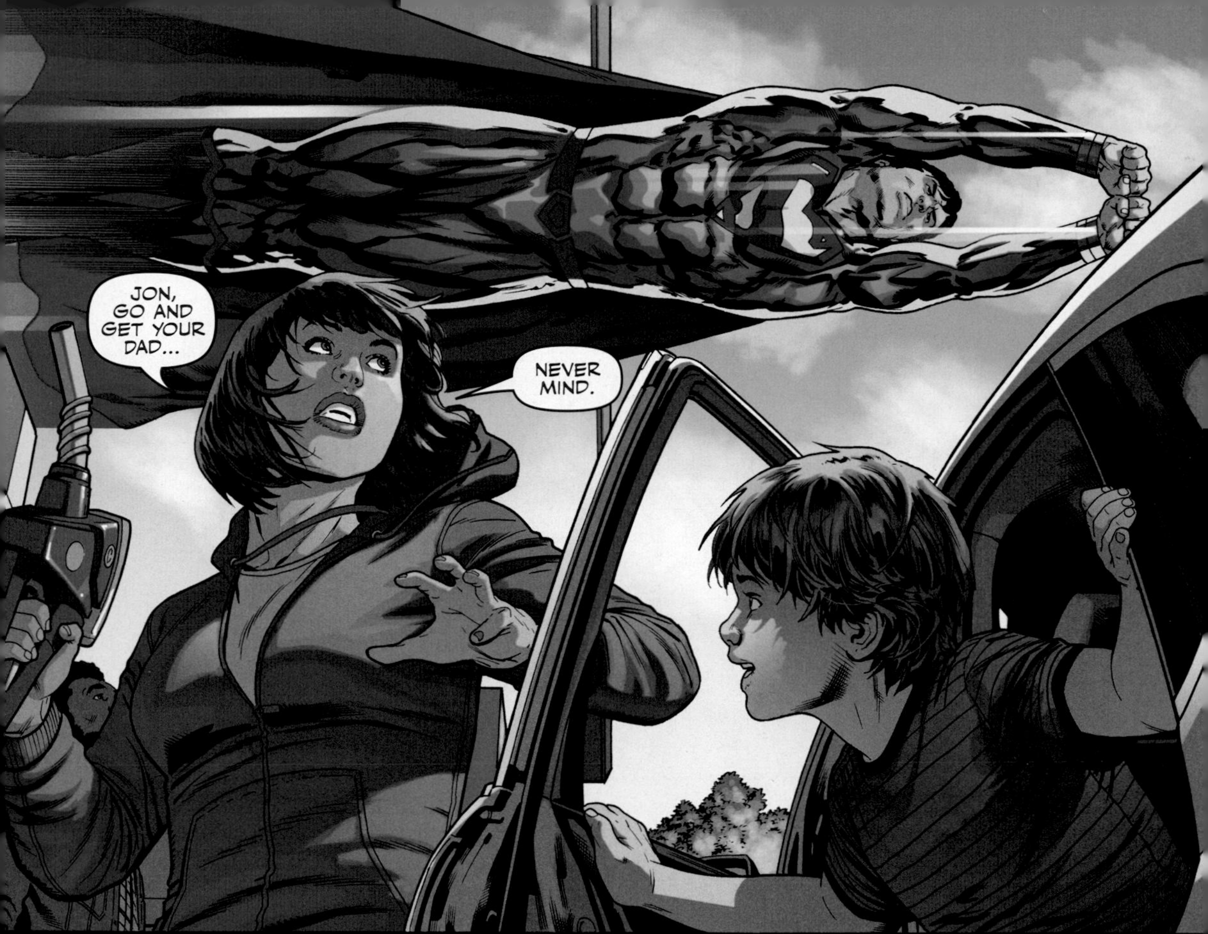
JON, GO AND GET YOUR DAD...
NEVER MIND.

TIMELESS PART 4

RYAN HITCH WRITER • FERNANDO PASARIN PENCILLER • MATT RYAN INKER
RAD ANDERSON COLORIST • RICHARD STARKINGS AND COMICRAFT LETTERING
RNANDO PASARIN, MATT RYAN & BRAD ANDERSON COVER • YANICK PAQUETTE & NATHAN FAIRBAIRN VARIANT COVER
EGO LOPEZ & AMEDEO TURTURRO ASSISTANT EDITORS • BRIAN CUNNINGHAM EDITOR
IPERMAN CREATED BY JERRY SIEGEL & JOE SHUSTER, BY SPECIAL ARRANGEMENT WITH THE JERRY SIEGEL FAMILY

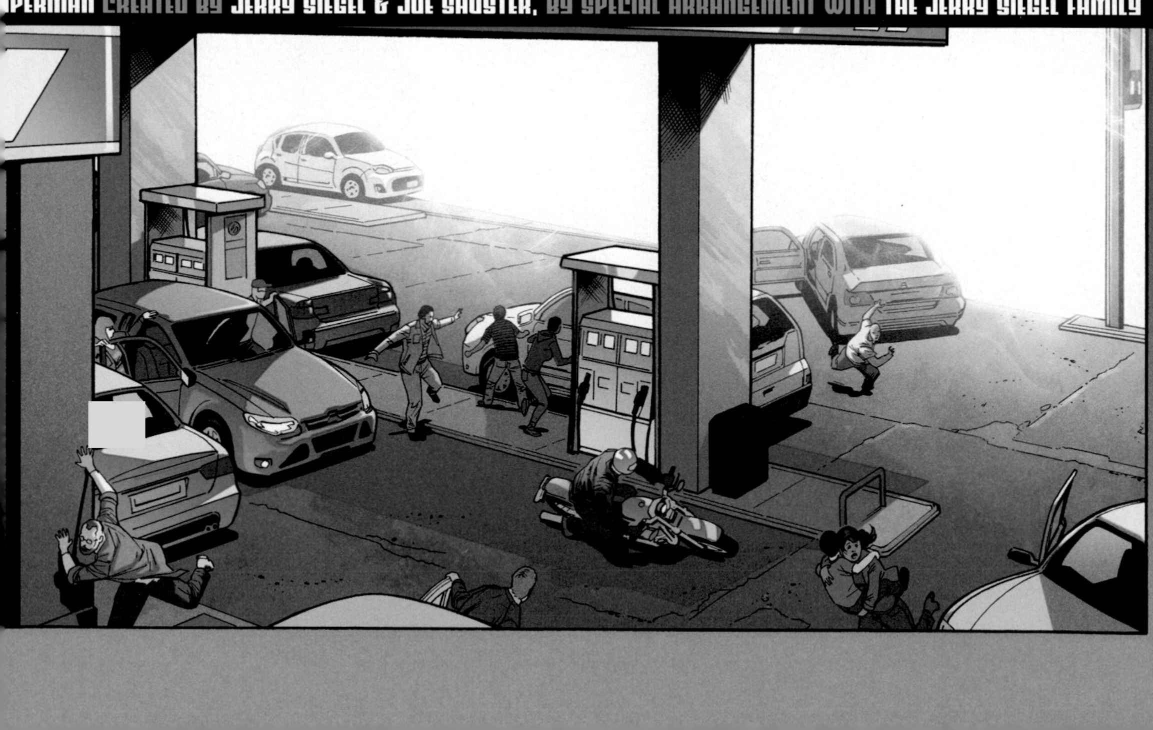

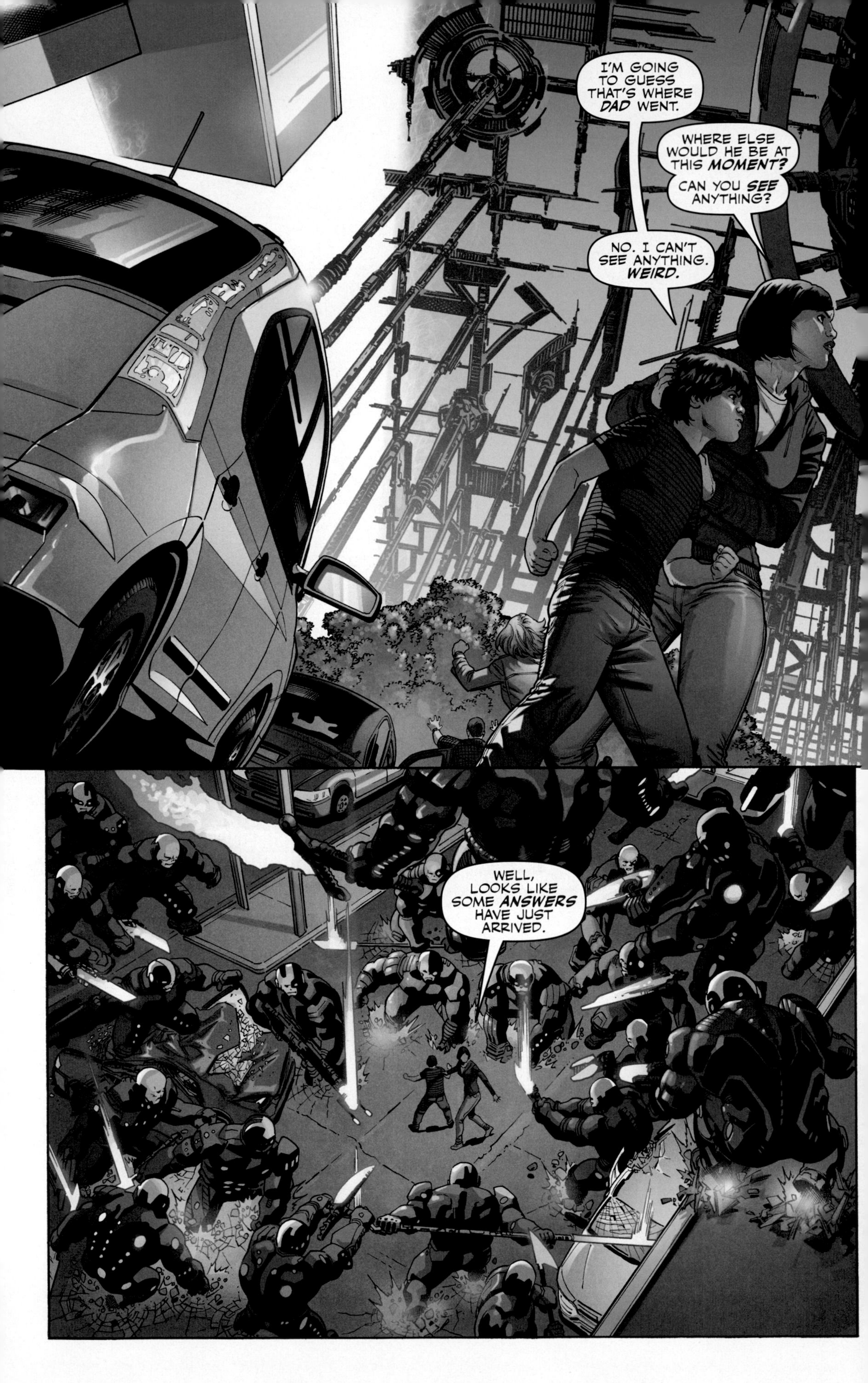
I'M GOING TO GUESS THAT'S WHERE DAD WENT.
WHERE ELSE WOULD HE BE AT THIS MOMENT?
CAN YOU SEE ANYTHING?
NO. I CAN'T SEE ANYTHING. WEIRD.
WELL, LOOKS LIKE SOME ANSWERS HAVE JUST ARRIVED.

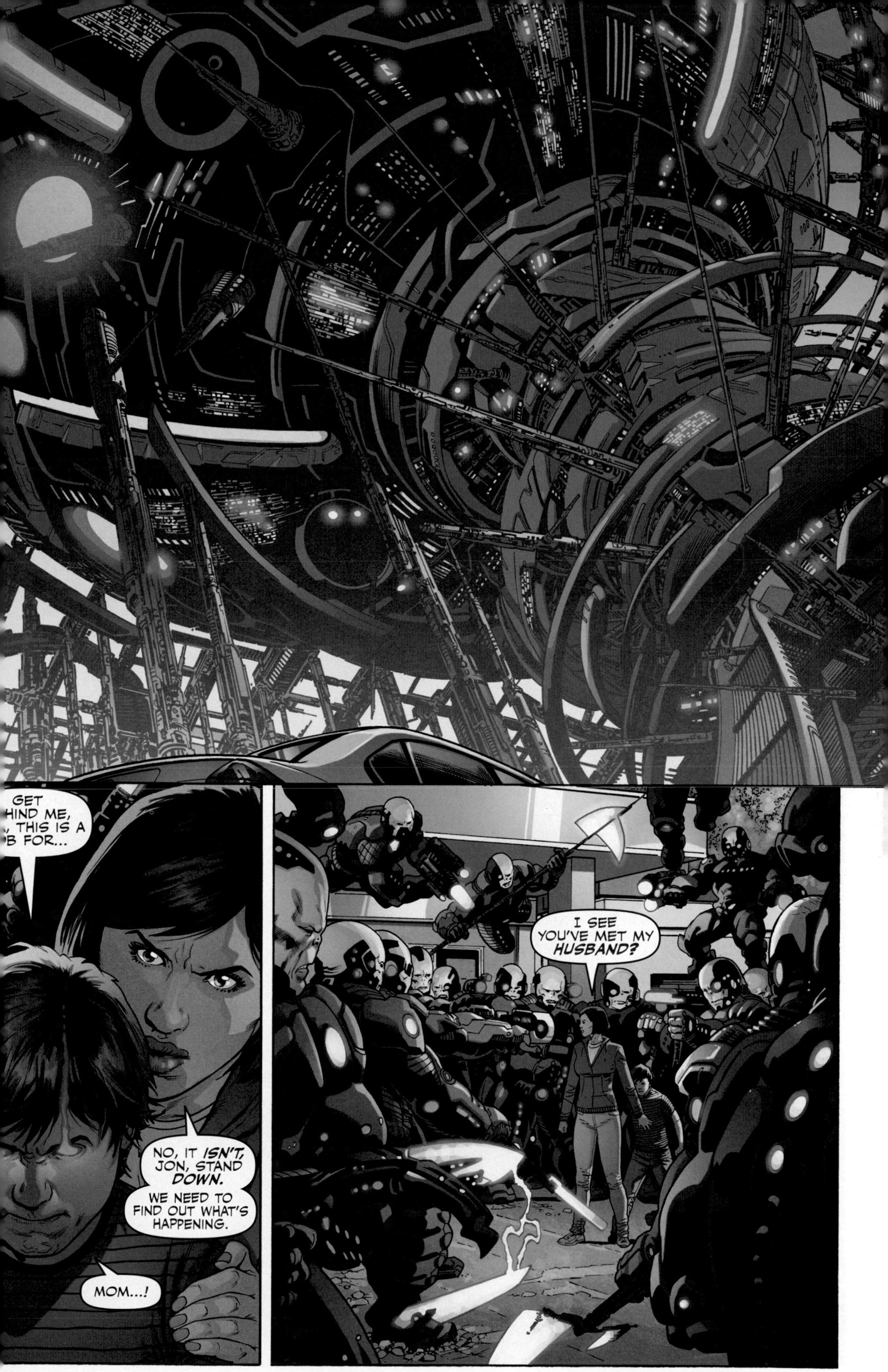
GET HIND ME, , THIS IS A B FOR...
NO, IT ISN'T, JON, STAND DOWN.
WE NEED TO FIND OUT WHAT'S HAPPENING.
MOM...!
I SEE YOU'VE MET MY HUSBAND?

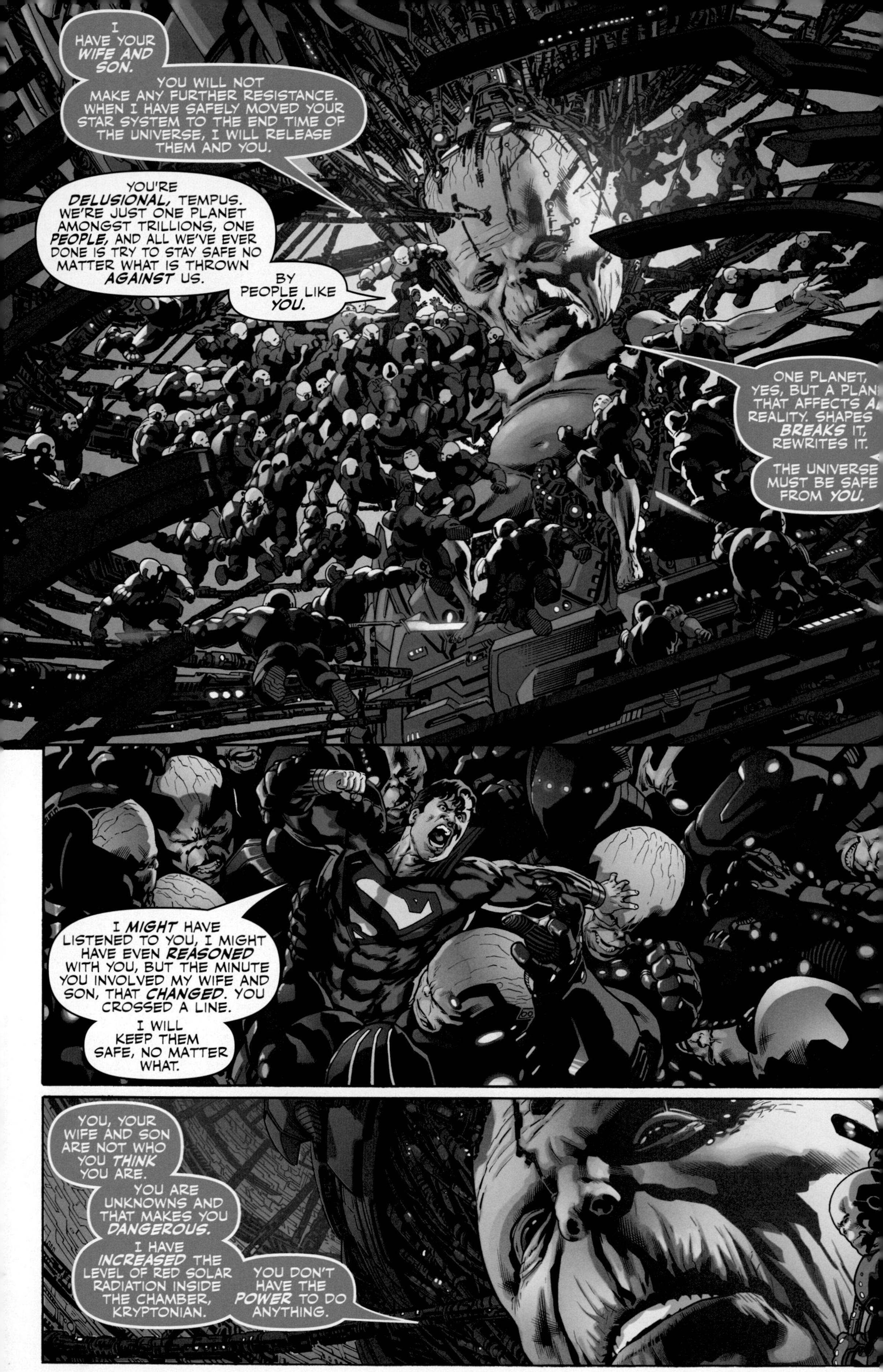

I HAVE YOUR WIFE AND SON.
YOU WILL NOT MAKE ANY FURTHER RESISTANCE. WHEN I HAVE SAFELY MOVED YOUR STAR SYSTEM TO THE END TIME OF THE UNIVERSE, I WILL RELEASE THEM AND YOU.
YOU'RE DELUSIONAL, TEMPUS. WE'RE JUST ONE PLANET AMONGST TRILLIONS, ONE PEOPLE, AND ALL WE'VE EVER DONE IS TRY TO STAY SAFE NO MATTER WHAT IS THROWN AGAINST US.
BY PEOPLE LIKE YOU.
ONE PLANET, YES, BUT A PLAN THAT AFFECTS A REALITY. SHAPES BREAKS IT, REWRITES IT.
THE UNIVERSE MUST BE SAFE FROM YOU.
I MIGHT HAVE LISTENED TO YOU, I MIGHT HAVE EVEN REASONED WITH YOU, BUT THE MINUTE YOU INVOLVED MY WIFE AND SON, THAT CHANGED. YOU CROSSED A LINE.
I WILL KEEP THEM SAFE, NO MATTER WHAT.
YOU, YOUR WIFE AND SON ARE NOT WHO YOU THINK YOU ARE.
YOU ARE UNKNOWNS AND THAT MAKES YOU DANGEROUS.
I HAVE INCREASED THE LEVEL OF RED SOLAR RADIATION INSIDE THE CHAMBER, KRYPTONIAN.
YOU DON'T HAVE THE POWER TO DO ANYTHING.

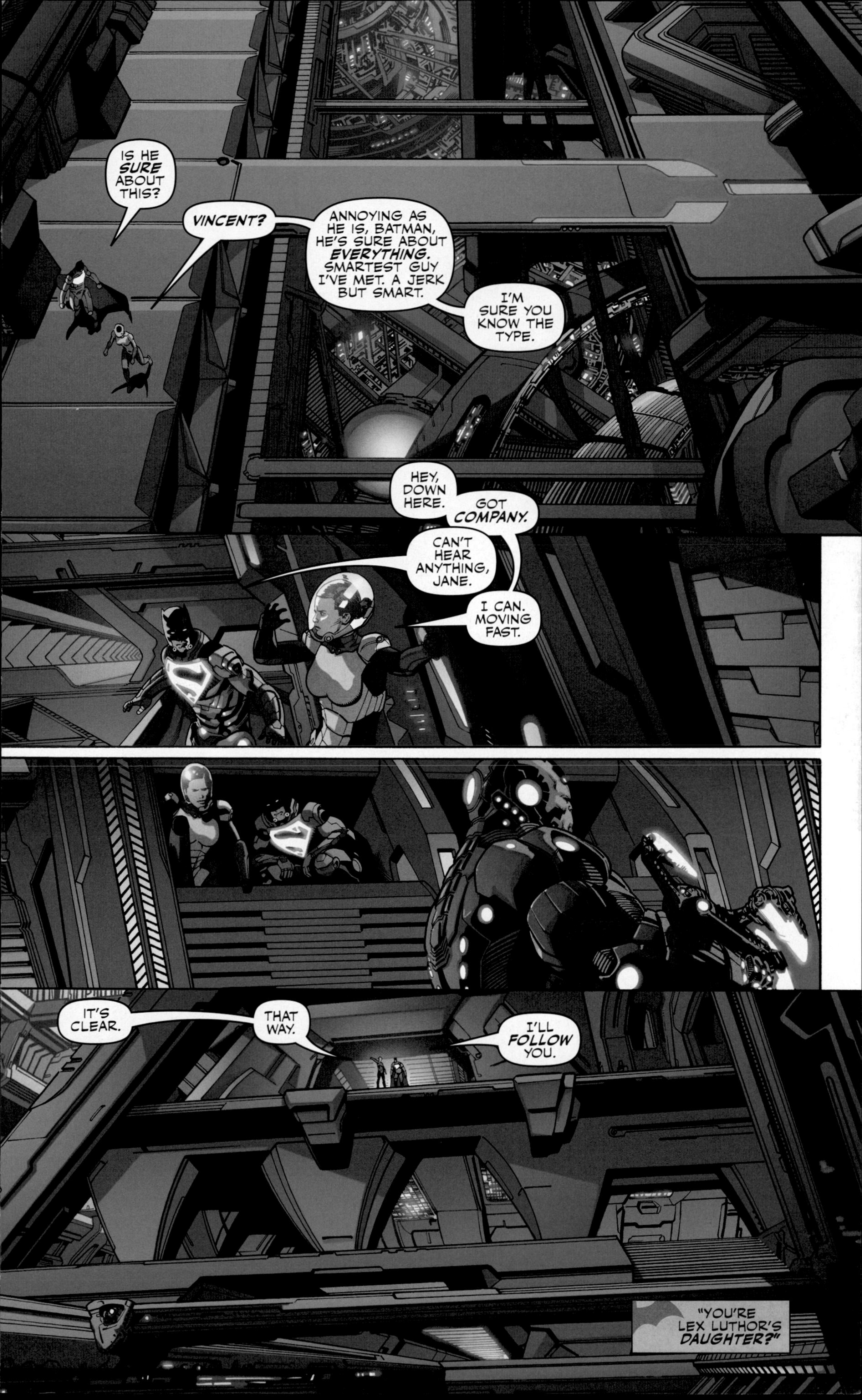
IS HE SURE ABOUT THIS?
VINCENT?
ANNOYING AS HE IS, BATMAN, HE'S SURE ABOUT EVERYTHING. SMARTEST GUY I'VE MET. A JERK BUT SMART.
I'M SURE YOU KNOW THE TYPE.
HEY, DOWN HERE.
GOT COMPANY.
CAN'T HEAR ANYTHING, JANE.
I CAN. MOVING FAST.
IT'S CLEAR.
THAT WAY.
I'LL FOLLOW YOU.
"YOU'RE LEX LUTHOR'S DAUGHTER?"

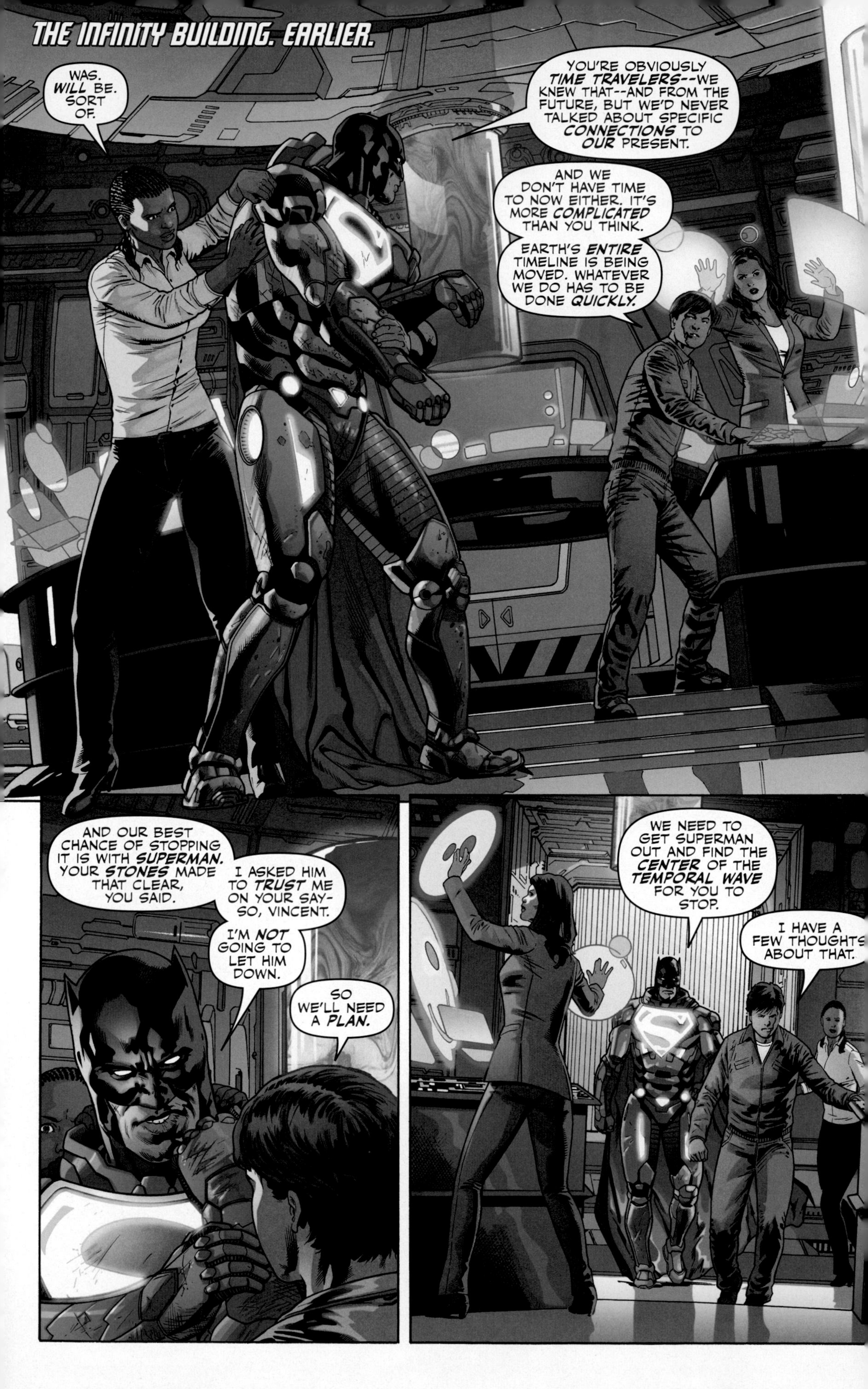
THE INFINITY BUILDING. EARLIER.
WAS. WILL BE. SORT OF.
YOU'RE OBVIOUSLY TIME TRAVELERS--WE KNEW THAT--AND FROM THE FUTURE, BUT WE'D NEVER TALKED ABOUT SPECIFIC CONNECTIONS TO OUR PRESENT.
AND WE DON'T HAVE TIME TO NOW EITHER. IT'S MORE COMPLICATED THAN YOU THINK.
EARTH'S ENTIRE TIMELINE IS BEING MOVED. WHATEVER WE DO HAS TO BE DONE QUICKLY.
AND OUR BEST CHANCE OF STOPPING IT IS WITH SUPERMAN. YOUR STONES MADE THAT CLEAR, YOU SAID.
I ASKED HIM TO TRUST ME ON YOUR SAY-SO, VINCENT.
I'M NOT GOING TO LET HIM DOWN.
SO WE'LL NEED A PLAN.
WE NEED TO GET SUPERMAN OUT AND FIND THE CENTER OF THE TEMPORAL WAVE FOR YOU TO STOP.
I HAVE A FEW THOUGHTS ABOUT THAT.

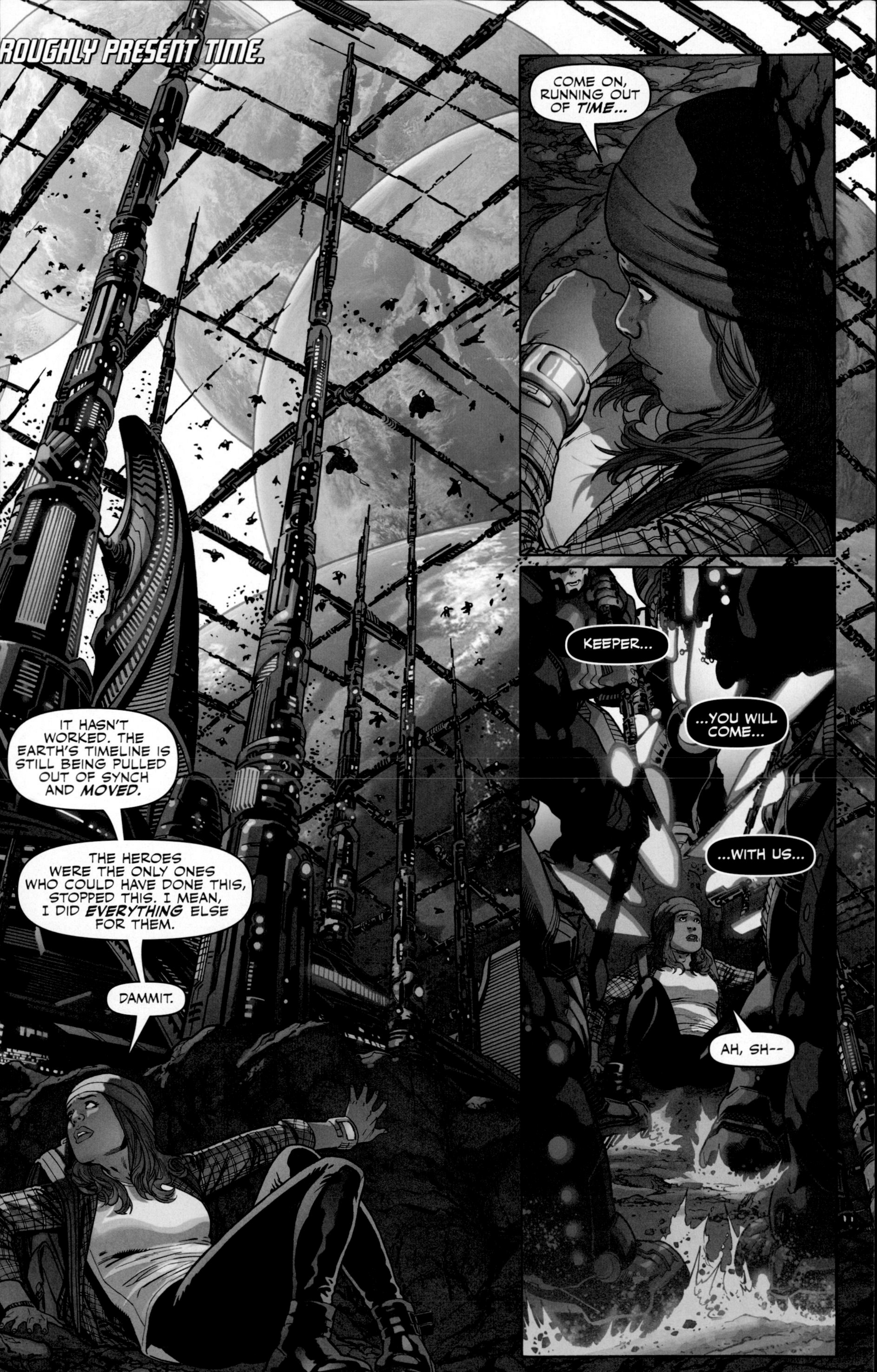
ROUGHLY PRESENT TIME.
COME ON, RUNNING OUT OF TIME...
IT HASN'T WORKED. THE EARTH'S TIMELINE IS STILL BEING PULLED OUT OF SYNCH AND MOVED.
THE HEROES WERE THE ONLY ONES WHO COULD HAVE DONE THIS, STOPPED THIS. I MEAN, I DID EVERYTHING ELSE FOR THEM.
DAMMIT.
KEEPER...
...YOU WILL COME...
...WITH US...
AH, SH--

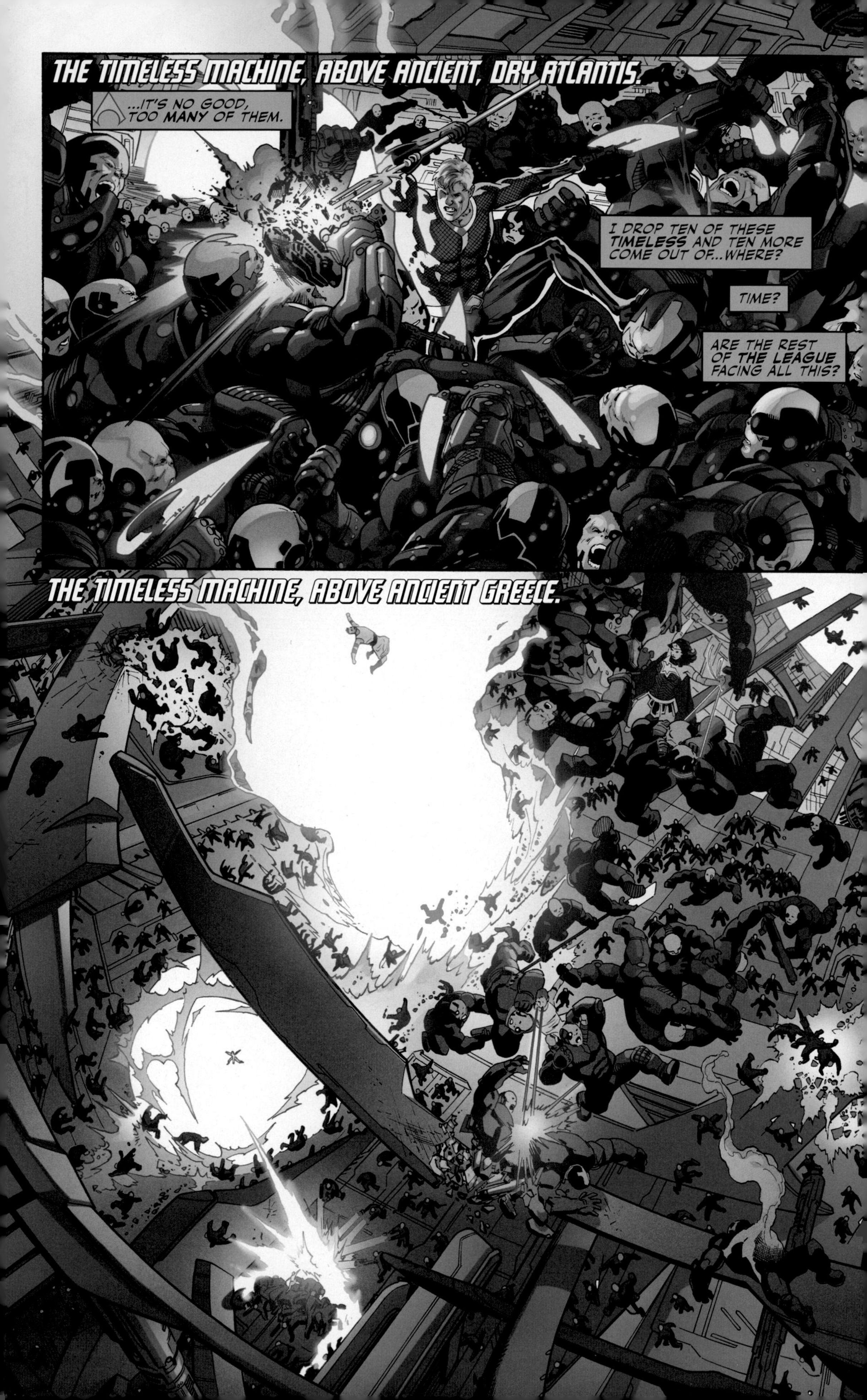
THE TIMELESS MACHINE, ABOVE ANCIENT, DRY ATLANTIS.
...IT'S NO GOOD, TOO MANY OF THEM.
I DROP TEN OF THESE TIMELESS AND TEN MORE COME OUT OF...WHERE?
TIME?
ARE THE REST OF THE LEAGUE FACING ALL THIS?
THE TIMELESS MACHINE, ABOVE ANCIENT GREECE.

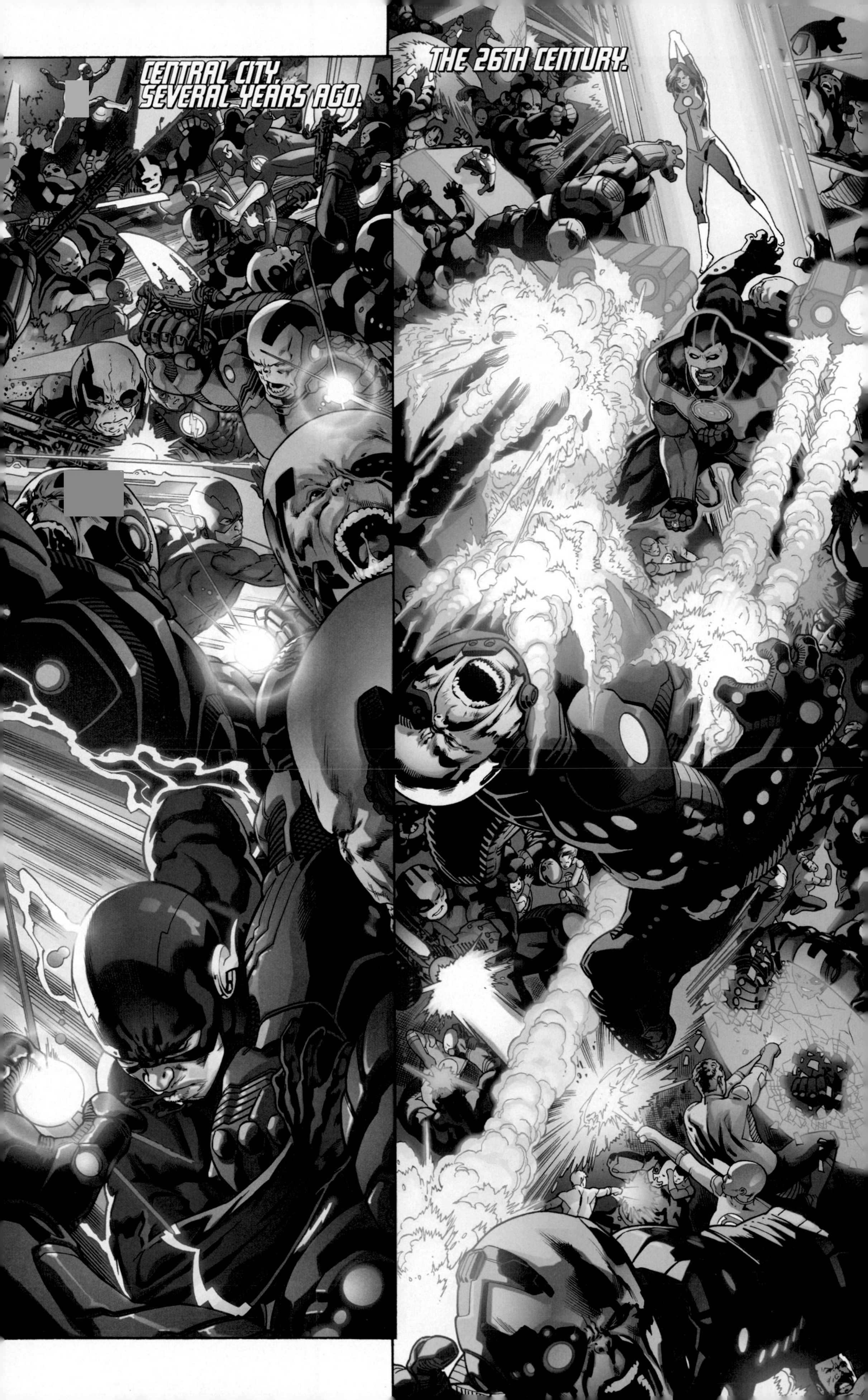
CENTRAL CITY, SEVERAL YEARS AGO.
THE 26TH CENTURY.

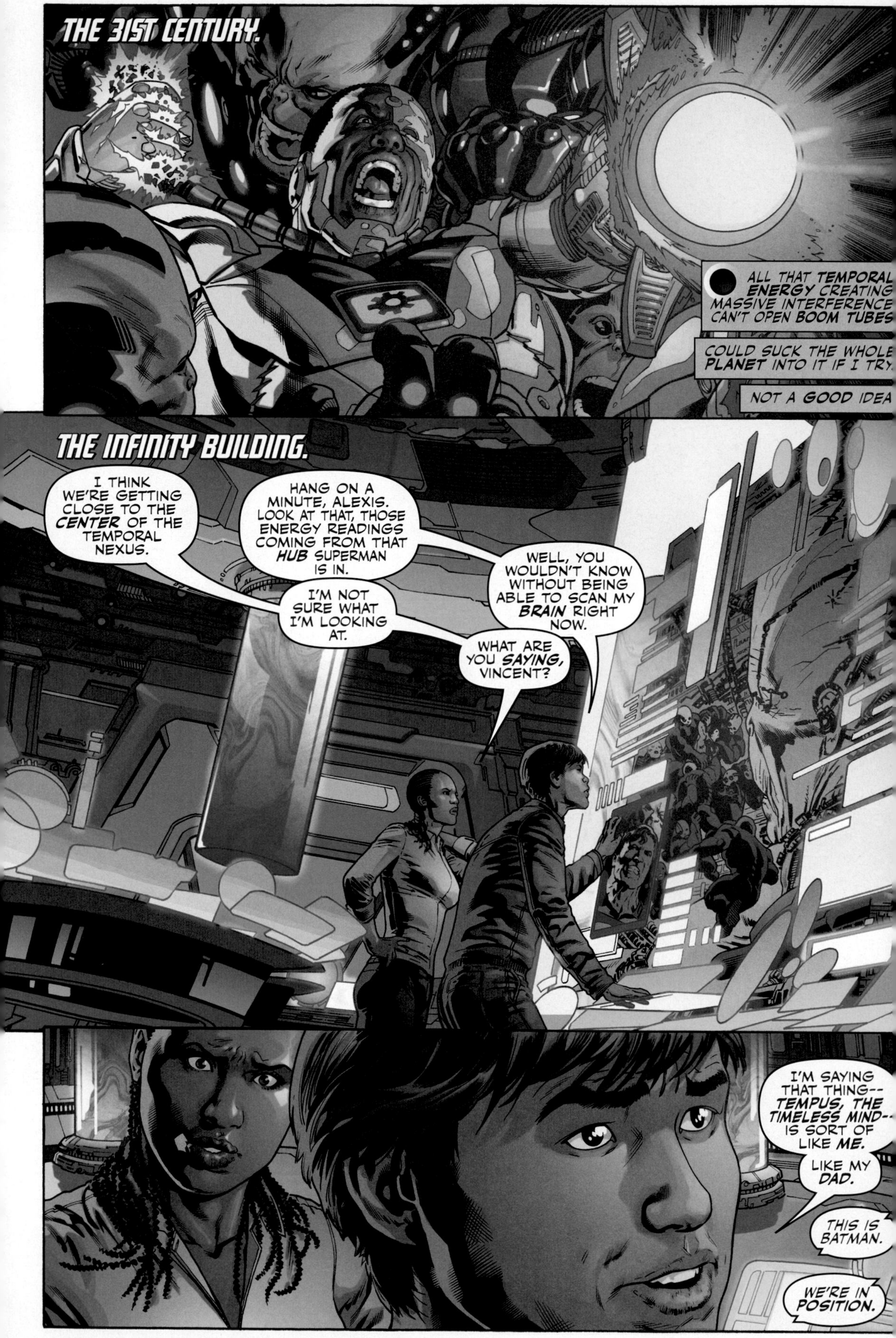
THE 31ST CENTURY.
ALL THAT TEMPORAL ENERGY CREATING MASSIVE INTERFERENCE. CAN'T OPEN BOOM TUBES.
COULD SUCK THE WHOLE PLANET INTO IT IF I TRY.
NOT A GOOD IDEA.
THE INFINITY BUILDING.
I THINK WE'RE GETTING CLOSE TO THE CENTER OF THE TEMPORAL NEXUS.
HANG ON A MINUTE, ALEXIS. LOOK AT THAT, THOSE ENERGY READINGS COMING FROM THAT HUB SUPERMAN IS IN.
I'M NOT SURE WHAT I'M LOOKING AT.
WELL, YOU WOULDN'T KNOW WITHOUT BEING ABLE TO SCAN MY BRAIN RIGHT NOW.
WHAT ARE YOU SAYING, VINCENT?
I'M SAYING THAT THING-- TEMPUS, THE TIMELESS MIND-- IS SORT OF LIKE ME.
LIKE MY DAD.
THIS IS BATMAN.
WE'RE IN POSITION.

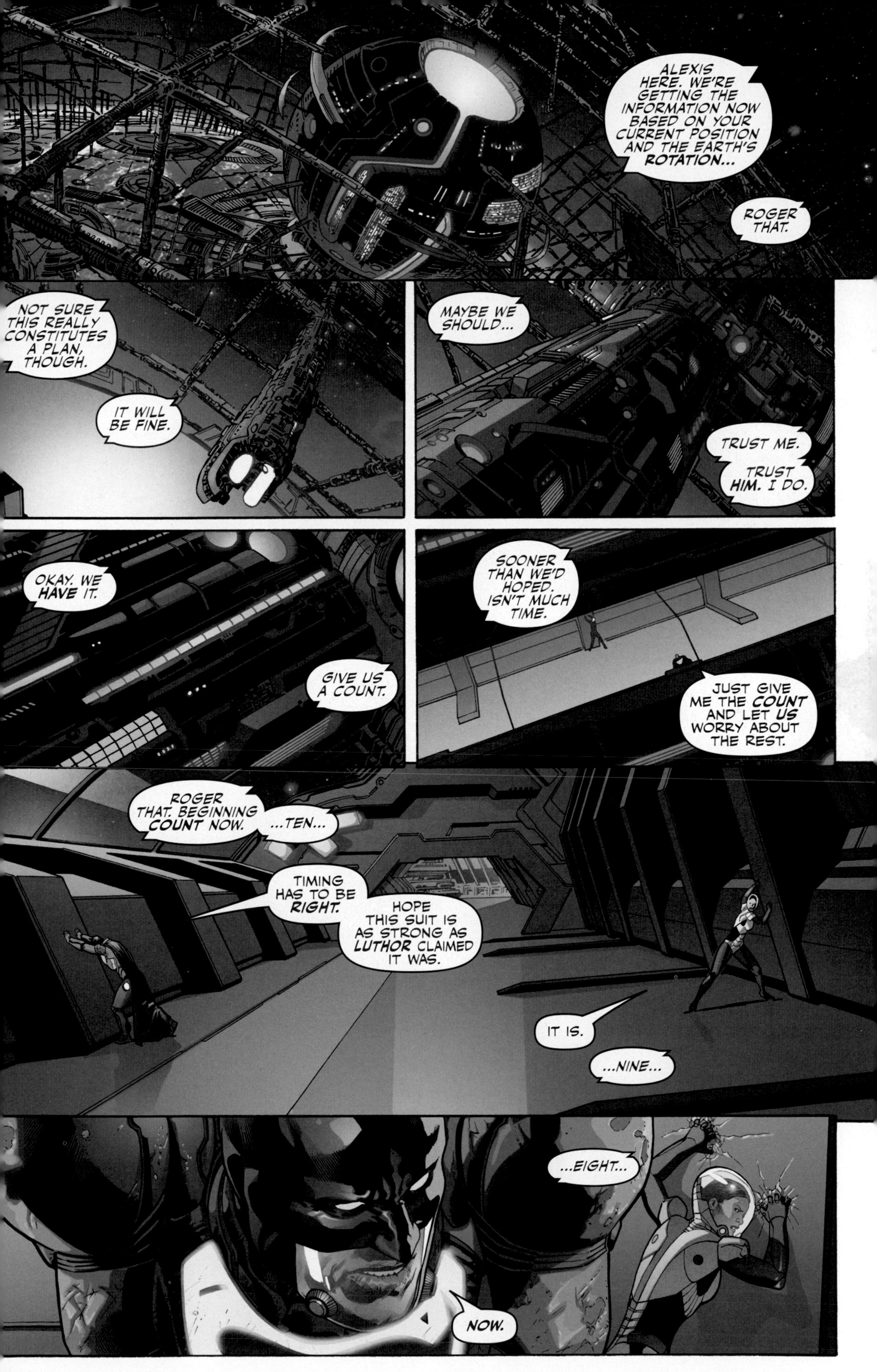
ALEXIS HERE. WE'RE GETTING THE INFORMATION NOW BASED ON YOUR CURRENT POSITION AND THE EARTH'S ROTATION...
ROGER THAT.
NOT SURE THIS REALLY CONSTITUTES A PLAN, THOUGH.
IT WILL BE FINE.
MAYBE WE SHOULD...
TRUST ME.
TRUST HIM. I DO.
OKAY. WE HAVE IT.
GIVE US A COUNT.
SOONER THAN WE'D HOPED. ISN'T MUCH TIME.
JUST GIVE ME THE COUNT AND LET US WORRY ABOUT THE REST.
ROGER THAT. BEGINNING COUNT NOW.
...TEN...
TIMING HAS TO BE RIGHT.
HOPE THIS SUIT IS AS STRONG AS LUTHOR CLAIMED IT WAS.
IT IS.
...NINE...
...EIGHT...
NOW.

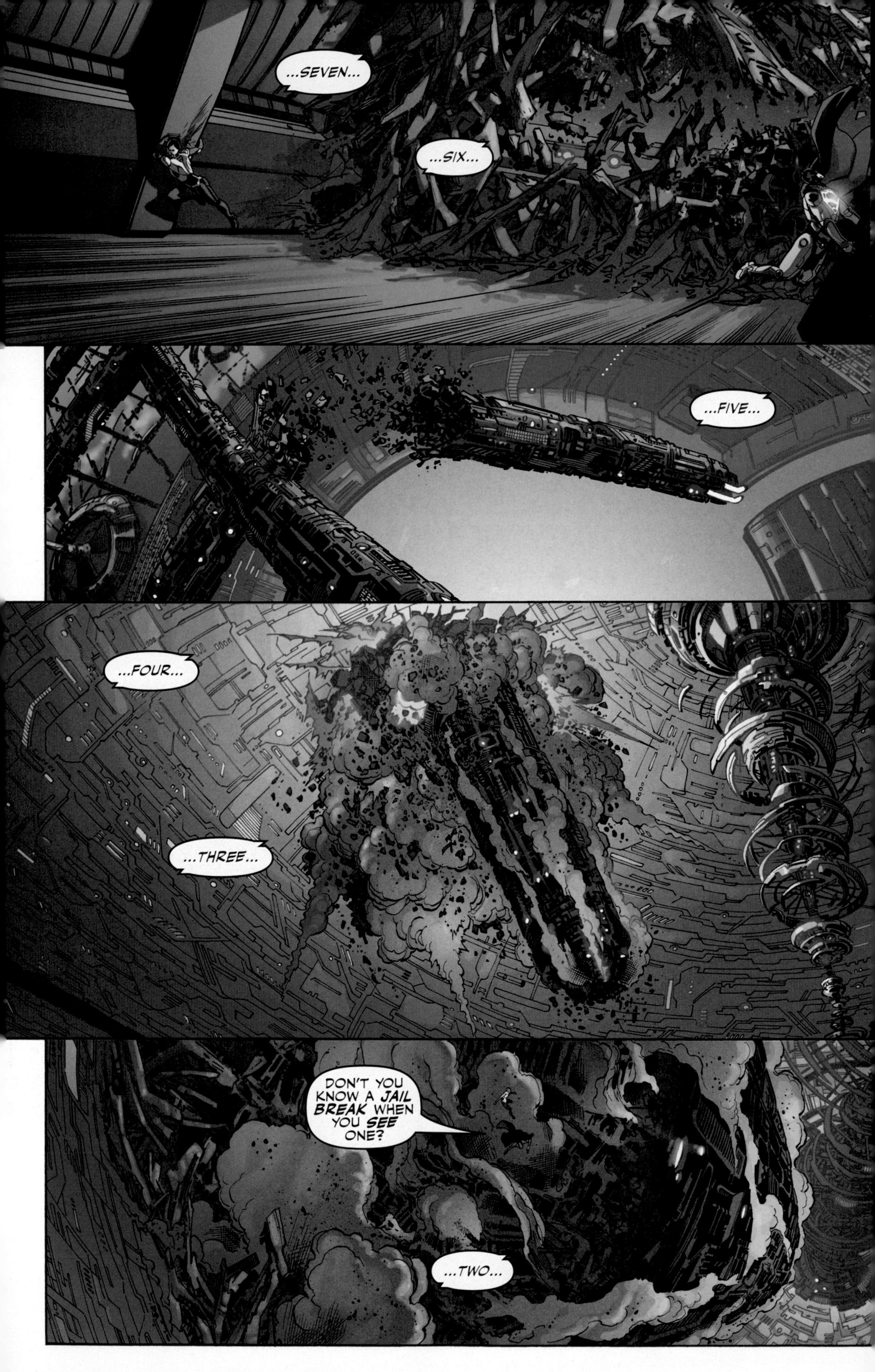

...SEVEN...
...SIX...
...FIVE...
...FOUR...
...THREE...
DON'T YOU KNOW A JAIL BREAK WHEN YOU SEE ONE?
...TWO...

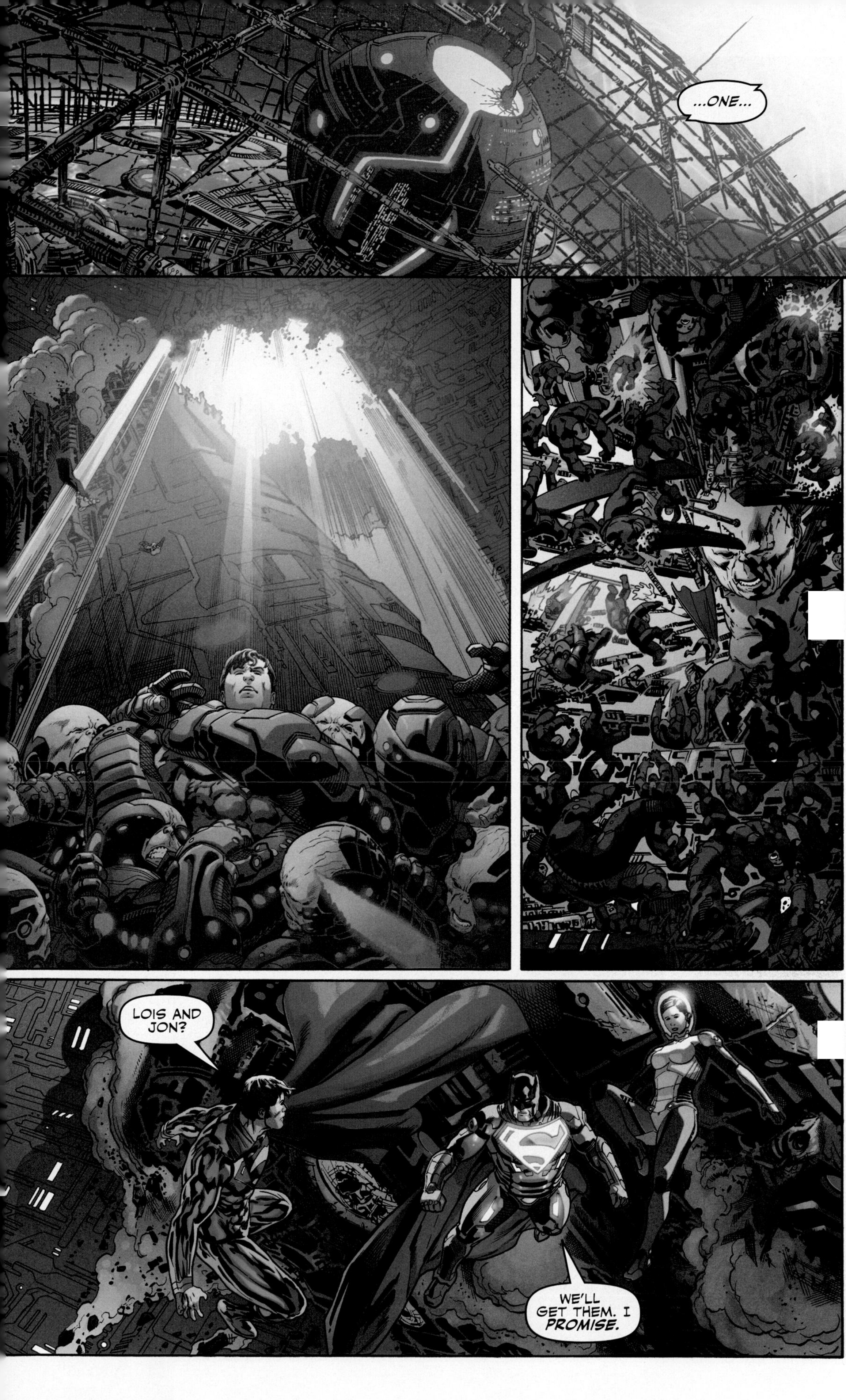
...ONE...
LOIS AND JON?
WE'LL GET THEM. I *PROMISE.*

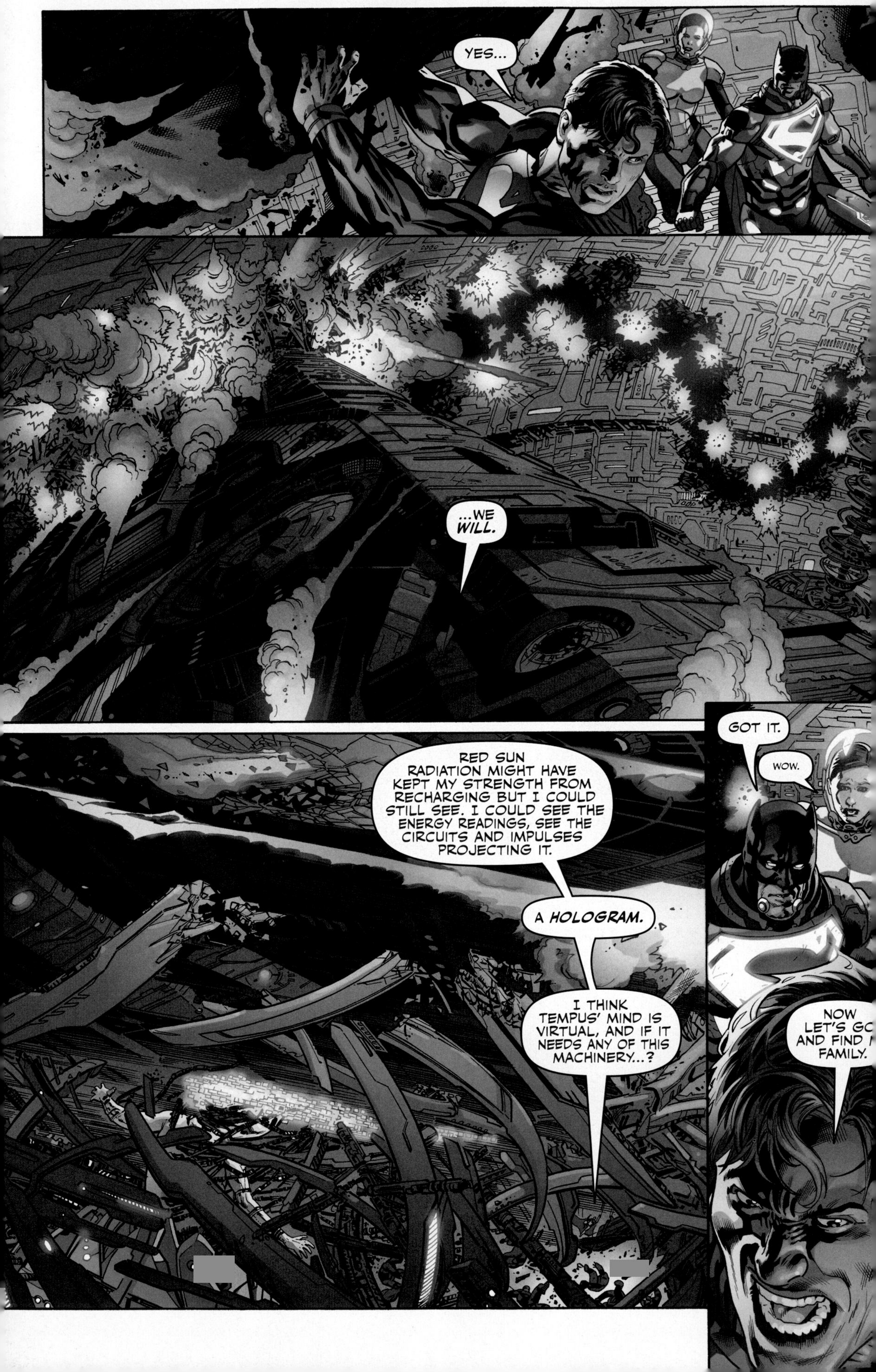
YES...
...WE *WILL.*
RED SUN RADIATION MIGHT HAVE KEPT MY STRENGTH FROM RECHARGING BUT I COULD STILL SEE. I COULD SEE THE ENERGY READINGS, SEE THE CIRCUITS AND IMPULSES PROJECTING IT.
A *HOLOGRAM.*
I THINK TEMPUS' MIND IS VIRTUAL, AND IF IT NEEDS ANY OF THIS MACHINERY...?
GOT IT.
WOW.
NOW LET'S GO AND FIND FAMILY.

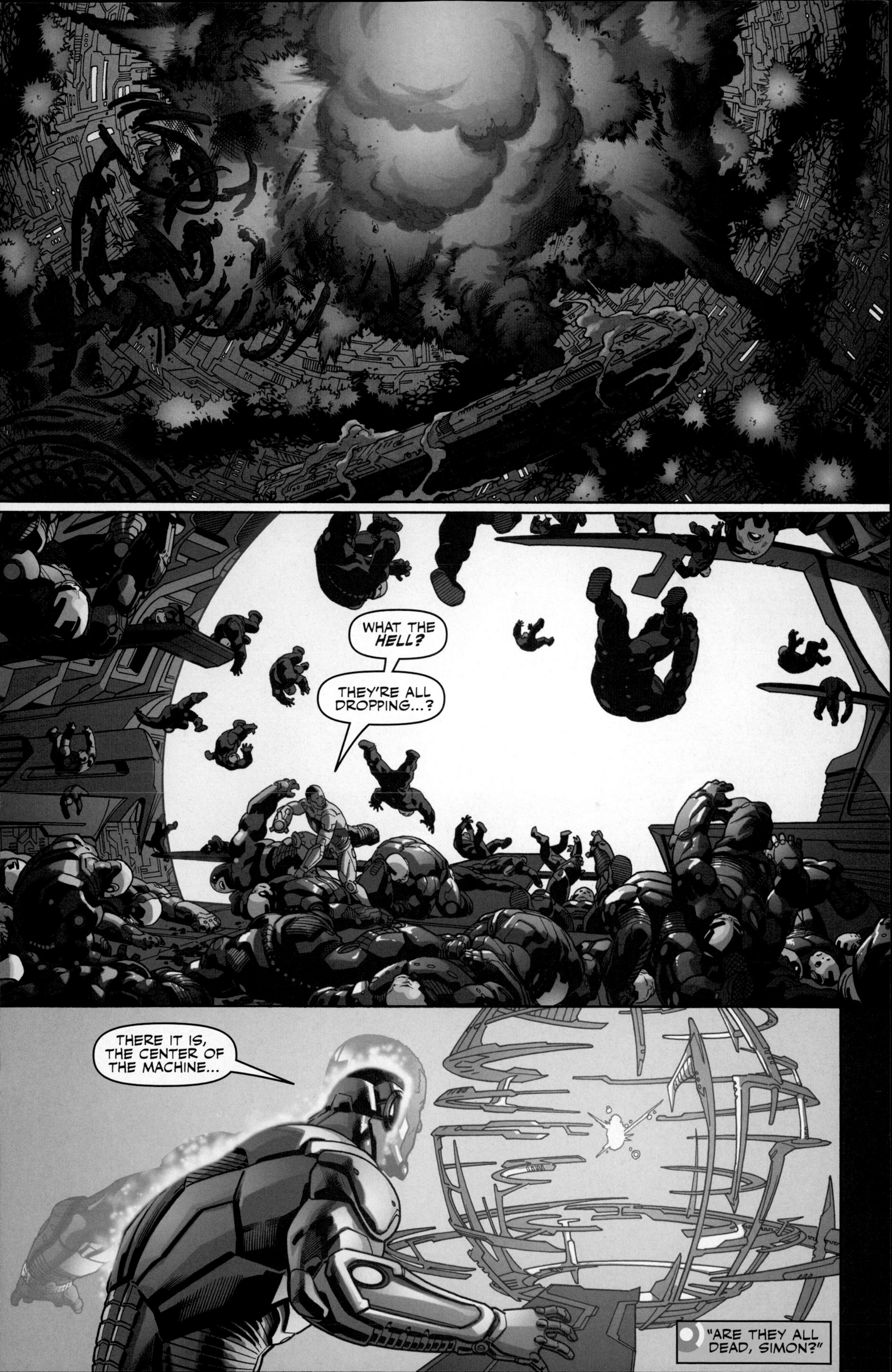
WHAT THE HELL?
THEY'RE ALL DROPPING...?
THERE IT IS, THE CENTER OF THE MACHINE...
"ARE THEY ALL DEAD, SIMON?"

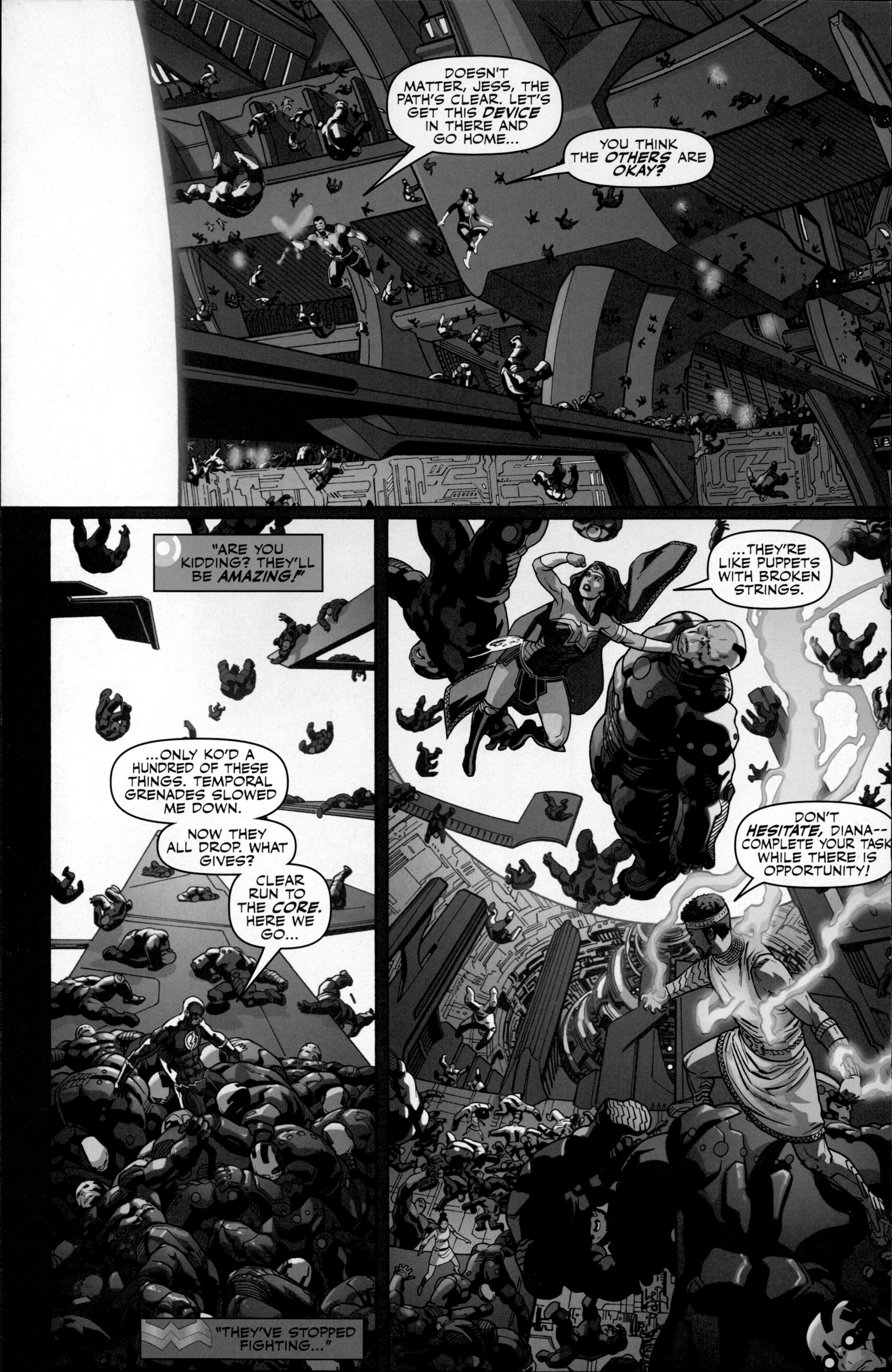
DOESN'T MATTER, JESS, THE PATH'S CLEAR. LET'S GET THIS *DEVICE* IN THERE AND GO HOME...
YOU THINK THE *OTHERS* ARE *OKAY?*
"ARE YOU KIDDING? THEY'LL BE *AMAZING!*"
...ONLY KO'D A HUNDRED OF THESE THINGS. TEMPORAL GRENADES SLOWED ME DOWN.
NOW THEY ALL DROP. WHAT GIVES?
CLEAR RUN TO THE *CORE.* HERE WE GO...
"THEY'VE STOPPED FIGHTING..."
...THEY'RE LIKE PUPPETS WITH BROKEN STRINGS.
DON'T *HESITATE,* DIANA-- COMPLETE YOUR TASK WHILE THERE IS OPPORTUNITY!

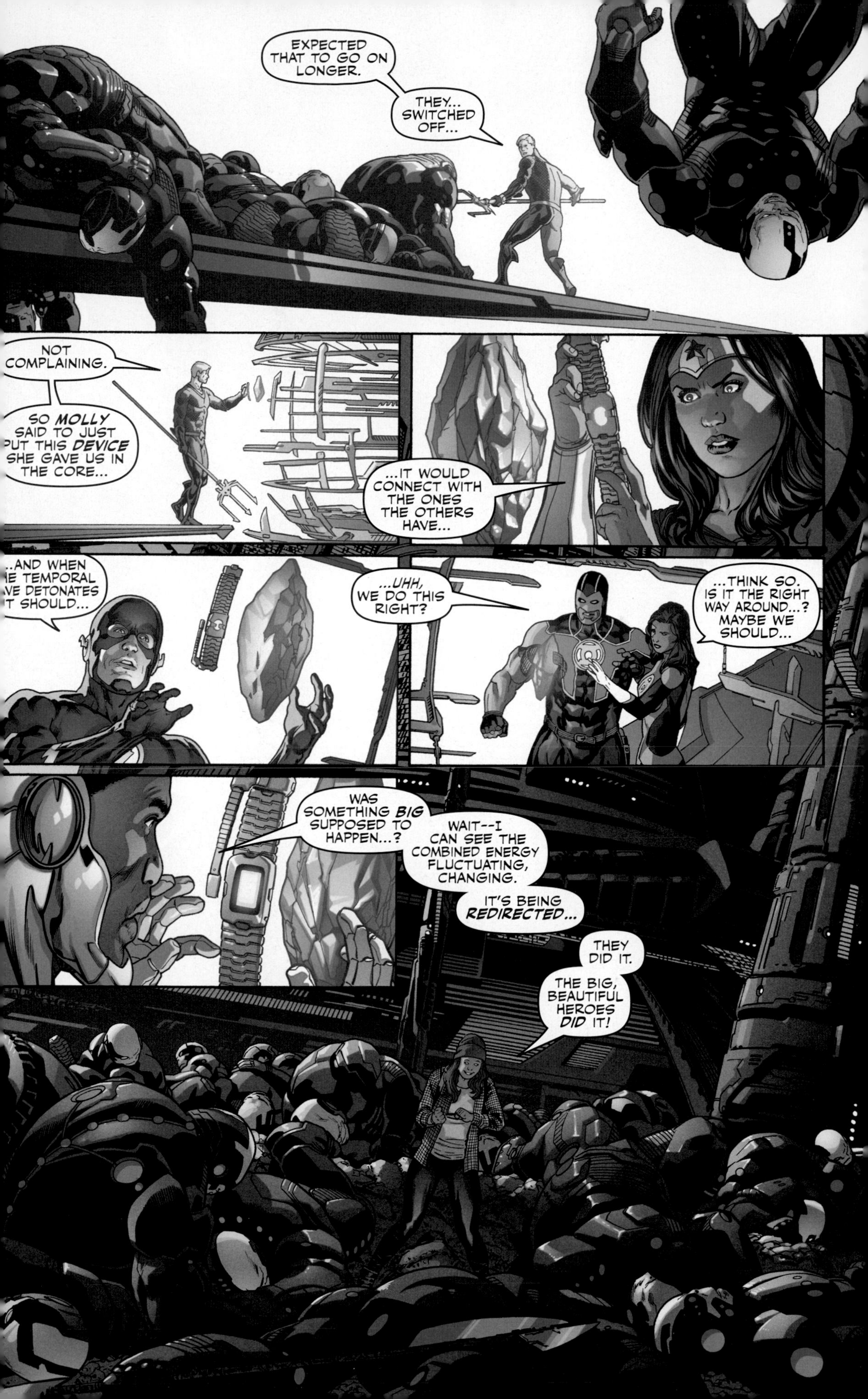

EXPECTED THAT TO GO ON LONGER.
THEY... SWITCHED OFF...
NOT COMPLAINING.
SO MOLLY SAID TO JUST PUT THIS DEVICE SHE GAVE US IN THE CORE...
...IT WOULD CONNECT WITH THE ONES THE OTHERS HAVE...
..AND WHEN THE TEMPORAL AVE DETONATES T SHOULD...
...UHH, WE DO THIS RIGHT?
...THINK SO. IS IT THE RIGHT WAY AROUND...? MAYBE WE SHOULD...
WAS SOMETHING BIG SUPPOSED TO HAPPEN...?
WAIT--I CAN SEE THE COMBINED ENERGY FLUCTUATING, CHANGING.
IT'S BEING REDIRECTED...
THEY DID IT.
THE BIG, BEAUTIFUL HEROES DID IT!

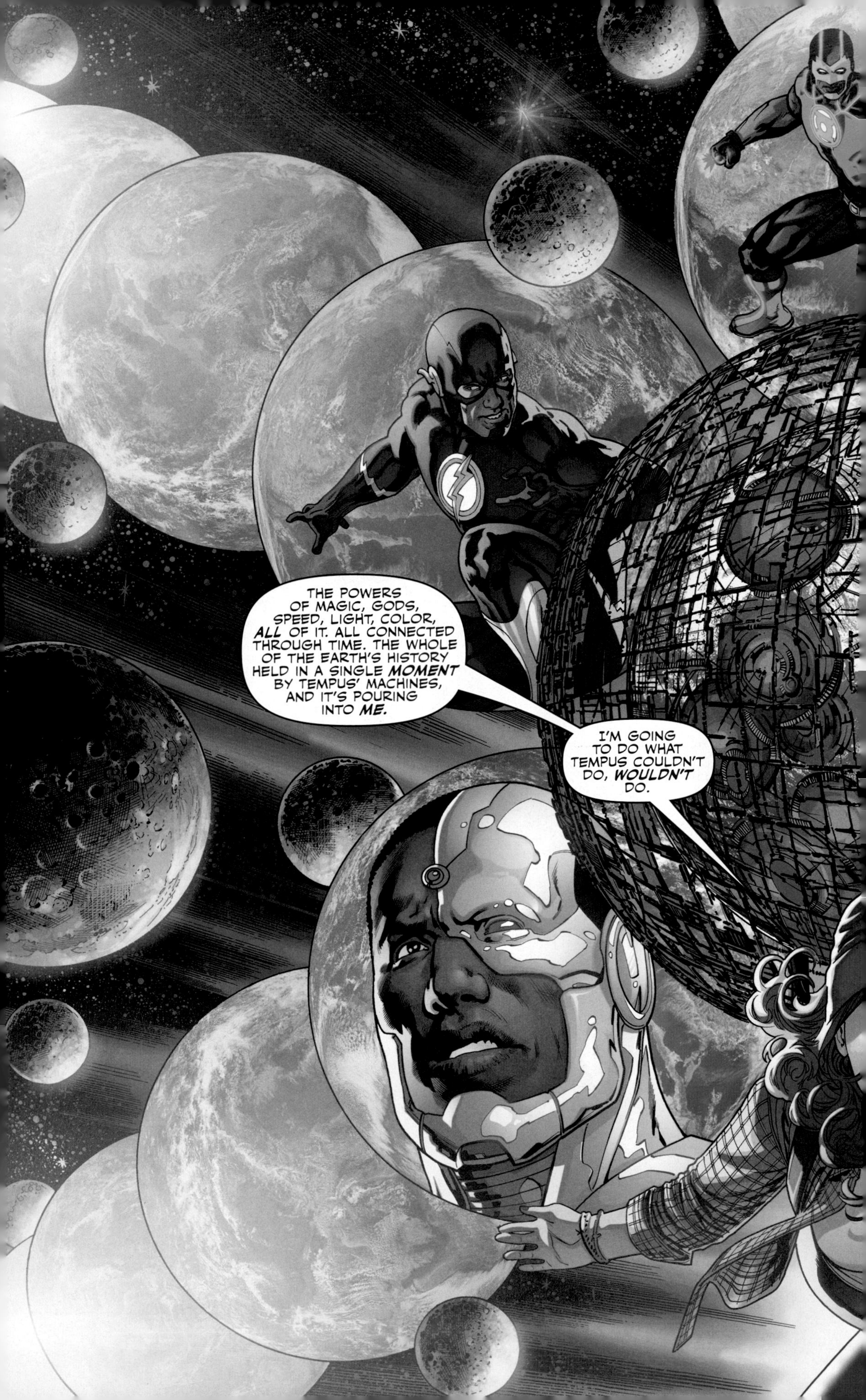
THE POWERS OF MAGIC, GODS, SPEED, LIGHT, COLOR, ALL OF IT. ALL CONNECTED THROUGH TIME. THE WHOLE OF THE EARTH'S HISTORY HELD IN A SINGLE MOMENT BY TEMPUS' MACHINES, AND IT'S POURING INTO ME.
I'M GOING TO DO WHAT TEMPUS COULDN'T DO, WOULDN'T DO.

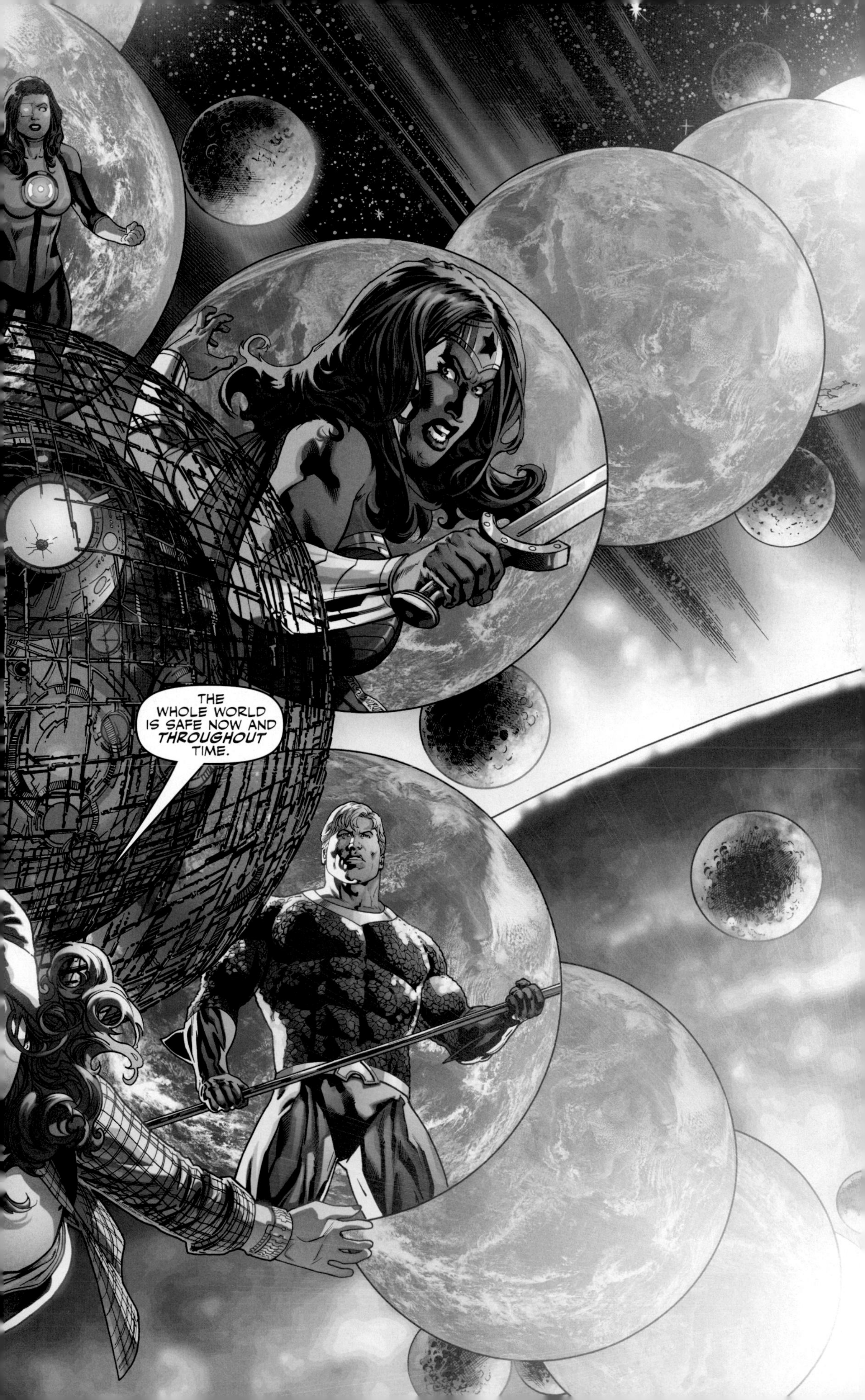
THE WHOLE WORLD IS SAFE NOW AND *THROUGHOUT* TIME.

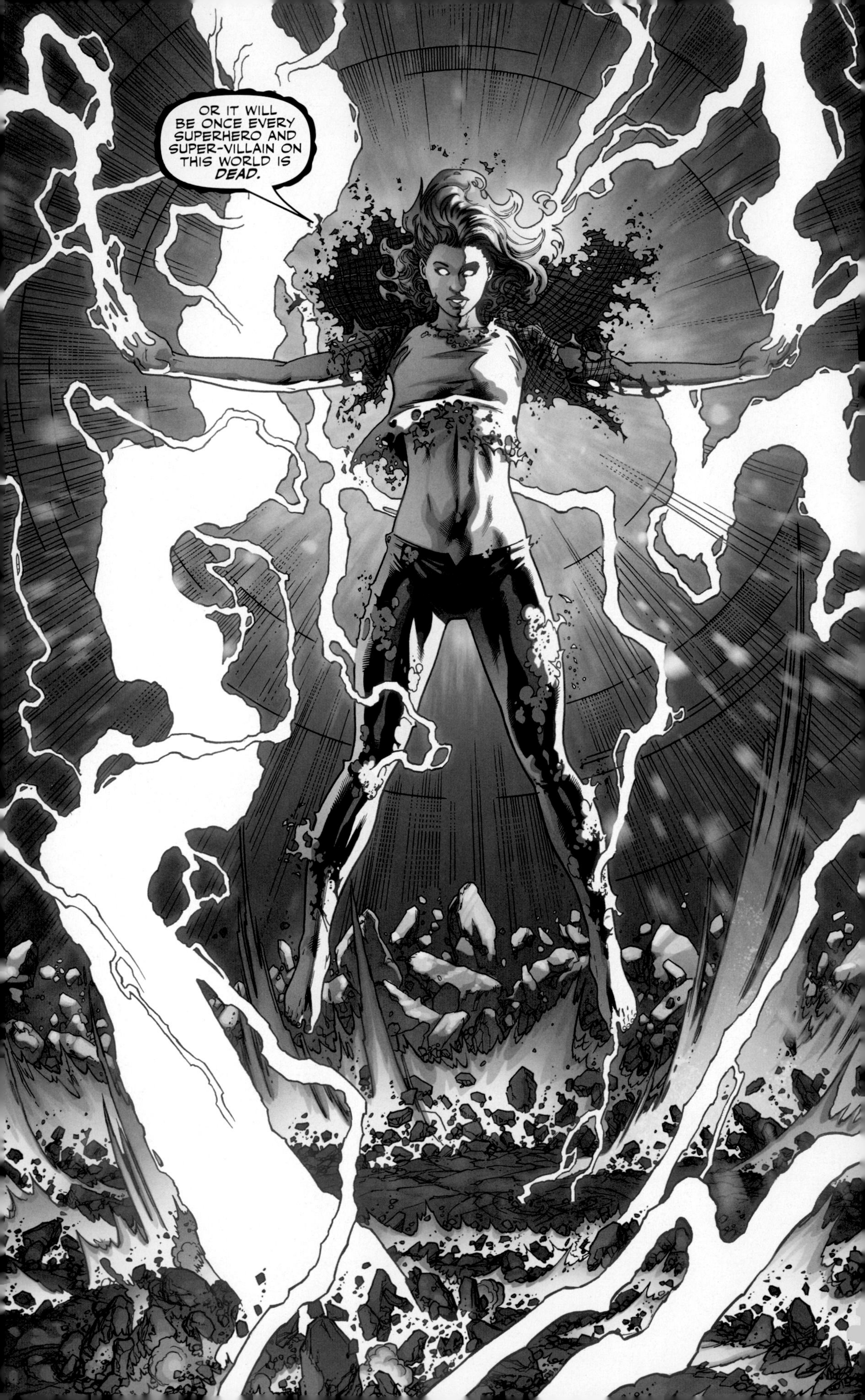
OR IT WILL BE ONCE EVERY SUPERHERO AND SUPER-VILLAIN ON THIS WORLD IS DEAD.

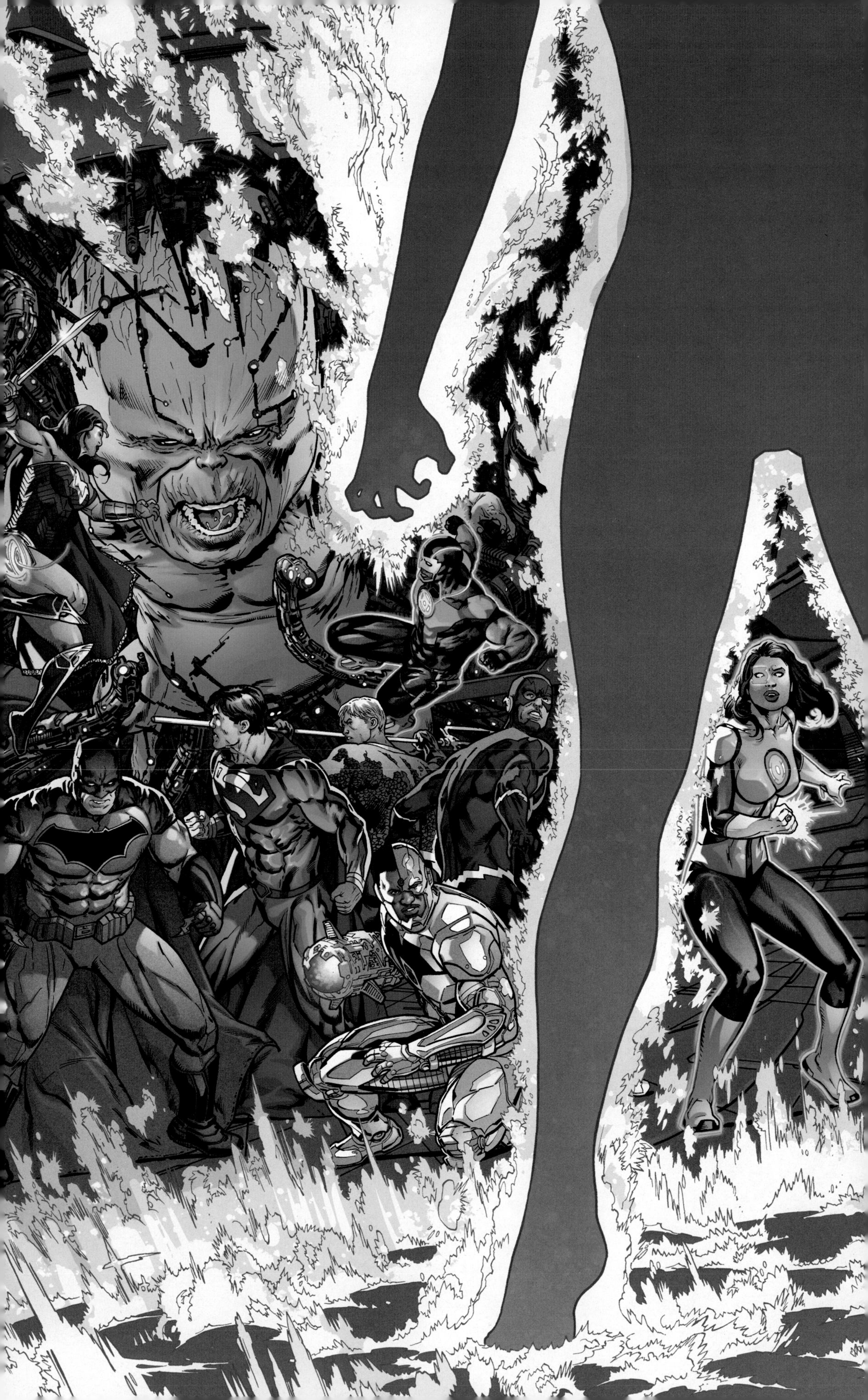

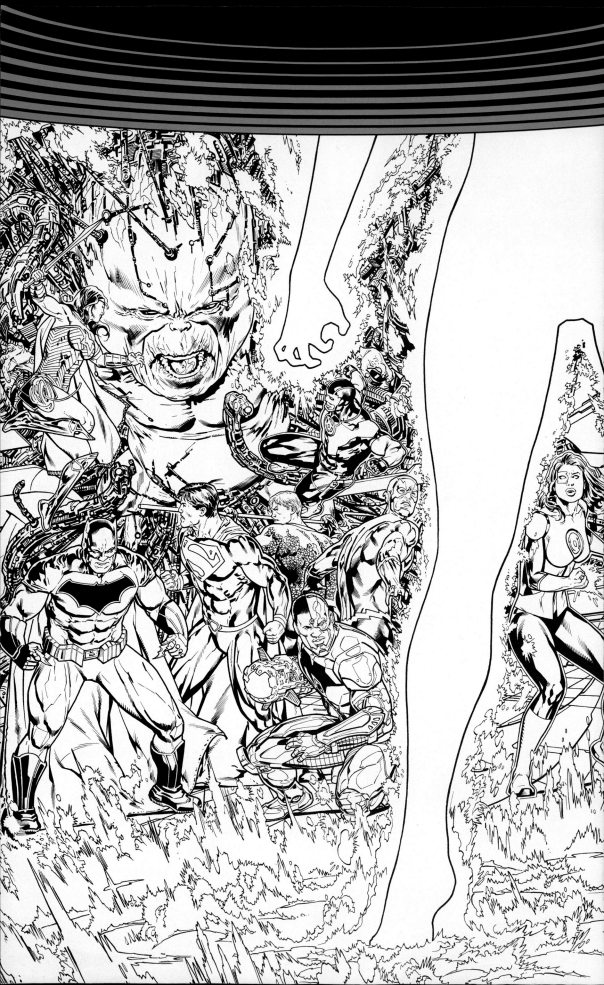

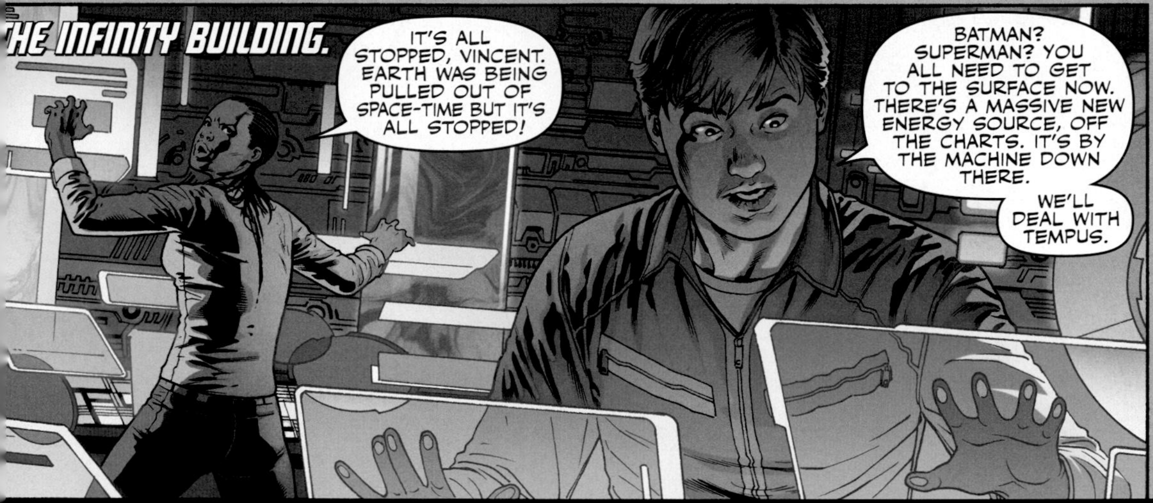
THE INFINITY BUILDING.
IT'S ALL STOPPED, VINCENT. EARTH WAS BEING PULLED OUT OF SPACE-TIME BUT IT'S ALL STOPPED!
BATMAN? SUPERMAN? YOU ALL NEED TO GET TO THE SURFACE NOW. THERE'S A MASSIVE NEW ENERGY SOURCE, OFF THE CHARTS. IT'S BY THE MACHINE DOWN THERE.
WE'LL DEAL WITH TEMPUS.

TIMELESS PART 5

RYAN HITCH WRITER • FERNANDO PASARIN PENCILLER • MATT RYAN INKER
RAD ANDERSON COLORIST • RICHARD STARKINGS AND COMICRAFT LETTERING
RNANDO PASARIN MATT RYAN & BRAD ANDERSON COVER • NICK BRADSHAW VARIANT COVER
IEGO LOPEZ & AMEDEO TURTURRO ASSISTANT EDITORS • BRIAN CUNNINGHAM EDITOR
UPERMAN CREATED BY JERRY SIEGEL & JOE SHUSTER, BY SPECIAL ARRANGEMENT WITH THE JERRY SIEGEL FAMILY.

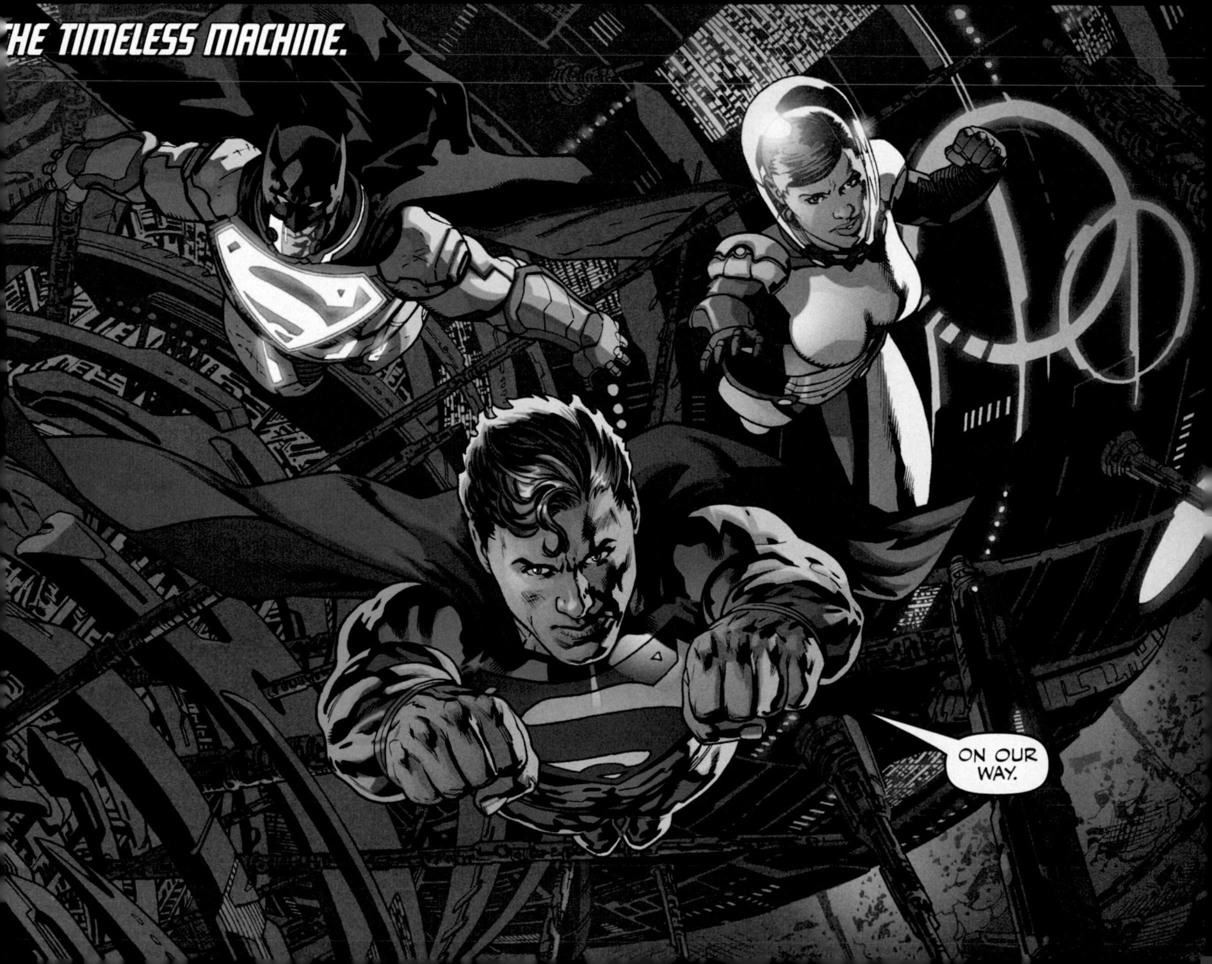
THE TIMELESS MACHINE.
ON OUR WAY.

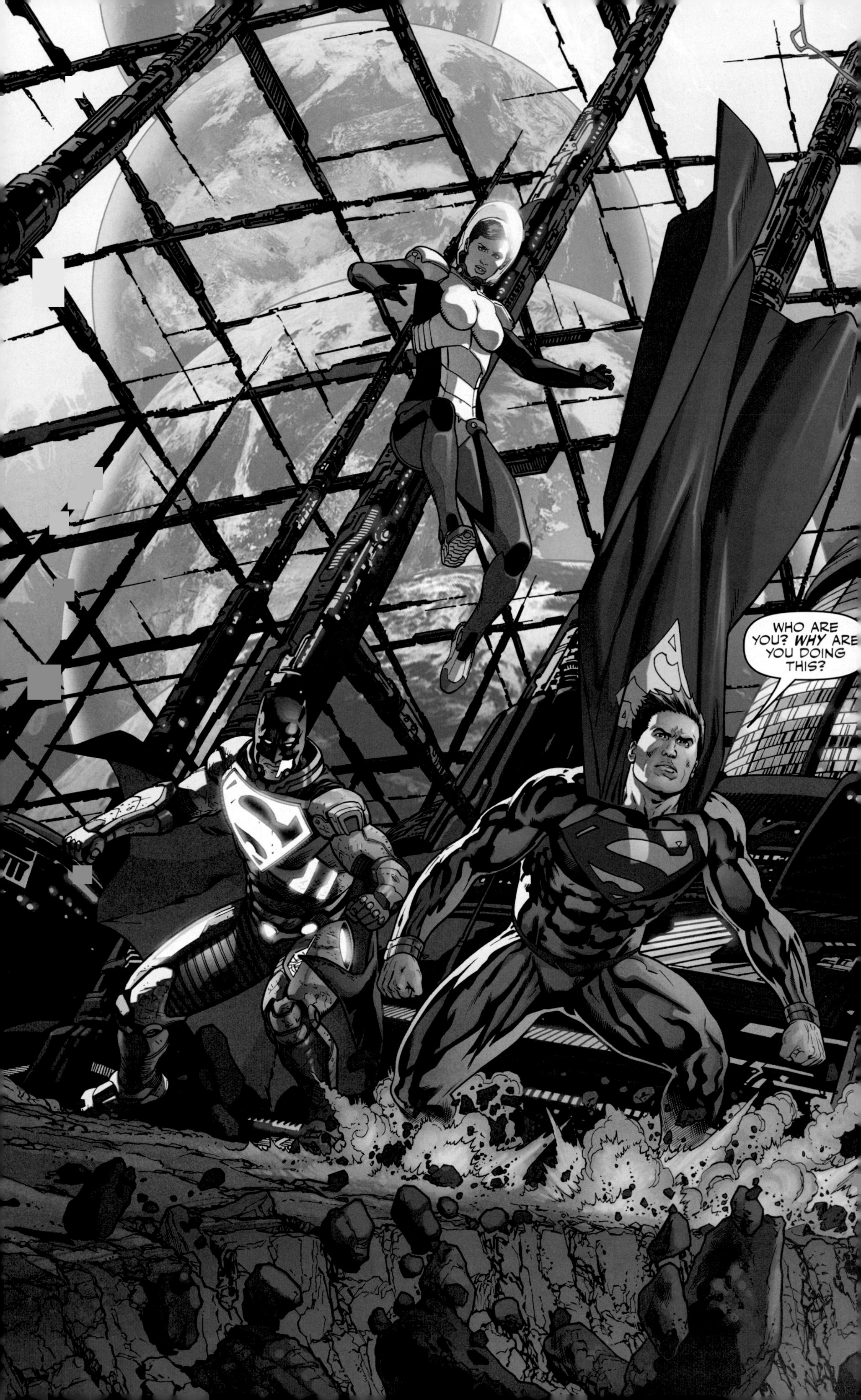
WHO ARE YOU? *WHY* ARE YOU DOING THIS?

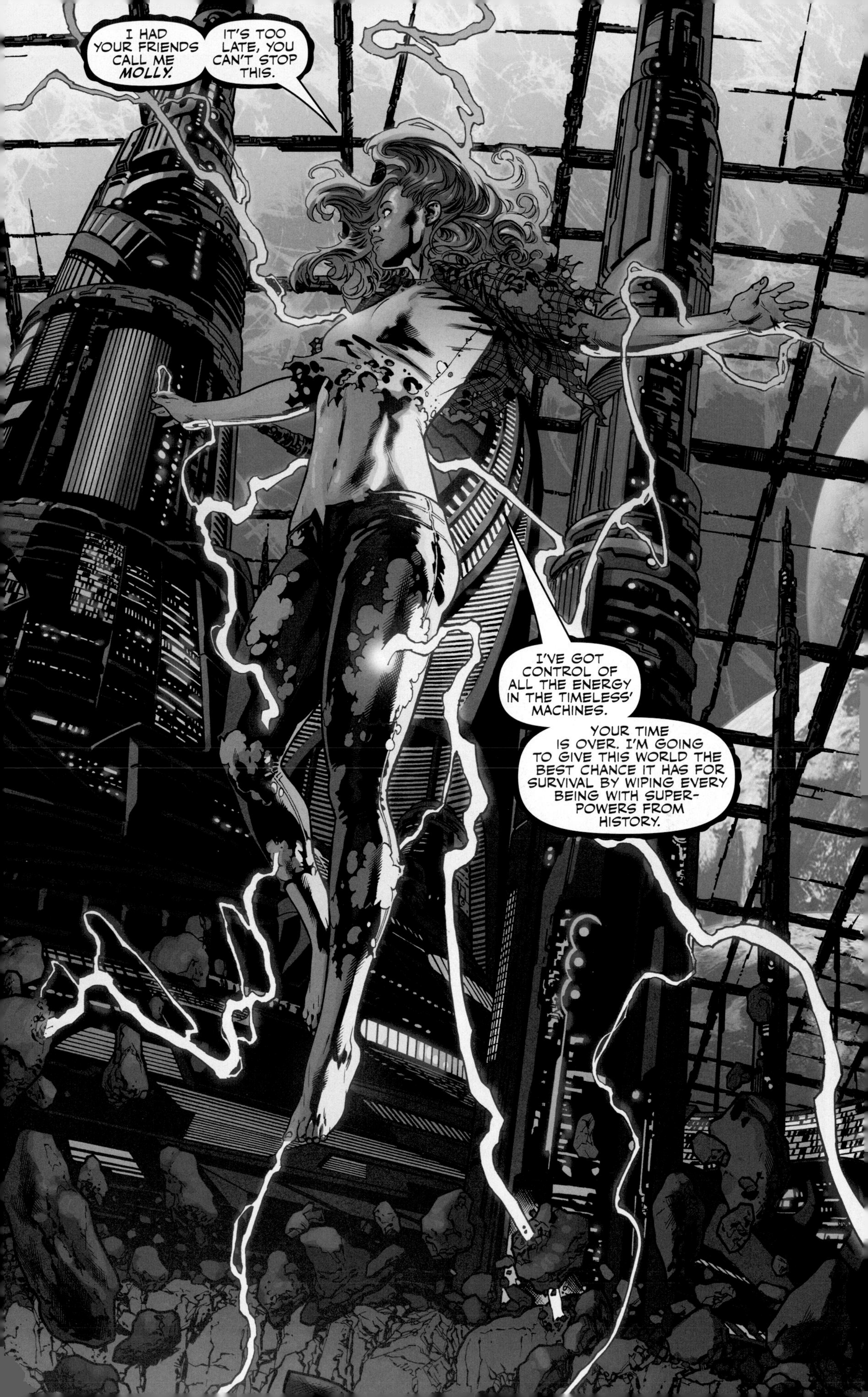
I HAD YOUR FRIENDS CALL ME *MOLLY.*
IT'S TOO LATE, YOU CAN'T STOP THIS.
I'VE GOT CONTROL OF ALL THE ENERGY IN THE TIMELESS' MACHINES.
YOUR TIME IS OVER. I'M GOING TO GIVE THIS WORLD THE BEST CHANCE IT HAS FOR SURVIVAL BY WIPING EVERY BEING WITH SUPER-POWERS FROM HISTORY.

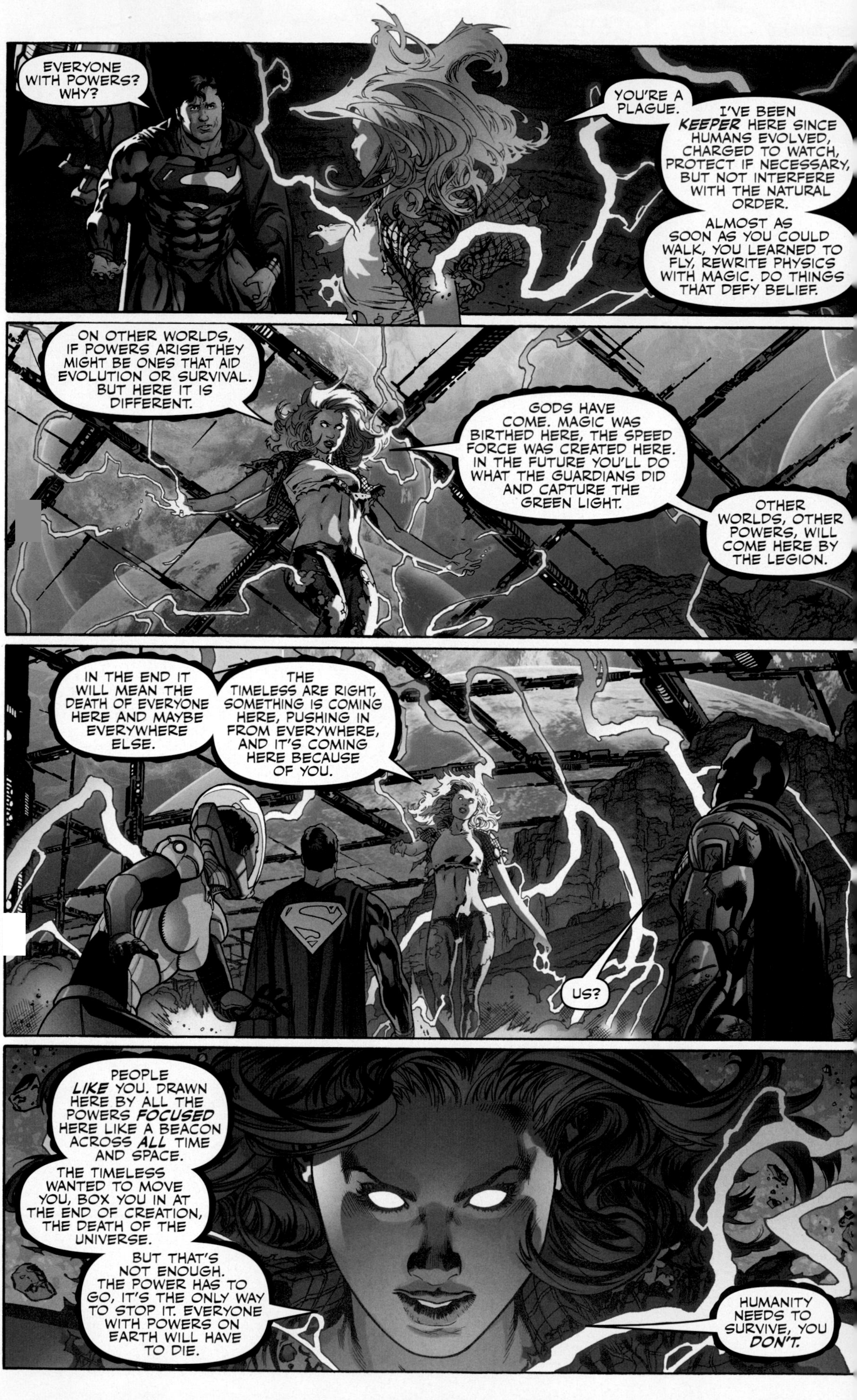
EVERYONE WITH POWERS? WHY?
YOU'RE A PLAGUE.
I'VE BEEN KEEPER HERE SINCE HUMANS EVOLVED, CHARGED TO WATCH, PROTECT IF NECESSARY, BUT NOT INTERFERE WITH THE NATURAL ORDER.
ALMOST AS SOON AS YOU COULD WALK, YOU LEARNED TO FLY, REWRITE PHYSICS WITH MAGIC. DO THINGS THAT DEFY BELIEF.
ON OTHER WORLDS, IF POWERS ARISE THEY MIGHT BE ONES THAT AID EVOLUTION OR SURVIVAL. BUT HERE IT IS DIFFERENT.
GODS HAVE COME. MAGIC WAS BIRTHED HERE, THE SPEED FORCE WAS CREATED HERE. IN THE FUTURE YOU'LL DO WHAT THE GUARDIANS DID AND CAPTURE THE GREEN LIGHT.
OTHER WORLDS, OTHER POWERS, WILL COME HERE BY THE LEGION.
IN THE END IT WILL MEAN THE DEATH OF EVERYONE HERE AND MAYBE EVERYWHERE ELSE.
THE TIMELESS ARE RIGHT, SOMETHING IS COMING HERE, PUSHING IN FROM EVERYWHERE, AND IT'S COMING HERE BECAUSE OF YOU.
US?
PEOPLE LIKE YOU. DRAWN HERE BY ALL THE POWERS FOCUSED HERE LIKE A BEACON ACROSS ALL TIME AND SPACE.
THE TIMELESS WANTED TO MOVE YOU, BOX YOU IN AT THE END OF CREATION, THE DEATH OF THE UNIVERSE.
BUT THAT'S NOT ENOUGH. THE POWER HAS TO GO, IT'S THE ONLY WAY TO STOP IT. EVERYONE WITH POWERS ON EARTH WILL HAVE TO DIE.
HUMANITY NEEDS TO SURVIVE, YOU DON'T.

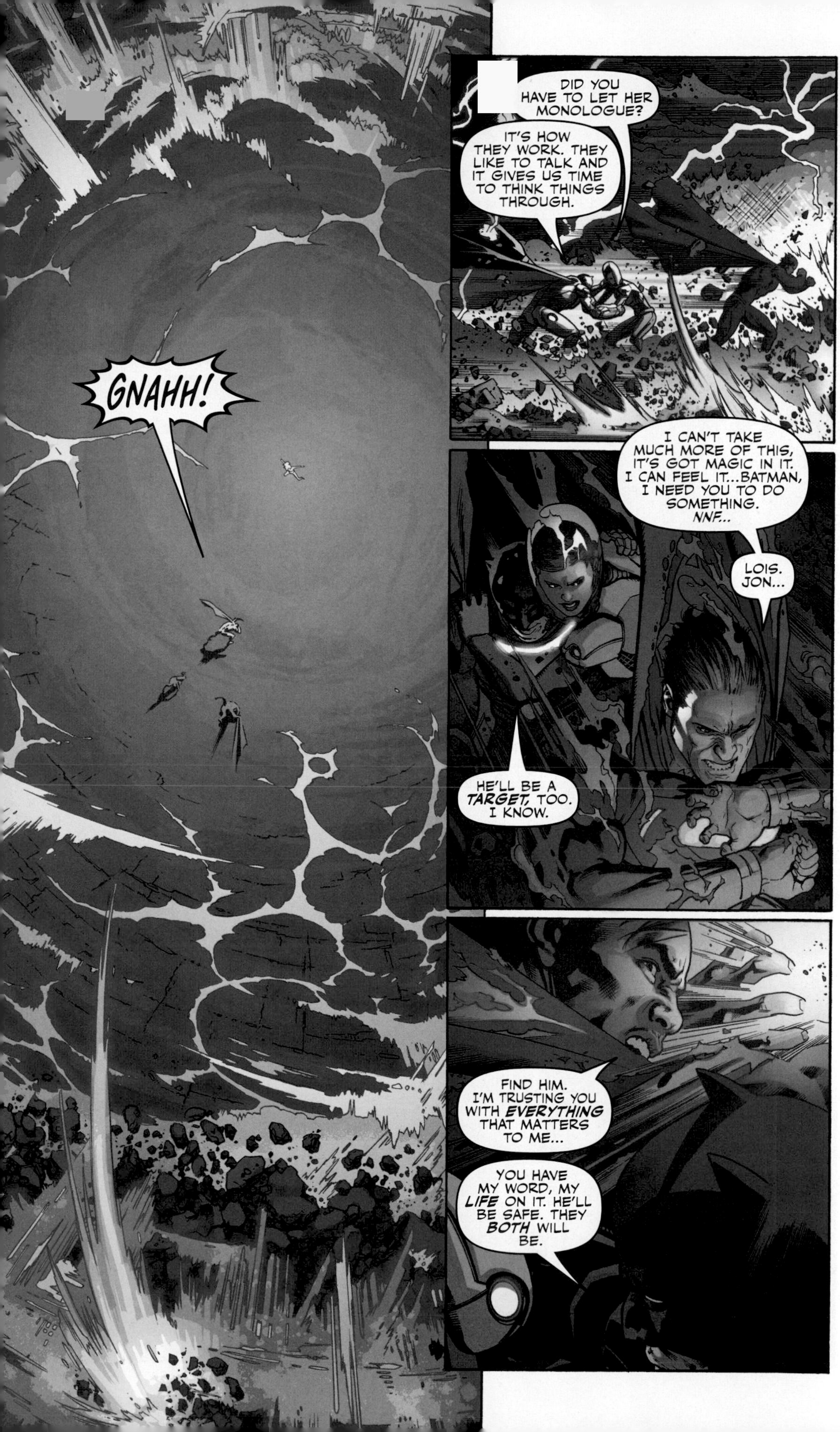
GNAHH!
DID YOU HAVE TO LET HER MONOLOGUE?
IT'S HOW THEY WORK. THEY LIKE TO TALK AND IT GIVES US TIME TO THINK THINGS THROUGH.
I CAN'T TAKE MUCH MORE OF THIS, IT'S GOT MAGIC IN IT. I CAN FEEL IT...BATMAN, I NEED YOU TO DO SOMETHING. *NNF...*
LOIS. JON...
HE'LL BE A *TARGET,* TOO. I KNOW.
FIND HIM. I'M TRUSTING YOU WITH *EVERYTHING* THAT MATTERS TO ME...
YOU HAVE MY WORD, MY *LIFE* ON IT. HE'LL BE SAFE. THEY *BOTH* WILL BE.

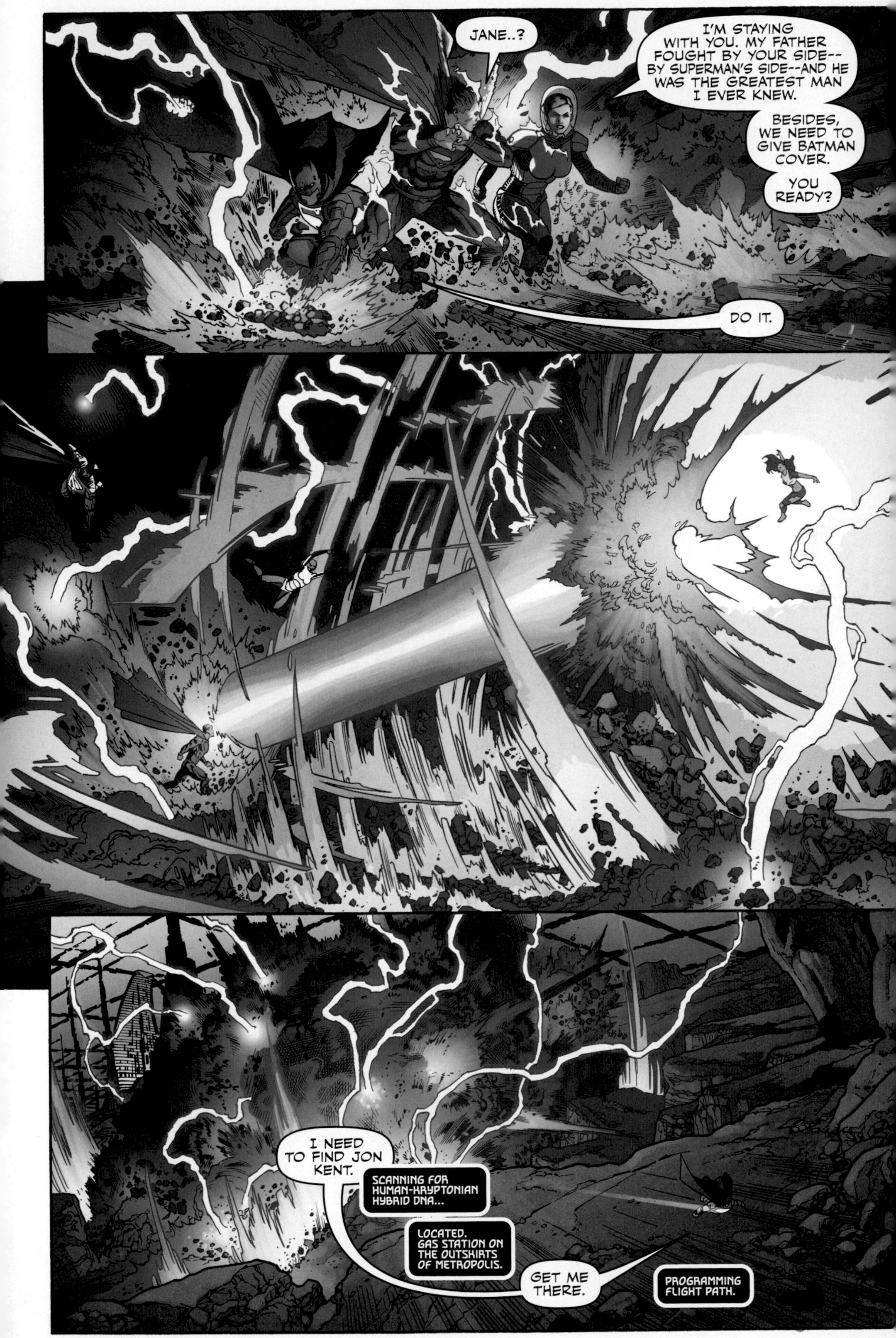
JANE..?
I'M STAYING WITH YOU. MY FATHER FOUGHT BY YOUR SIDE-- BY SUPERMAN'S SIDE--AND HE WAS THE GREATEST MAN I EVER KNEW.
BESIDES, WE NEED TO GIVE BATMAN COVER.
YOU READY?
DO IT.
I NEED TO FIND JON KENT.
SCANNING FOR HUMAN-KRYPTONIAN HYBRID DNA...
LOCATED. GAS STATION ON THE OUTSKIRTS OF METROPOLIS.
GET ME THERE.
PROGRAMMING FLIGHT PATH.

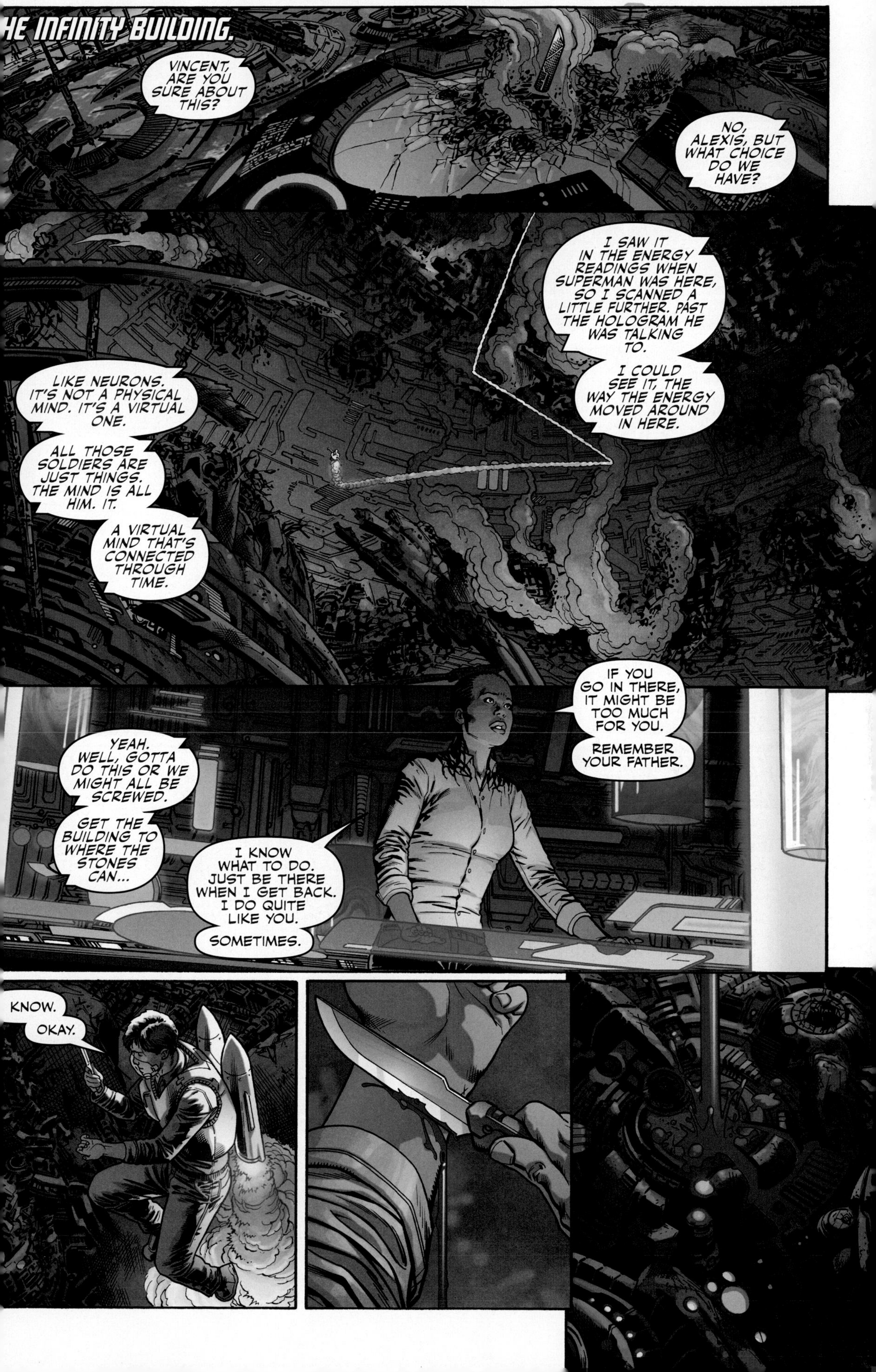
HE INFINITY BUILDING.
VINCENT, ARE YOU SURE ABOUT THIS?
NO, ALEXIS, BUT WHAT CHOICE DO WE HAVE?
I SAW IT IN THE ENERGY READINGS WHEN SUPERMAN WAS HERE, SO I SCANNED A LITTLE FURTHER. PAST THE HOLOGRAM HE WAS TALKING TO.
I COULD SEE IT, THE WAY THE ENERGY MOVED AROUND IN HERE.
LIKE NEURONS. IT'S NOT A PHYSICAL MIND. IT'S A VIRTUAL ONE.
ALL THOSE SOLDIERS ARE JUST THINGS. THE MIND IS ALL HIM. IT.
A VIRTUAL MIND THAT'S CONNECTED THROUGH TIME.
IF YOU GO IN THERE, IT MIGHT BE TOO MUCH FOR YOU.
REMEMBER YOUR FATHER.
YEAH. WELL, GOTTA DO THIS OR WE MIGHT ALL BE SCREWED.
GET THE BUILDING TO WHERE THE STONES CAN...
I KNOW WHAT TO DO. JUST BE THERE WHEN I GET BACK. I DO QUITE LIKE YOU.
SOMETIMES.
KNOW.
OKAY.

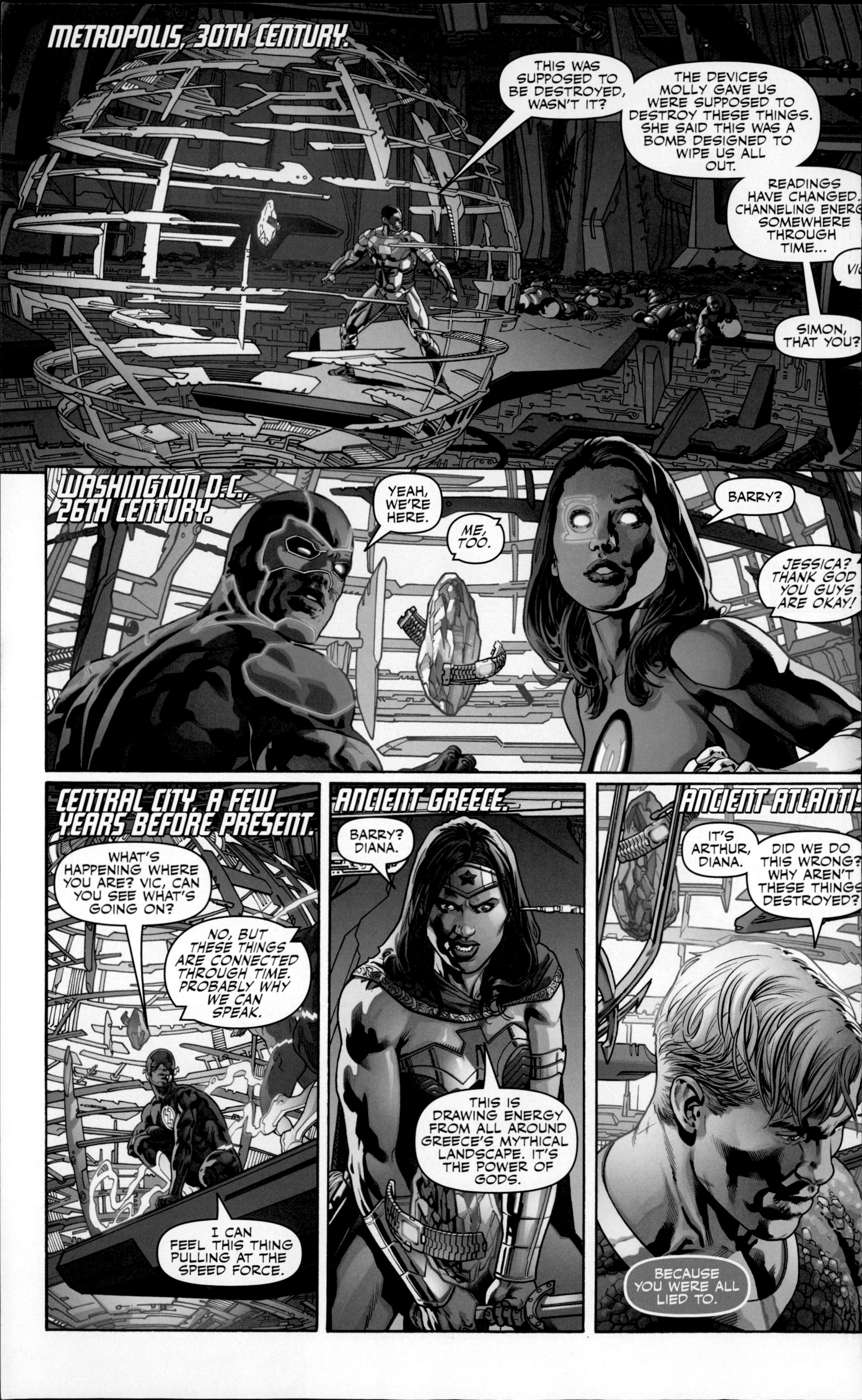
METROPOLIS, 30TH CENTURY.
THIS WAS SUPPOSED TO BE DESTROYED, WASN'T IT?
THE DEVICES MOLLY GAVE US WERE SUPPOSED TO DESTROY THESE THINGS. SHE SAID THIS WAS A BOMB DESIGNED TO WIPE US ALL OUT.
READINGS HAVE CHANGED. CHANNELING ENERG SOMEWHERE THROUGH TIME...
SIMON, THAT YOU?
WASHINGTON D.C., 26TH CENTURY.
YEAH, WE'RE HERE.
ME, TOO.
BARRY?
JESSICA? THANK GOD YOU GUYS ARE OKAY!
CENTRAL CITY, A FEW YEARS BEFORE PRESENT.
WHAT'S HAPPENING WHERE YOU ARE? VIC, CAN YOU SEE WHAT'S GOING ON?
NO, BUT THESE THINGS ARE CONNECTED THROUGH TIME. PROBABLY WHY WE CAN SPEAK.
I CAN FEEL THIS THING PULLING AT THE SPEED FORCE.
ANCIENT GREECE.
BARRY? DIANA.
THIS IS DRAWING ENERGY FROM ALL AROUND GREECE'S MYTHICAL LANDSCAPE. IT'S THE POWER OF GODS.
IT'S ARTHUR, DIANA.
DID WE DO THIS WRONG? WHY AREN'T THESE THINGS DESTROYED?
BECAUSE YOU WERE ALL LIED TO.

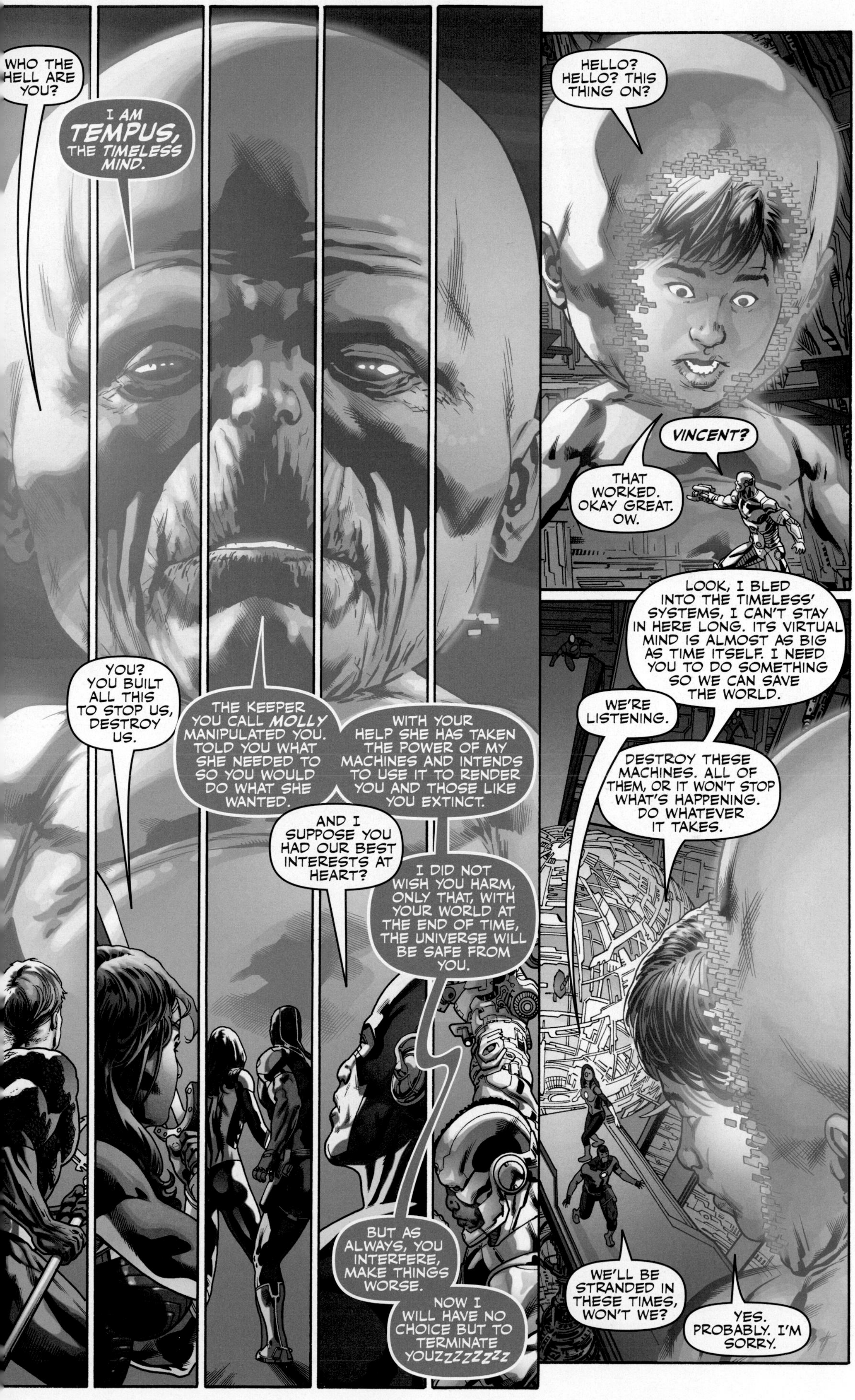
WHO THE HELL ARE YOU?
I AM TEMPUS, THE TIMELESS MIND.
YOU? YOU BUILT ALL THIS TO STOP US, DESTROY US.
THE KEEPER YOU CALL MOLLY MANIPULATED YOU. TOLD YOU WHAT SHE NEEDED TO SO YOU WOULD DO WHAT SHE WANTED.
WITH YOUR HELP SHE HAS TAKEN THE POWER OF MY MACHINES AND INTENDS TO USE IT TO RENDER YOU AND THOSE LIKE YOU EXTINCT.
AND I SUPPOSE YOU HAD OUR BEST INTERESTS AT HEART?
I DID NOT WISH YOU HARM, ONLY THAT, WITH YOUR WORLD AT THE END OF TIME, THE UNIVERSE WILL BE SAFE FROM YOU.
BUT AS ALWAYS, YOU INTERFERE, MAKE THINGS WORSE.
NOW I WILL HAVE NO CHOICE BUT TO TERMINATE YOUZZZZZZZ
HELLO? HELLO? THIS THING ON?
VINCENT?
THAT WORKED. OKAY GREAT. OW.
LOOK, I BLED INTO THE TIMELESS' SYSTEMS, I CAN'T STAY IN HERE LONG. ITS VIRTUAL MIND IS ALMOST AS BIG AS TIME ITSELF. I NEED YOU TO DO SOMETHING SO WE CAN SAVE THE WORLD.
WE'RE LISTENING.
DESTROY THESE MACHINES. ALL OF THEM, OR IT WON'T STOP WHAT'S HAPPENING. DO WHATEVER IT TAKES.
WE'LL BE STRANDED IN THESE TIMES, WON'T WE?
YES. PROBABLY. I'M SORRY.

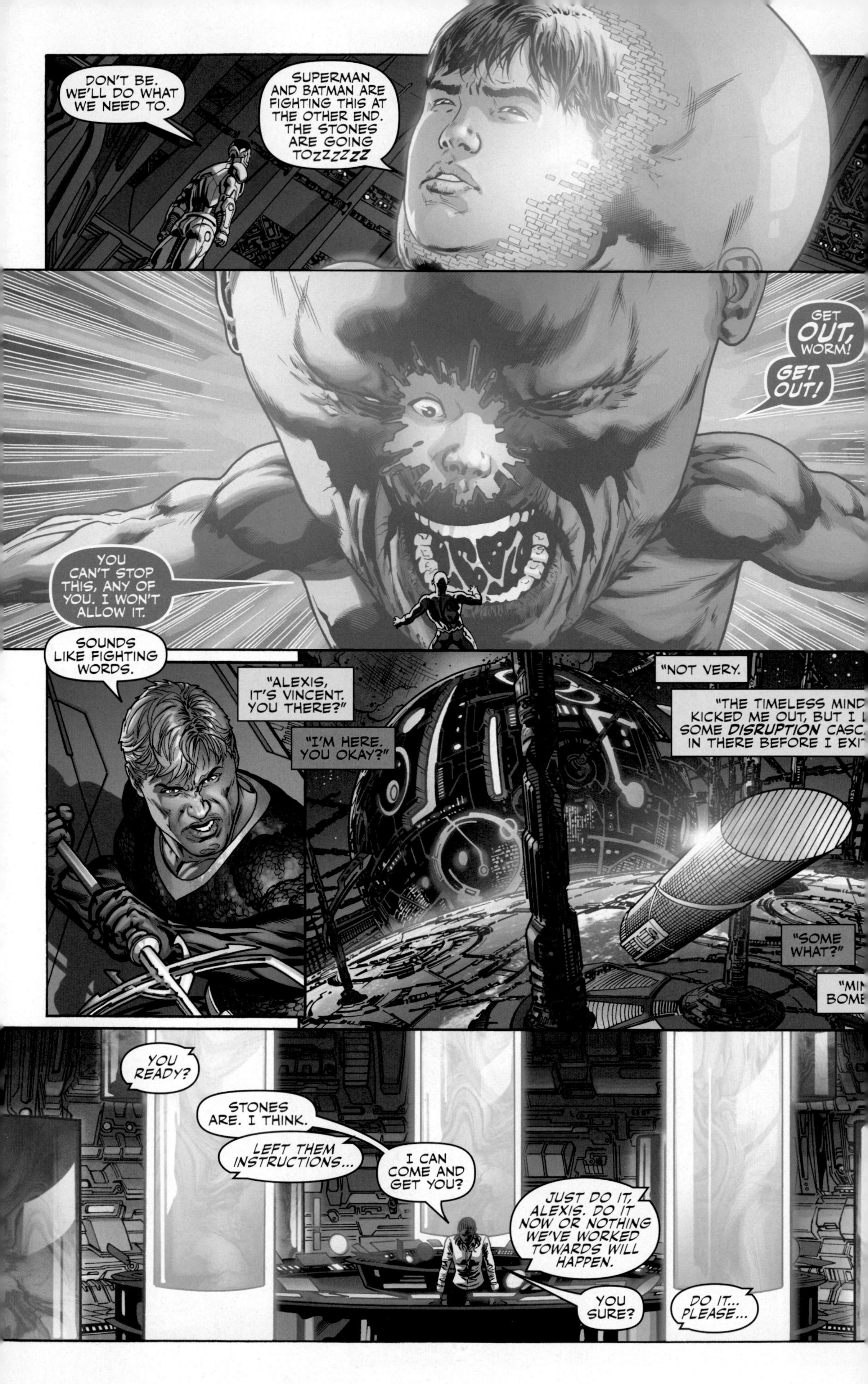
DON'T BE. WE'LL DO WHAT WE NEED TO.
SUPERMAN AND BATMAN ARE FIGHTING THIS AT THE OTHER END. THE STONES ARE GOING TOZZZZZZ
GET OUT, WORM!
GET OUT!
YOU CAN'T STOP THIS, ANY OF YOU. I WON'T ALLOW IT.
SOUNDS LIKE FIGHTING WORDS.
"ALEXIS, IT'S VINCENT. YOU THERE?"
"I'M HERE. YOU OKAY?"
"NOT VERY.
"THE TIMELESS MIND KICKED ME OUT, BUT I L SOME DISRUPTION CASC IN THERE BEFORE I EXIT
"SOME WHAT?"
"MIN BOMB
YOU READY?
STONES ARE. I THINK.
LEFT THEM INSTRUCTIONS...
I CAN COME AND GET YOU?
JUST DO IT, ALEXIS. DO IT NOW OR NOTHING WE'VE WORKED TOWARDS WILL HAPPEN.
YOU SURE?
DO IT... PLEASE...

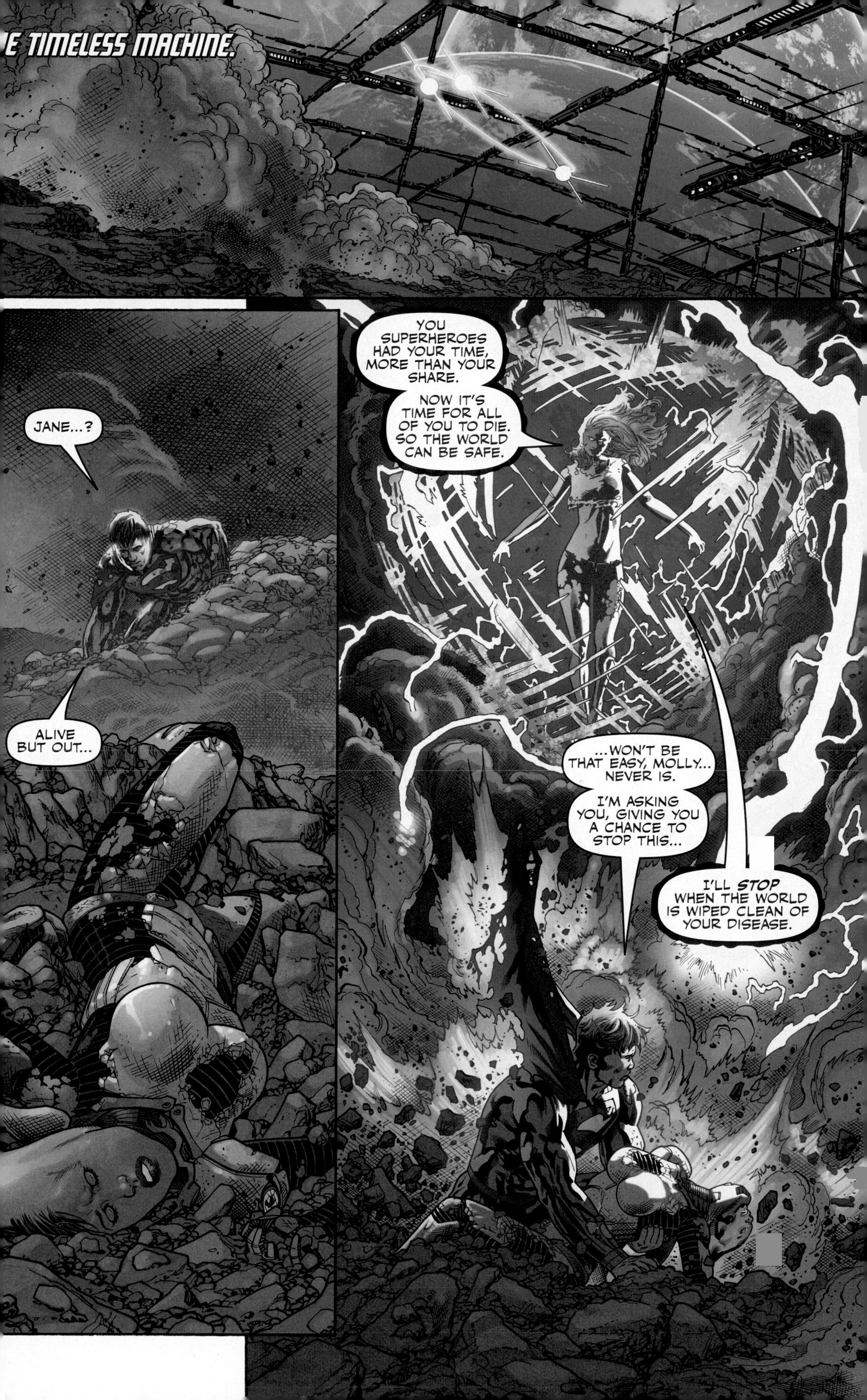
E TIMELESS MACHINE.
JANE...?
ALIVE BUT OUT...
YOU SUPERHEROES HAD YOUR TIME, MORE THAN YOUR SHARE.
NOW IT'S TIME FOR ALL OF YOU TO DIE. SO THE WORLD CAN BE SAFE.
...WON'T BE THAT EASY, MOLLY... NEVER IS.
I'M ASKING YOU, GIVING YOU A CHANCE TO STOP THIS...
I'LL STOP WHEN THE WORLD IS WIPED CLEAN OF YOUR DISEASE.

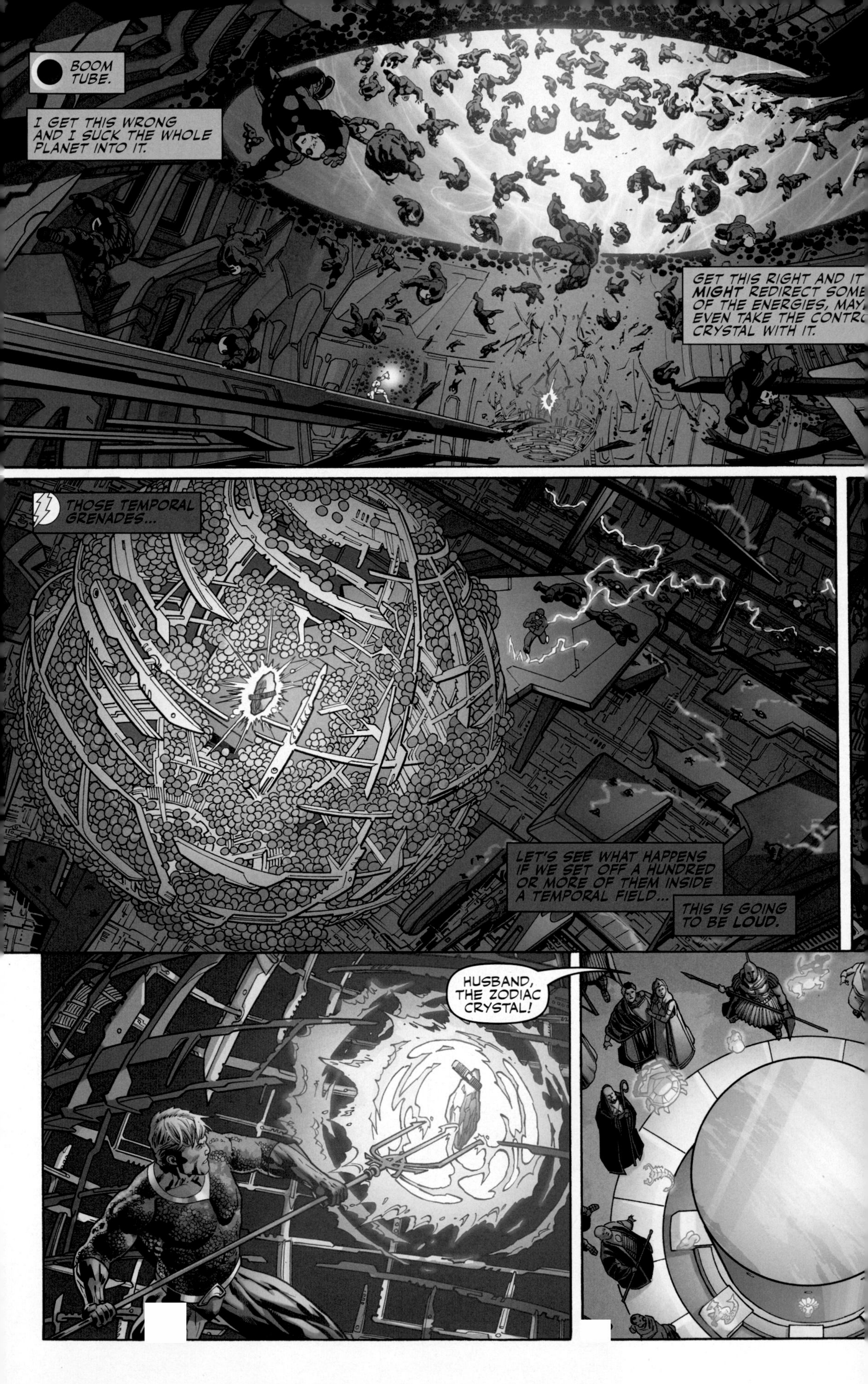
BOOM TUBE.
I GET THIS WRONG AND I SUCK THE WHOLE PLANET INTO IT.
GET THIS RIGHT AND IT MIGHT REDIRECT SOME OF THE ENERGIES, MAY EVEN TAKE THE CONTRO CRYSTAL WITH IT.
THOSE TEMPORAL GRENADES...
LET'S SEE WHAT HAPPENS IF WE SET OFF A HUNDRED OR MORE OF THEM INSIDE A TEMPORAL FIELD...
THIS IS GOING TO BE LOUD.
HUSBAND, THE ZODIAC CRYSTAL!

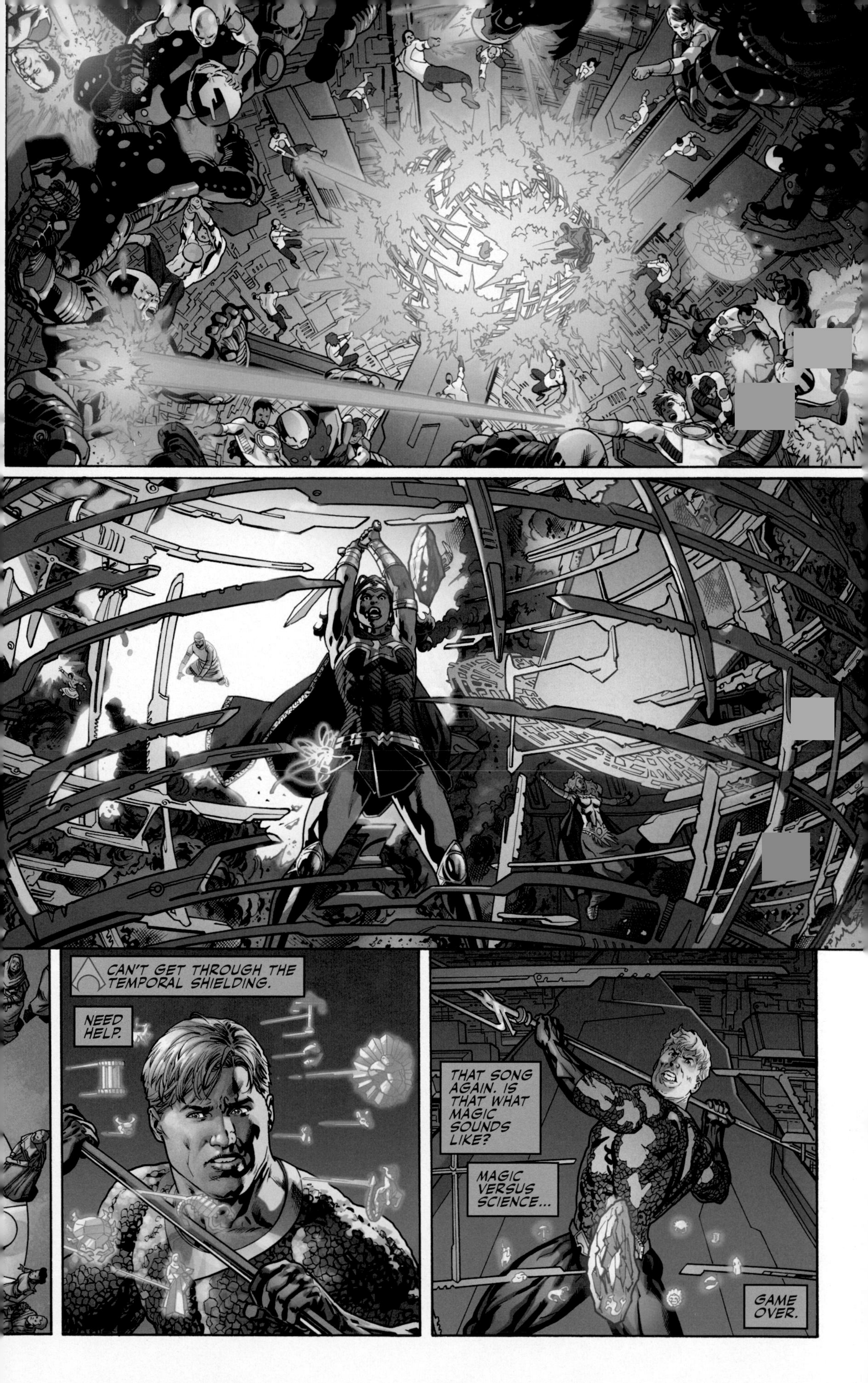
CAN'T GET THROUGH THE TEMPORAL SHIELDING.
NEED HELP.
THAT SONG AGAIN. IS THAT WHAT MAGIC SOUNDS LIKE?
MAGIC VERSUS SCIENCE...
GAME OVER.

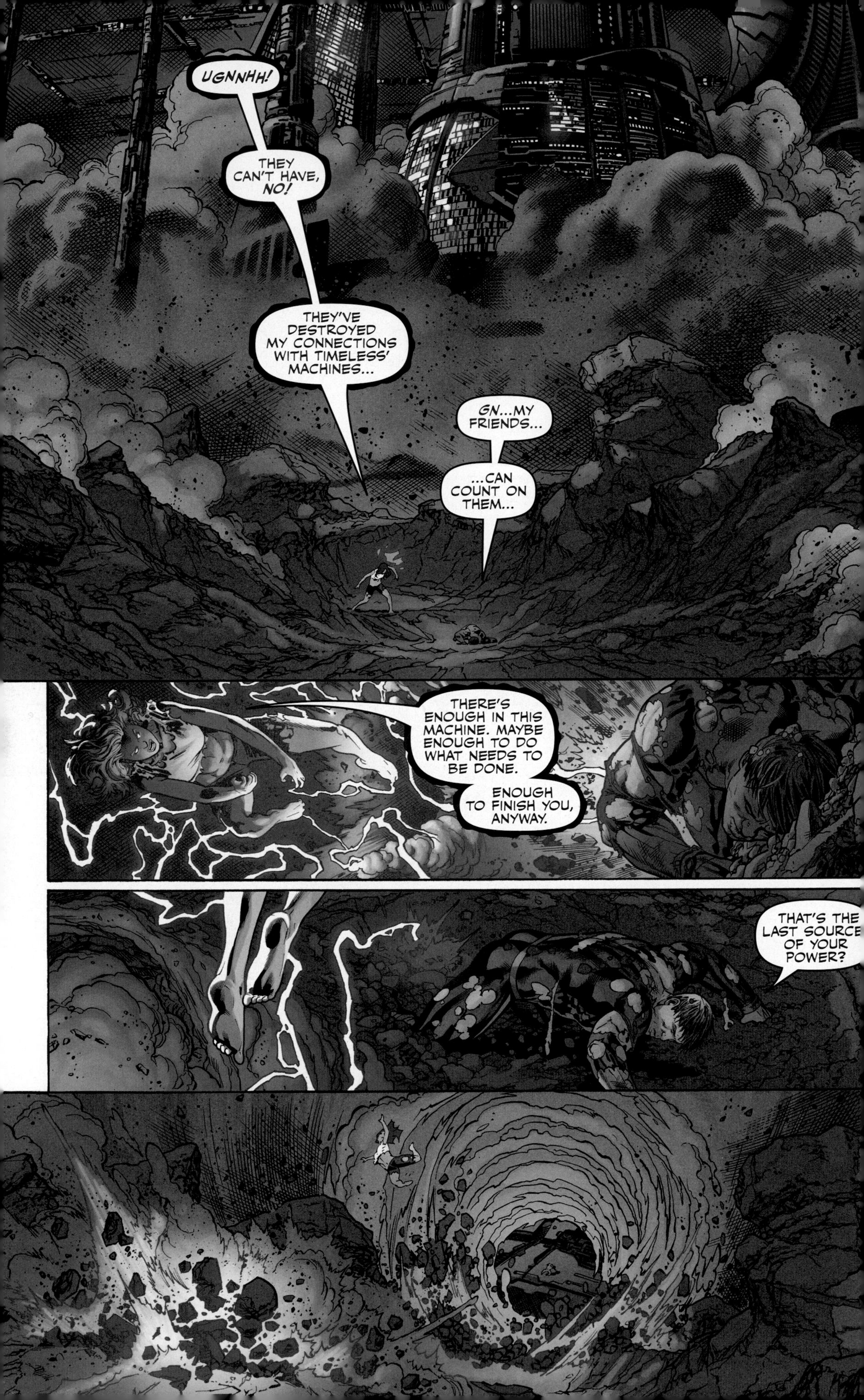
UGNNHH!
THEY CAN'T HAVE, NO!
THEY'VE DESTROYED MY CONNECTIONS WITH TIMELESS' MACHINES...
GN...MY FRIENDS...
...CAN COUNT ON THEM...
THERE'S ENOUGH IN THIS MACHINE. MAYBE ENOUGH TO DO WHAT NEEDS TO BE DONE.
ENOUGH TO FINISH YOU, ANYWAY.
THAT'S THE LAST SOURCE OF YOUR POWER?

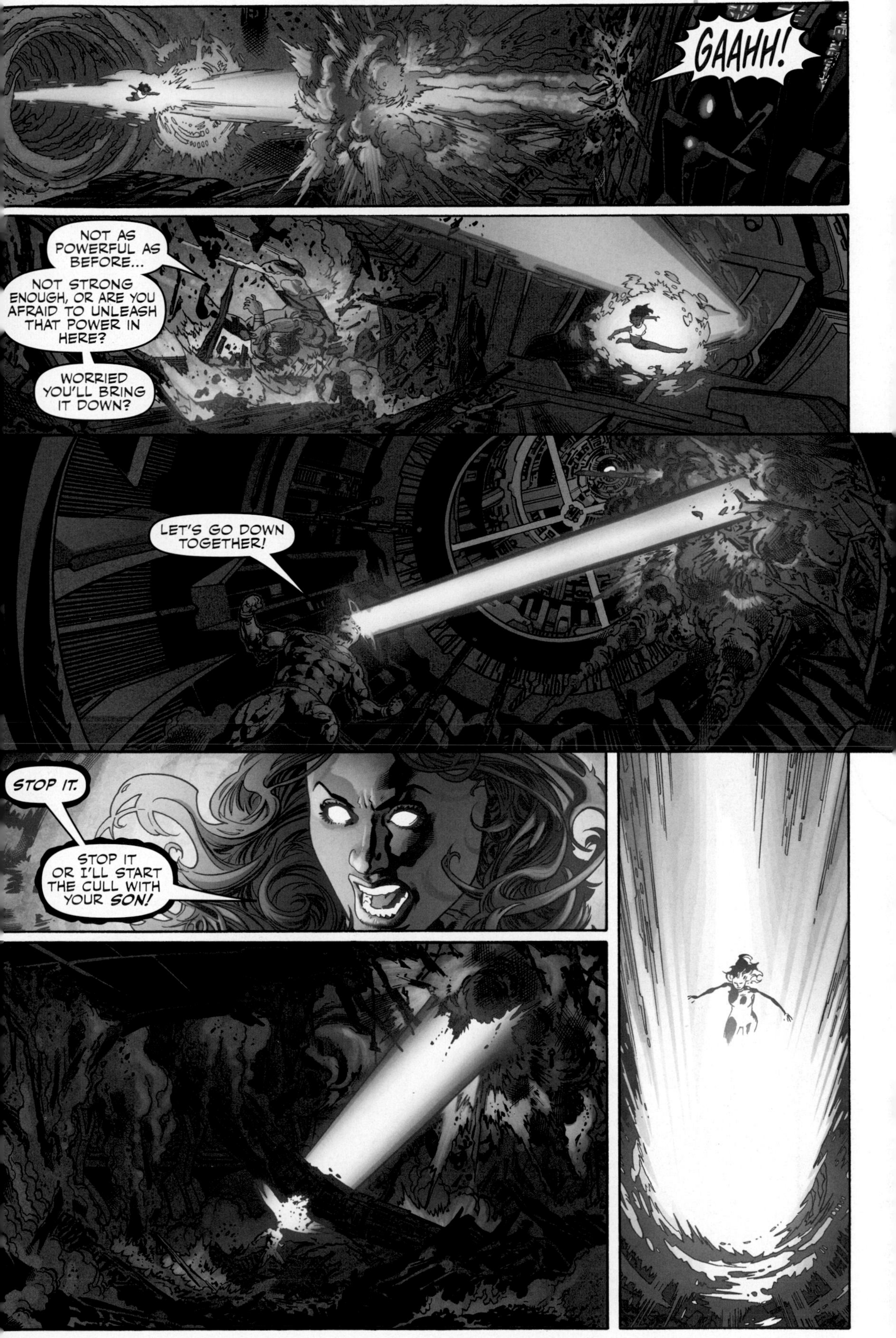
GAAHH!
NOT AS POWERFUL AS BEFORE...
NOT STRONG ENOUGH, OR ARE YOU AFRAID TO UNLEASH THAT POWER IN HERE?
WORRIED YOU'LL BRING IT DOWN?
LET'S GO DOWN TOGETHER!
STOP IT.
STOP IT OR I'LL START THE CULL WITH YOUR SON!

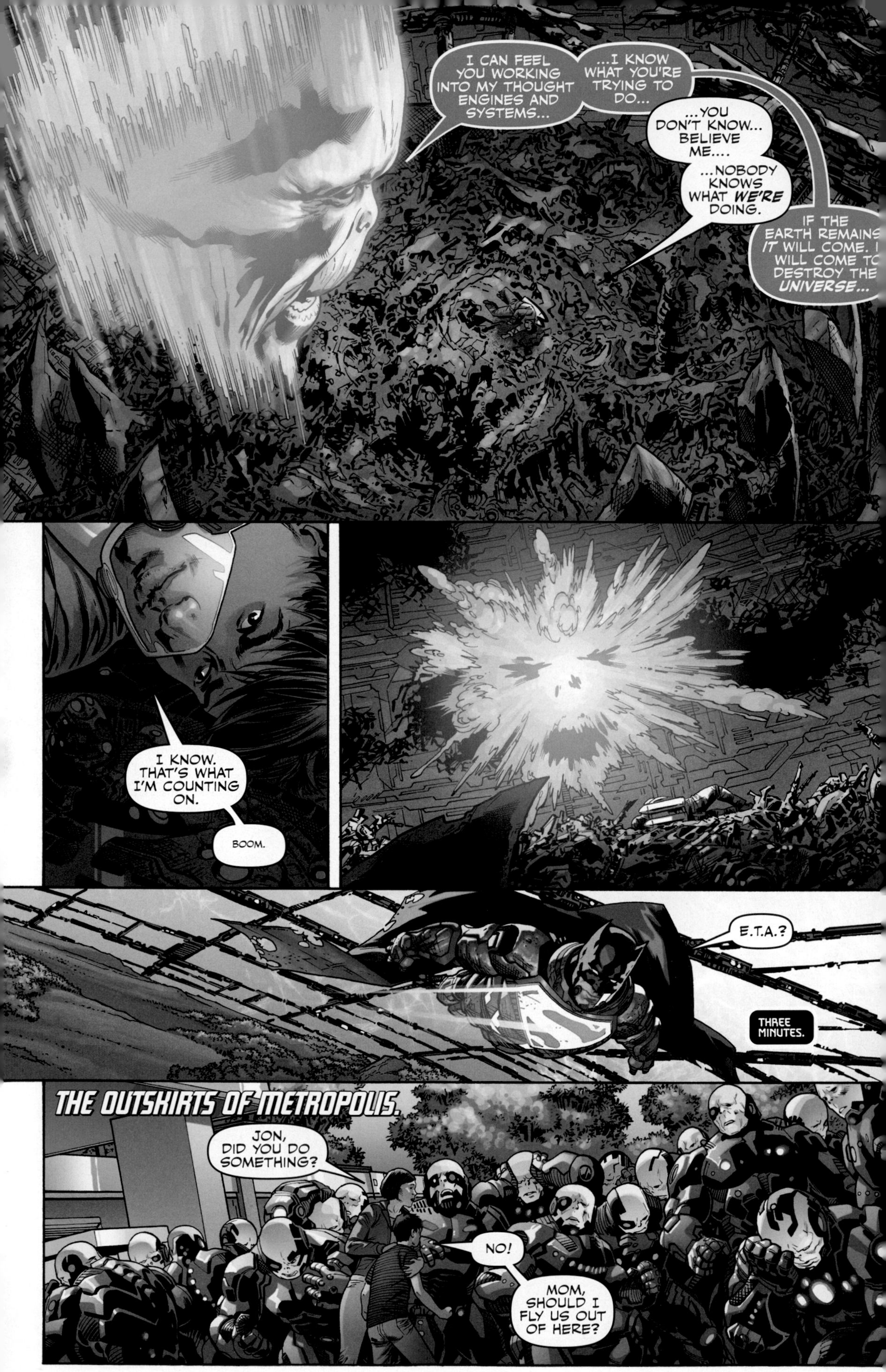
I CAN FEEL YOU WORKING INTO MY THOUGHT ENGINES AND SYSTEMS...
...I KNOW WHAT YOU'RE TRYING TO DO...
...YOU DON'T KNOW... BELIEVE ME....
...NOBODY KNOWS WHAT WE'RE DOING.
IF THE EARTH REMAINS IT WILL COME. IT WILL COME TO DESTROY THE UNIVERSE...
I KNOW. THAT'S WHAT I'M COUNTING ON.
BOOM.
E.T.A.?
THREE MINUTES.
THE OUTSKIRTS OF METROPOLIS.
JON, DID YOU DO SOMETHING?
NO!
MOM, SHOULD I FLY US OUT OF HERE?